Martina Hrabová | The Le Corbusier Galaxy

Designed cover image: František Sammer, early 1930s. Contact print, 3.2 × 4.5 cm. SAAA.

Martina Hrabová

Drawing on the author's discovery of an unknown, long-forgotten collection of photographs in an Indian ashram, this book offers an exciting, new view of the international community of young architects who served as Le Corbusier's assistants in the inter-war years. A collection of some 500 snapshots, assembled by the Czech architect František Sammer between 1931 and 1939, had been stored unnoticed for more than 70 years in an unlikely location – the Sri Aurobindo Ashram in Pondicherry, India. Sammer was one of Le Corbusier's closest assistants from the early 1930s. Later, Sammer worked in the Soviet Union, Japan and India. During, and after, his time in Paris, he personally took or collected these photographs, which he then deposited at the ashram when he left to fight in World War II. The images offer a remarkable view of the international community of people who worked in Le Corbusier's *atelier* in the 1930s. Among those featured in the photographs are Charlotte Perriand, Pierre Jeanneret, Jane West (the first American woman to work for Le Corbusier), Gordon Stephenson, Antonin Raymond, Junzo Sakakura and Josep Lluís Sert. Given the travels and international background of these individuals, the photographs are from different countries around the world, including the USSR, England, France, Czech Republic, Greece, USA (Tennessee, Montana, California and New Mexico), Japan and India. *The Le Corbusier Galaxy* successfully brings together serious archival research with a fascinating narrative, and it captures the human dimension of modern architecture, which is all too often neglected in today's accounts.

Martina Hrabova is an art historian who specializes in the history of modern architecture. She obtained her PhD in art history from the Charles University in Prague, where her dissertation addressed new findings on Le Corbusier's connections with the former Czechoslovakia. She is a recipient of numerous grants and fellowhips, including a Fulbright Fellowship, a French Government grant and the Canadian Centre for Architecture Visiting Scholarship. She has published articles in *JSAH, Room One Thousand and Art/Umění*. The Czech-language edition of her book *Galaxie Le Corbusier* received the prestigious 2022 Josef Krása prize for the best art book in the Czech Republic. She is currently an Assistant Professor at the Department of Art History at Palacký University in Olomouc.

The Le Corbusier Galaxy

František Sammer
and a global network of avant-garde architects

Martina Hrabová

First published in English 2025
by Routledge
4 Park Square, Milton Park, Abingdon, Oxon OX14 4RN

and by Routledge
605 Third Avenue, New York, NY 10158

Routledge is an imprint of the Taylor & Francis Group, an informa business

© 2025 Martina Hrabová

Translated by Derek Paton

The right of Martina Hrabová to be identified as author of this work has been asserted in accordance with sections 77 and 78 of the Copyright, Designs and Patents Act 1988.

All rights reserved. No part of this book may be reprinted or reproduced or utilised in any form or by any electronic, mechanical, or other means, now known or hereafter invented, including photocopying and recording, or in any information storage or retrieval system, without permission in writing from the publishers.

Trademark notice: Product or corporate names may be trademarks or registered trademarks, and are used only for identification and explanation without intent to infringe.

British Library Cataloguing-in-Publication Data
A catalogue record for this book is available from the British Library

ISBN: 9781032678580 (hbk)
ISBN: 9781032678221 (pbk)
ISBN: 9781032678597 (ebk)

DOI: 10.4324/9781032678597

Foreword by Mary McLeod
Index and bibliography by Magda van Duijkeren-Hrabová
Book design by Jiří Příhoda
Typeset in John Sans Text and Lite © Stormtype Foundry
Pre-print preparation of reproductions by Jakub Hrab

Publisher's Note
This book has been prepared from camera-ready copy provided by the author.

Contents

- 8   Foreword by Mary McLeod
- 12   Introduction
- 20   Author's Note
- 22   Letter for the Reader

24   The Research Diary

39   The Le Corbusier Galaxy

- 41   The Le Corbusier Galaxy
- 42   'Livre noir'
- 45   Sammer's photograph collection
- 45   35 rue de Sèvres, Paris, 1931
- 48   The family from the atelier
- 51   Architect-photographer
- 51   Summer 1931
- 52   In the gravitational field of the galaxy
- 55   The Depression as a bonding agent
- 57   A professional in a crew of amateurs, 1932
- 60   The female element
- 63   On marriage
- 66   Urban planning
- 70   Leaving 35 rue de Sèvres, Spring 1933
- 71   Spain and the Maghreb
- 78   West Kirby
- 84   CIAM IV
- 84   The architects brigade from Paris: 'The Le Corbusier Group'
- 88   Moscow
- 89   Merging with the masses
- 94   35 rue de Sèvres outside Paris
- 98   The Grand Tour, Autumn 1934
- 108   A life worth living
- 114   The land of 1,001 Sakakuras
- 120   The Soviet Union, 1935–37
- 124   Paris, January–February 1937
- 128   Japan revisited
- 132   India
- 136   Real war
- 138   Great Britain, 1946–1947
- 140   Returning
- 145   The galaxy reflected in the 'Livre noir'

155   Excursuses

- 156   Excursus 1: Great Britain, 1931
- 160   Excursus 2: Spain and the Maghreb, 1933
- 170   Excursus 3: Japan, 1935
- 176   Excursus 4: The Caucasus, summer 1936

- 180   Timeline
- 188   Acknowledgements
- 192   Bibliography
- 198   Index
- 204   Abbreviations
- 206   Image credits

To my grandmother

'In those days we were still fired by the faith of the Nineteen-Twenties, a time when the colours of painters were more luminous and optimistic than they had ever been before or ever have been since. We were confident that our generation was destined to bridge at last the gulf between inward and outward reality. We saw clearly enough what had to be done in planning, in architecture, and in art, to achieve our aim. The road to our goal lay straight before us, and we would not admit we were already a prey to dread, and that we stood on the brink of the world-wide catastrophe which was to reduce us, like our age itself, to silence'.

Sigfried Giedion, 'CIAM at Sea. The Background of the Fourth (Athens) Congress', *Architect's Year Book* 3, 1949, p. 39.

| **Foreword**

Mary McLeod

"We were going to change the world."

This statement, written in 1994 by American sculptor Agnes Larsen to British-born architect Gordon Stephenson, captures the immense hope and idealism—and deep sense of collective endeavor—of a circle of close friends associated with Le Corbusier and Pierre Jeanneret's atelier in the early 1930s. Besides Stephenson, it included Alex Adam, Charlotte Perriand, Junzo Sakakura, Josep Lluís Sert, Jane West and František Sammer (Larsen's former lover and husband). It was an international group of young, passionate, and often impoverished architects and friends from Britain, France, Japan, Spain, the United States and Czechoslovakia, who, after leaving the atelier at 35 rue de Sèvres, would go on to practice in numerous countries across the world. They stayed in touch with each other, often trading photos, postcards and drawings, until the end of their lives. Together, they comprised what might be considered a kind of international architectural avant-garde—not a cohort of heroic masters but rather a group of creative and highly-skilled professionals, who enjoyed working collaboratively and shared with one another the joys of everyday life and discoveries of new places and cultures. Most of all, they were deeply committed to both modern architecture and social change; for them, the two were one and the same.

This marvellous book, what Le Corbusier might have called a 'box of miracles', gives us a glimpse into this little-known world, in which personal and professional lives were closely intertwined. Meticulously researched, imaginatively assembled, and clearly narrated by Martina Hrabová, it tells a story through a montage of newly-discovered photographs, postcards, family letters and memoirs, not just of their architecture but also of their leftist politics, travels, skiing and hiking trips and festive meals, testifying to the desire of this young avant-garde group to experience life in its fullest. Although there's not a single photo of Le Corbusier, this collective portrait offers, as well, a fresh, more personal dimension of the Swiss-French master, showing him to be warmer and more supportive than that of many of the prevailing stereotypes of this complex, brilliant and sometimes opportunistic man. He comes across as a concerned mentor, genuinely interested in his young assistants, asking them about their personal lives (perhaps a little too much), encouraging them to travel and experience new adventures and offering to help them find paid employment. In turn, these young assistants, though rarely paid, seemed to be genuinely fond of him; they were intensely loyal and even protective (as in the polemic battles in the USSR), wanting him to share in their own discoveries, most of all of Japan. While they sometimes differed or disagreed with him, especially about politics, they continued to revere his vision of modern architecture and to embrace his constant search for a new, more liberated way of living, one that rejected bourgeois conventions and academic traditions.

If, as the book title suggests, this galaxy of friends orbited around Le Corbusier, Hrabová's own study centres around František Sammer, an exceptionally talented, highly competent, politically committed young Czech architect. Like many of the protagonists in Hrabová's account, he had an itinerant life. He worked for Le Corbusier from 1931 to 1933, drawing urban plans for Algiers and Stockholm, installing an exhibition stand in Cologne with Perriand and supervising construction of the Swiss Pavilion, the Salvation Army building and the apartment building at 24 rue de Nungesser-et-Coli in Paris; he then worked in Moscow from 1933 to 1937, briefly in Tokyo in 1937 and then in Pondicherry [now Puducherry], India from 1938 to 1942, detailing and supervising construction of Antonin Raymond's Golconde dormitory building. In 1942, he joined the British regiment in India, fighting in Bengal and Burma, and received multiple honors for his courageous service. After recovering from serious war injuries in Britain, Sammer returned to Pilsen, his hometown in Czechoslovakia to practice in state agencies, often choosing to work on planning projects rather than buildings in order to avoid complying with the stylistic mandates of socialist realism. His letters to friends and family members suggest what a remarkable man he must have been—kind, generous, interested in diverse cultures and ways of life, highly principled and not afraid to take risks and to adhere to his political ideals. For example, in a letter from Moscow of September 1934, after sending 'greetings to Pierre and Corbu', he wrote, 'Charlotte, come with Pierre—We need you here to work for us! You have no idea how much I have recently been thinking about all the energy you waste with all those annoyances of the Boulogne type and so forth. Here, we do real work'. [see p. 89] And in a letter from Moscow that same year to his father, he explained that he saw 'the future of humanity [...] in social revolution and socialism' and declared, 'For a long time now, I have not ironed my trousers. My spouse [Larsen] doesn't care to iron for me either. Together with my trouser creases, my bourgeois views of life are also vanishing'. [see p. 91]

While Sammer's fascinating life deserves Hrabová's careful study in its own right, this book also makes clear how unconventional and courageous his circle of friends were–and how often their personal and political lives intersected. One can understand immediately why adventuresome young women like West and Perriand would be drawn to Le Corbusier and Jeanneret's atelier and, while there, felt strongly supported and respected by this group of young men with whom they worked and enjoyed many and lively evenings and sporting expeditions together. One also sees how they reinforced each other's leftist politics, and how they departed from and sometimes aligned with those of Le Corbusier. For example, in a letter in 1933 to Karel Teige, trying to court his favor, Sammer wrote: 'It is a great shame that Corbu cannot read your book [*Minimum Dwelling*]. You know, I pity his intelligence, which is much greater than that of the everyday bourgeois. I hope that he will change a bit once he has carefully read Bukharin's *Materialism historique*, which Charlotte Perriand and I gave him. Recently, he and a few gentlemen have still been publishing a ridiculous bulletin, *Prélude* (the prelude to action). If you are interested, I can send it to you for a laugh'. [see p. 88] However, only a year earlier, Sammer seemed to admire and enjoy working on the neo-syndicalist publication *Plans* with Le Corbusier. Nor did Sammer's Marxist sympathies keep Le Corbusier from inviting him to return to work in the atelier after the war. In the end, Sammer chose another course, still hoping to change the world by working in socialist Czechoslovakia. Soon that dream too would fade, as it would for many of this circle, even as they sought to make good architecture and to improve, if more modestly, people's lives.

Hrabová's impressive study is filled with new archival details and factual information but what the reader will appreciate most is the chance to experience firsthand the fervent belief and passionate commitment to modern architecture's social mission that these young architects held. As Larsen wrote more than 20 years after Sammer's death, they had genuinely hoped to make the world a more egalitarian and joyful place, a goal that was tragically shattered by World War II and the onset of the Cold War.

Mary McLeod
New York City, August 2024

Introduction

In this book I invite the reader to look behind the scenes of the history of modern architecture. I present an intimate portrait of a largely unknown Czech architect, František (François) Sammer (1907–1973), within the context of the great works of internationally renowned artists, and in an innovative way usher the reader into the world of Le Corbusier's work. Using photos from Sammer's collection, I reconstruct the social network that emerged in the atelier, and reveal the importance and value of the friendship amongst leading actors in avant-garde architecture of the first half of the twentieth century, as well as those who remained in their shadows. This community, the 'Le Corbusier Galaxy', had a remarkable vitality, and in its own way remains active even today in the network of people who keep the legacy of this famous architect alive.

The incentive to write this book was provided by my discovery of a collection of photographs assembled by Sammer, which I discovered in Pondicherry, India, in 2016. After arriving in this French enclave in 1939, Sammer soon became part of the community of the Sri Aurobindo Ashram there. In 1942, he enlisted in the British Army, leaving all his belongings with the ashram for safekeeping, including his collection of photographs. Dating from 1931 to 1939, the collection provides a portrait of the social circle of the Le Corbusier and Pierre Jeanneret studio at 35 rue de Sèvres, Paris, known as the 'atelier'. For two years Sammer was one of its closest collaborators, and after leaving Paris, he was involved in large projects in the Soviet Union, Japan and India. He remained in close touch with friends from the atelier; they wrote each other letters, visited each other, and Sammer also often followed their advice about where to travel. This book is the result of more than ten years of my research in the Czech Republic, France, the United States, Canada, Great Britain and India. It presents Sammer's international career and, through him, contributes significantly to what we know about Le Corbusier. I identify the people, times and places in these photographs chiefly with the help of primary sources and place them as part of the history of the international avant-garde.

Who was František (François) Sammer?

Sammer is an unusual figure in the history of modern architecture. His contribution and importance cannot be properly assessed by the number of his designs actually built or by the number of winning competition entries, nor can his significance be fully understood using only formal analysis of his architectural works. He did not write anything about himself, and before this publication, apart from my article from 2016,[1] no scholarly publication had been written about him. Although few of his architectural or urban plans were carried out, his legacy is clear in his extensive, unpublished correspondence and contemporary documents, mainly in Czech, French and English, which, for decades, remained deposited and unnoticed in various archives around the world. It is in this legacy that Sammer's extraordinary importance for the history of architecture lies.

The story of František Sammer unfolds from his work with great figures and visionaries of the modern movement between the two world wars. Le Corbusier in Paris; Nikolai Kolli, the Vesnin brothers and Moisei Ginzburg in Moscow; and Antonín Raymond in Tokyo. All quickly recognized his technical abilities and talent, entrusting him with work in their architectural studios and with supervising the execution of their plans. The evidence shows that Sammer was actively involved in the creation of groundbreaking works of modern architecture in the twentieth century. In the studio of Le Corbusier and his cousin Pierre Jeanneret, he played a major role in the work on the Pavillon Suisse of the Cité internationale universitaire de Paris, the Cité de refuge (Armée de Salut) building and the Immeuble Molitor apartment house at 24 rue Nungesser-et-Coli in Paris. He also worked on the competition entry for the Palace of the Soviets in Moscow and projects for Algeria. In Moscow he helped to supervise the construction of Le Corbusier's Centrosoyuz; in the studio of Nikolai Kolli he played a big part in the planning of the Kirovskaya Metro station (today, Chistye prudy); and in collaboration with Moisei Ginzburg, he was involved in planning a number of Soviet sanatoriums. He also helped Antonin Raymond design the Golconde dormitory in Pondicherry, and served as the on-site supervising architect while it was being built.

In addition to his professional qualities, Sammer had a remarkable feel for the human dimension of his profession and a gift for making true friends even in the highly competitive environment of architectural offices.

This aspect of Sammer's legacy provides us with insight into the history of modern architecture from a more unusual perspective. Sammer was an integral part of the social network of the international avant-garde and was close friends with leading figures of the movement. His historic legacy thus provides a look behind the scenes of major modernist projects, into the origin of new ideas, and into a community of people who were turning the ideas of some of the biggest names in the history of twentieth-century architecture into real buildings.

The others

Through Sammer, one discovers often-overlooked figures of the modern movement, people who have been overshadowed by the heroic figures of the story. Particularly revelatory in this regard is Sammer's contribution to the atelier from 1931 to 1933, the nature, importance and impact of which are the main topic of this publication. Sammer was one of the most prominent of the 15 or more Czechoslovak architects who worked there. In the renowned studio at 35 rue de Sèvres, he attained a high

---

1| Martina Hrabová, 'Between Ideal and Ideology: The Parallel Worlds of František Sammer', *Umění / Art* LXIV, No 2, 2016, pp. 137-166.

position. He was one of the few to receive a monthly salary, and was close to the key members of this community. It was at 35 rue de Sèvres that the basis of Sammer's approach to the profession was formed and where some of his most important personal ties were formed, which helped him to shape future decisions. These ties survived for the rest of his life.

The wealth of the primary sources in Sammer's legacy reveals the durability of the relationships and the close connections amongst members of Le Corbusier's circle. Through these documents one discovers the nature of the international community of the people who worked daily on the execution of Le Corbusier's ideas, and who, after being initiated and gaining this experience, further developed as independent architects. The sources linked with Sammer provide details about the operation of the atelier at the height of its activity in the early 1930s. They draw attention to an important phenomenon which, in the works of architectural historians, has often been eclipsed by the figure of Le Corbusier himself – that of the team of young people who put his ideas into practice.

The Le Corbusier Galaxy

The name I have chosen for the social network of Le Corbusier and Jeanneret's studio is borrowed from the designer Charlotte Perriand, who described the charismatic force of the atelier as the 'Le Corbusier Galaxy'.[2] In astronomy the term describes a system of stars and other components mutually bound by gravity and orbiting around a common centre. The individual parts are in motion, but that motion always takes place in relation to each other and the common core. I use the term 'galaxy' metaphorically for the circle of people linked by the milieu at 35 rue de Sèvres. I look at this social group as a system of people – stars – who orbited around the charismatic Le Corbusier and his studio – that is, the core with its strong gravitational pull. I pay particular attention to the 'Livre noir', the Black Book in which drawings were registered with the dates of their origin and the names of the individual draughtsmen. This unique source, deposited at the Fondation Le Corbusier, Paris, provides authentic period testimony about the individual studio members' involvement in certain projects and also provides us with a guide to the community of architects in the studio, and how they changed over time.

Sammer worked in the atelier at the side of Le Corbusier and his closest collaborators – Pierre Jeanneret, Charlotte Perriand, Junzo Sakakura and Josep Lluís Sert. Thanks to Sammer's legacy, this book also presents figures, who, in connection with Le Corbusier, have previously not been subjects of scholarly interest. It introduces the British architects Gordon Stephenson and Alex Adam, and it also highlights the largely neglected topic of women architects in the Le Corbusier and Jeanneret atelier and the perception of the movement for the 'New Woman' among the assistants there. For example, it provides new information about Charlotte Perriand, especially concerning her interest in the Soviet Union and Japan. Thanks to the sources that I found while researching Sammer's inter-war career, I have been able to assess information from Perriand's autobiography and provide precise dates of her visits to the Soviet Union. In addition, a special place in the book is accorded to the architect Jane West (later Clauss), the first American woman in the atelier. During her time there, she and Perriand were the only female collaborators at 35 rue de Sèvres. The book also introduces Agnes Larsen, an American sculptor of Norwegian origin, who was Sammer's partner at the time. Through Larsen, although she was not a member of the atelier, the reader gains valuable information about the community of friends and collaborators.

---

2 | For more details see p. 42 and n. 10 in the main text.

Sammer's collection of photographs

Sammer's collection comprises about 500 photos, the vast majority of which are contact prints of negatives made strictly for personal use and enjoyment, not for publication. The photographs are small, often of atypical dimensions, and are made with various cameras and by different people, either when with Sammer or sent to him in letters. By the time when the photographs in this collection were being made, lightweight folding cameras were readily available, as were the means to make contact prints in improvised conditions. It is hard to tell who took most of these photos. Consequently, the name of the photographer is given in the book only where I have succeeded in identifying him or her. To give the reader a better idea of the true size of the photographs from Sammer's collection, the dimensions of each one reproduced here is listed. The photographs that were most likely by Sammer are usually contact prints from 3 × 4 cm and 6 × 9 cm negatives. I was unable, however, to obtain more detailed information about his cameras. Sammer made his prints either on Velox paper or on the cheaper paper available in the Soviet Union and other places he travelled.

The snapshots from travels, shared experiences and everyday life often resemble photographs made today with smart phones. During my research I was often asked what the importance of these 'ugly pictures' was. The answer is that it is often the imperfection, authenticity and frankness of the photos in Sammer's collection that make them most informative. Thanks to these qualities, the photos are free of the period criteria regarding aesthetics, and provide an unfettered, more personal view of important figures in the modern movement.

Photographs as instruments to revive the past

Presenting the human side of the story, I do not attempt to achieve a technical analysis of the photos or their stylistic classification. I use the collection chiefly as an instrument to help identify the social network emerging from Le Corbusier and Jeanneret's atelier, and as evidence of the longevity of that network even after some of the members had left Paris. The photos thus tend to carry the story along, serving as a means of reviving past moments, rather than as self-contained artefacts. This book seeks to contribute to our understanding of the architects' travels, amateur photography and ways of conveying information, and it functions as a wide-ranging guide to the transnational community associated with Le Corbusier's circle. The method employed here by necessity differs from traditional approaches taken in the history of art and architecture.

Several publications that look at the importance of private and seemingly less important photographs or film footage from the milieu of the international avant-garde provided me with the inspiration and courage to step out of the usual ways of thinking about such a topic. Tim Benton's work, especially his *LC FOTO: Le Corbusier Secret Photographer* (2013),[3] is of key importance in this regard. In his book Benton analyzes in detail Le Corbusier's photographs and film footage, for the first time presenting stills from films Le Corbusier left unprocessed. New material was also presented by Véronique Boone in the exhibition 'Dans l'intimité de l'Atelier du 35, rue de Sèvres', which was held at the Fondation Le Corbusier, Paris, in 2017.[4] In stills from private film footage of the assistant Ernest Weissmann, it was possible to trace many moments in the life of the atelier during the big projects of the late 1920s and early 1930s. A refreshing look at pictorial sources as the medium of a story is provided by Chris Blencowe and Judith Levine in *Moholy's Edit: The Avant-Garde at Sea, August 1933* (published in 2019).[5] By means of detailed analysis of film footage taken by László Moholy-Nagy at the fourth of the International Congresses of Modern Architecture (CIAM), Blencowe and Levine offer unusual insight into the course of an otherwise well-known event in the history of modern architecture. The im-

[3] Tim Benton, *LC FOTO: Le Corbusier Secret Photographer*, Zurich: Lars Müller, 2013.

[4] '*Dans l'intimité de l'Atelier du 35, rue de Sevres'. Point de vue d'un amateur, Ernest Weissmann. Bobines inédites, 1929-1930*, curator Véronique Boone, Maison La Roche, Fondation Le Corbusier, Paris, 30 May–1 July 2017. The amateur films of Ernest Weissmann are the subject of a new publication by Véronique Boone, *Le Corbusier on Camera: The Unknown films of Ernest Weissmann*, Basel: Birkhäuser, 2024.

[5] Chris Blencowe and Judith Levine, *Moholy's Edit: The Avant-Garde at Sea, August 1933,* Zurich: Lars Müller, 2019.

portance that looking at the free time and private records of its members has for increasing our understanding of the avant-garde is also demonstrated in the spectacular publication by a group of authors led by Almut Grunewald, *The Giedion World: Sigfried Giedion and Carola Giedion-Welcker in Dialogue* (2019).[6] Their book reveals the world of two art historians, authorities on the modern movement, whose private and professional lives were inseparably interwoven, and it thus helps to complete the historical picture.

The connections between the private and the professional, the intimate and great creative acts, is one of the chief messages of Sammer's legacy. I identified the photographs from his collection with the help of a voluminous set of letters and documents from related archives. The various sources work together to cast light on the past, and together form a whole of a conceptual nature. Sammer's collection of photographs provides period testimony from different places around the world, for instance, the Soviet Union in the 1930s or Paris during the preparations for the Exposition internationale des arts et des techniques dans la vie moderne in 1937. The message is sometimes conveyed almost like comics; for example, when documenting Sammer and Larsen's travels in Spain and the Maghreb (undertaking the visit to Josep Lluís Sert in Barcelona, a sojourn in Toledo, photographs from Tétouan and other places in northern Morocco, or the sequence of photos from boarding the *M.S. Dempo* in Gibraltar), visits to Antonin Raymond at his summer residence in the Japanese seaside town of Hayama, or in the photos documenting work on a competition entry for Antwerp. That project, which Sammer created in spring 1933 in the British town of West Kirby with two former assistants from 35 rue de Sèvres, Gordon Stephenson and Alex Adam, together with Bill Holford, was in competition with one created by the Le Corbusier and Jeanneret atelier.

At several points the book reveals the unknown physical appearance of the architects and their works. For the first time, the reader can become acquainted with a portrait of Alex Adam, who is described in a photograph in the archive of Charlotte Perriand as an 'unknown friend'. Besides the photo documentation of the project for Antwerp, Sammer's collection includes photographs of other competition entries in which Stephenson had been involved (an entertainment centre in Bexhill and council offices in Slough, England). There are also photos, perhaps sent to Sammer by Jane West, of the interior of her and her husband Alfred Clauss's home in Knoxville, Tennessee, which provide previously unpublished documentation of the modern design of the furnishings of the house. Sammer's collection also presents a new portrait of Agnes Larsen and her works. A photograph of one of her sculptures was taken in Paris by an assistant in the Le Corbusier and Jeanneret atelier, Andreas Feininger, who later became a renowned photographer.

The photos from Sammer's collection also provide new documentation of some projects of Charlotte Perriand's (variants of a photomontage of a project for a hotel in the mountains and different views of the interior of her studio in Montparnasse, Paris). In some cases, the publication presents parallels between photos that were taken by Le Corbusier and Perriand in places where, on their recommendation, Sammer had also been. Like Le Corbusier, Sammer sought to capture the architecture and life of the locals in the villages of the Maghreb. The documentation of Sammer's travels in Greece in 1934, a year after CIAM IV, is especially notable. From the character of the photographs it is clear that Sammer was well acquainted with the photos taken by participants in the congress. Moreover, he also had a keen interest in monuments of classical antiquity, which stemmed from knowledge gained from Le Corbusier during conversations in the atelier and from his publications.

6| Almut Grunewald (ed.), *The Giedion World: Sigfried Giedion and Carola Giedion-Welcker in Dialogue*, Zurich: Scheidegger & Spiess, 2019.

The possibility of capturing motion in a single photograph or a sequence, together with an eye for detail and the textures of materials, all brought with them new ways to explore reality, thus offering inspiration for further creative work. Amongst the subjects that this circle of avant-garde artists found interesting were everyday life, social problems, vernacular architecture, sport and life in the great outdoors. In Sammer's collection we come across, in particular, records of fleeting moments, impressions, random passers-by and locals. This way of looking at things sometimes prevailed over documenting a famous monument or a new modernist building (like the Casa Bloc in Barcelona or the Izvestia building in Moscow). Through Sammer's collection, the book offers glimpses of what seems to be the germination of some important creations in the history of modern architecture.

A system of power lines
Sammer's collection contains few photos of modern architecture; indeed, it does not contain even a single photograph of Le Corbusier. Yet the collection is directly linked with the famous architect because it has its roots in the ties among members of his studio. The photographs have remained in this collection like memory traces of friends and acquaintances from Le Corbusier's circle. As such, the documentary evidence may be better understood by using the sociologist Pierre Bourdieu's theory of the 'intellectual field'. He argues that making of art is a socially conditioned act, dependent on the community it comes out of: 'The intellectual field, which cannot be reduced to a simple aggregate of isolated agents or to the sum of elements merely juxtaposed, is, like a magnetic field, made up of a system of power lines. In other words, the constituting agents or systems of agents may be described as so many forces which, by their existence, opposition or combination, determine its specific structure at a given moment in time.'[7] It is that system of power lines and elements attracted by a magnetic force, as in a galaxy in the universe, which forms the core of this book. The book is not, however, limited to a certain moment in time. I trace the bonds originally formed in the Le Corbusier and Jeanneret atelier throughout their long existence. Some of these bonds are in fact still alive today.

Sammer was able to stay in touch with his friends from the atelier even after the Second World War, when he returned to his native Czechoslovakia. His contacts from the years between the wars survived despite the censorship and persecution he faced at home, particularly in the totalitarian state during the 1950s owing to his international career. Whenever possible, especially during the political 'Thaw' in the second half of the 1960s, he resumed contact with colleagues abroad and again tried to work with them. In the spring of 1973, at the most oppressive point of the re-established hard-line Communist regime, and only several months before his death, Sammer received a letter from the vice-president of the Geneva-based Association Internationale Le Corbusier (AILC), Pierre-André Emery, requesting help in drawing up a list of assistants at the atelier. The basis of the list was the 'Livre noir'. Emery's letter included photocopies of the pages from the 'Livre noir' with Sammer's signature together with those of other atelier members, about whom Emery sought current information. Sammer provided a surprisingly comprehensive answer, and whenever he lacked the necessary information, he told Emery to whom he should turn. I present this as evidence of the vitality of the relations established in the atelier, which by their nature went far beyond being merely the contacts of colleagues in the workplace.

7| Pierre Bourdieu, 'Intellectual Field and Creative Project', in Michael F. D. Young (ed.), *Knowledge and Control: New Directions for the Sociology of Education*, London: Collier Macmillan, 1971, p. 161. I thank Mary McLeod for bringing this source to my attention.

| Author's Note

This book is based on numerous unpublished primary sources in various languages. Apart from the correspondence in Czech, these are documents written in French, English, Russian and Japanese. Unless otherwise stated, all translations were translated into English by Derek Paton.

František Sammer lived in a multilingual environment and learned the languages he used in the course of both everyday life and architectural practice. Sometimes, in the case of documents in foreign languages, it results in a certain clumsiness, which I see as an authentic testimony of the times and Sammer's in a transnational itinerary. In some places, therefore, I approach the translation more freely, in an effort to keep Sammer's message. The original texts from the foreign language sources, except for those in Czech, are quoted in full in footnotes, and the reader can check the translations or descipher their own interpretation of Sammer's meanings in the original texts.

Similarly to the reproduced photographs, the book treats the written contemporary sources as authentic evidence and sees the value even in minor imperfections and errors that, in some places, contradict current ideas about proper literary language. In the transcripts and translations of letters, I retain the long dashes (pauses), in some cases used extensively, as a signature feature of contemporary handwriting and, in Sammer's case, a favourite tool for giving flow to his texts. We have interfered with the text only by altering the spelling and wording of some names of people and places, when leaving them untouched would impair clarity.

Where a sketch or handwriting by another writer is present in the letters, I indicate the deviations by a note in brackets. Phonetic or colloquial entries are left as Sammer wrote them to preserve authenticity, such as the designation of Le Corbusier as *Corbusier, Corbusiér, Korbík, Corb.* and *Corbu*, or Nikolai Kolli as *Colley, Coly* and *Colly*. Family names have been retained in all their different versions, for example, František is given as *Frantík, François* and *Francek*; Sammer's sister Miloslava as *Milča* and *Milána*; and his brother Jan as *Honza* and *Jenda*. Where Sammer referred to Le Corbusier's and Jeanneret's atelier as the Office, I retain the capital letter to preserve the importance he obviously assigned to the word.

All references to literature and sources provided in the captions of illustrations and glosses (short quotations) refer to the footnotes in the main text.

Letter for the Reader

Dear Reader,

The main part of this book is written as a story with chapters arranged chronologically. I therefore recommend reading it in the order it is presented, from the beginning to the end.

On the individual pages of the book, several levels of content intertwine with one another. The main text is complemented by a good many footnotes containing factual details. Another level is the rich pictorial message, which in some cases provides information independent of the main text. The illustrations are accompanied by captions and in some cases by glosses (short quotations) from related primary and secondary sources.

The book comprises three main parts. The main text is preceded by the Research Diary, in which I describe how my research progressed, the circumstances related to the discovery of Sammer's collection of photographs and what followed immediately afterwards. The main text is then followed by four Excursuses, sections containing additional information found in archives, together with pictorial documentation of Sammer's travels and his companions on some of the journeys.

To facilitate orientation, the book has at the back a List of Abbreviations, a Timeline, a Bibliography and an Index of People, Places and Concepts.

I sincerely wish you an inspirational read
Martina Hrabová

| The Research Diary

**Avery Hall, Columbia University, New York City,
March 2013**

We met in a cellar snack bar. A school of architecture and a fantastic library. Though it is on another continent, the library has European materials, periodicals and items that I would hardly find in one place elsewhere. Ask for the 'Black Book'. Mary McLeod reveals what I should look for in Paris. The 'Livre noir', also called the 'Log Book'. You'll find a list of drawings there. At the Le Corbusier atelier, drawings were each appended with an entry number, a description of the project and the name of the person who drew it.

**The Museum of Modern Art, New York City,
June 2013**

An exhibition opening, a big event, the greatest architect of the twentieth century is presented at this institution comprehensively for the first time. A visionary full of paradoxes. He fought against tradition and at the same time sought inspiration there. He advocated radical urban-planning projects, yet had a feel for the landscape. Jean-Louis Cohen conceived the exhibition as an atlas. *An Atlas of Modern Landscapes*; that, too, is a possible perspective.

**Fondation Le Corbusier, Paris,
Autumn 2013**

For a couple of years now I have been travelling to the Fondation in search of documents about the architects who came to Le Corbusier from Czechoslovakia. They were well trained technically and they admired the charismatic architect. He was the main one to come up with the ideas and was always thinking ahead. But he could not really make axonometric drawings.

I have the 'Livre noir' in my hands for the first time. I am looking for Czech names. I am expecting well-known ones, those about which something has already been written. Instead, I find architects I have never heard of before. Dozens of drawings bear the abbreviaton SAM. František Sammer – of Czechoslovak nationality – who was at the studio from 1931 to 1933.

He drew everything, from implementation details to perspectives, which Le Corbusier then used in his publications. Some of them Sammer did alone; some he did with other draughtsmen; and sometimes he even worked with Pierre Jeanneret and Charlotte Perriand. He drew superbly and sometimes added commentary to the technical details. A fine, neat, minuscule handwriting. At the moment I have no inkling how much of it I will be deciphering.

**Bus Station, Pilsen,
Spring 2014**

I am waiting for the bus. The station is ugly but at the moment it doesn't bother me. I have found something. The Pilsen City Archives has letters. Again, the minuscule handwriting – everything Sammer sent to his native Pilsen. From France, England, Spain, Russia, Japan, Africa, India. God knows from where else. And then the letters in English and in French, from near and dear ones, from loved ones and famous people, from all four corners of the world. Le Corbusier, Charlotte Perriand, Antonin and Noémi Raymond, Jean Bossu, Junzo Sakakura, Pierre-André Emery, Mirra Alfassa (called the Mother in the Sri Aurobindo Ashram) and other names, abbreviations, conjectures.

In front of me on the table of the Pilsen City Archives lies a whole world, unsuspected links and stories. I have found something. It is a key. A series of access codes to the context of the history of the avant-garde. It is part of the mosaic, the pieces of which have been scattered in all directions, to incredibly distant places. The whole picture

< The family of František Sammer in 1909. From the left: Růžena (his mother, née Hlavatá), František, Josef (his brother), Miloslava (Milča, his sister) and Jan (his father). Archiv města Plzně (City of Pilsen Archives – AMP), František Sammer Papers.

will be difficult to put back together. A long time ago I reconciled myself to the fact that history is somehow fiction. At any given moment a reading of the available fragments brings another interpretation. Again and again, each time from the beginning, there arises a story that is dependent on the lottery of time and place. I have found something and must continue looking. Now, it is also my story.

317 Eanes School Rd, Austin, Texas, May 2014

I'm sitting on the doorstep and in the heat my hands are sticking to the keyboard. I have cactus prickles in my back that won't come out. I am hosted by Christopher Long and his wife Gia Marie Houck who claim that everyone who comes to Texas has to be photographed by a cactus. And almost everyone gets pricked. I am cooling myself with a glass of ice water and deciphering the letters. I still don't know what Sammer looked like. Again, I attempt to identify him in a photograph of people immersed in a pool somewhere in India. On the monitor I enlarge the head of one of them. Could that be him? Christopher claims it is. Look, the wet, smiling man has ears like the child in the studio photograph from the archive in Pilsen!

Is this, then, the only remaining photo of Sammer? Surely, he has some relatives, someone who's survived him, some family that didn't burn everything after he died. That has happened before, a few years ago, when I was researching another architect. For years I had been talking with his relatives, who, one suitcase after another, one envelope after another, gradually burned almost all his papers. They didn't have good memories of him.

How was Sammer remembered by those closest to him? I can't resist the temptation and open an online telephone directory. I look for all the Sammers in Pilsen and the surrounding area. There are about five of them. Better than a hundred or none. When I'm back in the Czech Republic, I'll ring them all. Now, I prefer to look at the cacti in the garden. I'm sweating. I'll wait to see if a deer passes by like yesterday.

Most of all, I'd like to take shelter in the cool of the air-conditioned house, but for a while longer I stare at the letters. Suddenly, I see it. For some people he's František and for others François. As soon as he's away from home, he's usually François. When I google 'François Sammer', completely new information turns up, another angle, a different portrait of the man. Specific works, details about his life, photo-

> František Sammer (third from the left) with friends at a pool in Pondicherry. Written on the back: Robert, Gabriel, François, [Févert], Yvette, Debost. Souvenir de 1940! AMP.

graphs. These traces don't lead to Paris or even to Prague or Pilsen. Most of the recollections and documents related to Sammer were published in India. It is probably even hotter there now than in Texas.

They're here. Deer and their young. They try to bite through the cactus to the water inside. I observe them, motionless, and remain glued to the keyboard. I cannot dream that in less than two years I will be sweating even more. On the other side of the world. In places where there is no air-conditioning, and where, instead of deer, wild dogs and holy cows gobble up the last scraps.

Libeň, Prague,
June 2014

Now's the time. Again, I open up a telephone directory on Google and ring the first number with the surname Sammer. Bull's-eye, right from the start. Yes, we live in Pilsen, at the Slovany housing estate, which was built by our uncle. His son will be able to tell you more. He lives in Prague. Here's his phone number. The baton is passed. I ring the son and make an appointment to meet.

He makes his living as a train driver. The freight railway station in the Prague district of Žižkov. I'm a train enthusiast, says Sammer's son Petr, who sometimes calls himself Hubička the train dispatcher, after the character from the Czechoslovak film, which won an Oscar in 1967. Hubička from *Closely Watched Trains* was a dispatcher at a small railway station. Petr Sammer also spends his free time with trains and tracks. He builds models and then takes them to conventions and competitions. He was 17 when his father died. An only child, a beloved son, whom his father told about his travels instead of bedtime stories.

Yes, yes, at Le Corbusier's he was very close to a young woman, Charlotte Perriand, who designed the reclining lounge chair. Dad told me about that again and again, how she came up with it; he drew me the details. Agnes Larsen, yes. He lived with her at the time. And does the name Jane West mean anything to you? He also got along well with her. During the war he fought in Burma. He was working on a construction of a big bridge over the River Shanga. The Japanese shot him in the lungs and it took a year before he got to a doctor. In order to survive he had a mongoose in his tent. The little carnivore saved him from venomous snakes. India? His whole life he wanted to return there. It broke him. That's also why he died early, because he could no longer go to India. I have his watch with a watchband stained from sweating in the jungle, a silver cigarette case with a dragon, a medal for valour and also a pebble from Pondicherry. Each of us had one, explains Petr. Shortly before the death of his father, and then his mother, their pebbles cracked apart. This one is mine, the only one still whole.

What if this is all just a dream? Am I watching *The Bridge on the River Kwai* or *Casablanca* or am I reading Kipling?

To:
Sri Aurobindo Ashram Archives Pondicherry, India,
July 2014

For the first time in my life, I am writing to India. I don't know whether to write in English or whether anyone will answer my email. I am writing to the Sri Aurobindo Ashram Archives in Pondicherry, looking for another piece of the mosaic. I am asking about documents related to Sammer.

He lived in Pondicherry for four years, where, until he signed up with the British Army, he supervised the building of a dormitory designed by the Czech architect Antonin Raymond. From the letters in Pilsen, I knew that this experience was vitally important for him. The head of the ashram wrote to him until the end of his life and he always wanted to return to India. There must be something in the ashram, at least the letters that he wrote to the people closest to him after he left.

Pondicherry. Puducherry. Pondy. Sri Aurobindo. Sri Sri bindo. The words run through my head and I cannot free myself of them. A former French colony on the south-east coast of India, a bit above Sri Lanka. Sri Aurobindo was a philosopher and a spiritual leader, an icon of the hippies in the 1960s. He founded the ashram, which has operated for almost a hundred years. For a few decades now, his legacy has also been preserved by a large archive.

Sammer's name is well known in Pondy. But they do not have anything special related to him. I ask them to look. I am convinced that there must be something there, somewhere. A few days later comes a reply.

Letter from Pondicherry,
July 2014

Dear Martina,
Our Research Library has a box of miscellaneous material from Sammer. [...] It includes some correspondence as well as photographs and postcards from his travels. The correspondence appears to be mostly in Czech. [...] This could conceivably be a missing link in your research. [...] If you think this material will be important for your research, it would certainly be best if you could come here on a research trip. [...] In any case, your feedback about the content and value of this material will be helpful for us in deciding how to treat it. Until now the box has been stored in a secondary collection and 'Sammer' has been listed in our database with no further information.

They did the work. They searched the repositories outside the main archive. It took two days, and in the mildewy cabinets in an old non-air-conditioned building on the edge of the white colonial city, they found BOX 1061. Those are Sammer's things, documents and letters. Almost all of them are in Czech, so no one in Pondy probably understands their contents. They can scan some material, but with things that are unimportant for the ashram that could be more difficult.

[...] The photographs would be more of a problem. I think you would have to come here in person to look through them all. [...] We have envelopes full of hundreds of pictures – and none of these seem to have been taken while Sammer was at the Ashram. We are hardly in a position even to evaluate which ones are significant. Many of them are quite tiny. [...] Pictures of people are mixed with pictures of places including a number of postcards. Glancing through them I noticed pictures that appear to have been taken in Greece, Egypt, the US and India. The person and/or place are sometimes identified on the back and they are occasionally dated – I noticed a few dates from 1931 to 1937.

Regards,
Richard Hartz

The material is not connected with the ashram and there is a lot of it. That makes it complicated.

Valencia to Barcelona,
November 2015

A motorway along the sea. From the coach I catch shards of a blurry horizon. I am travelling from Valencia, where there was a big conference. Fifty years since the death of Le Corbusier; it is a peculiar reason for celebrations. Two days, dozens of papers in three parallel panels, shoulder to shoulder, one expert next to another. Corbu's eyeglasses signpost the way to the canteen and the lavatories. It is a world unto itself, another planet, perhaps even a galaxy.

But not even Le Corbusier operated alone in his universe. He was surrounded by people and in the 1930s a camera was often present amongst them. It never ceases to amaze me how one person could set in motion such a strong whirlwind. During his life and also after his death. With his work he covered the whole world, from Europe to South America, and to Africa and Asia, 'La planète comme chantier' – 'The planet as a building site', that is, among other terms, how Jean-Louis Cohen analyzed his work.

Le Corbusier was also in Spain, and Spaniards worked for him. The great Josep Lluís Sert – Sammer knew him well too.

A warm reception by my friend Sert. Trips to the surrounding area, fish and crabs and grapes and oranges for lunch, the best things I have ever eaten in my whole life.

Thus wrote Sammer from his travels around Spain. In Valencia he gained an inkling of Andalusia. And Barcelona? That was *functioning disorder and filthy splendour*. The mosaic is being put together, but is still incomplete. What Sammer took photographs of there and what he read in the letters from his native Pilsen are things I will learn only later.

On board a Boeing, Prague–Dubai–Chennai,
5 January 2016

I never wanted to go to India. During the last two years, however, everything has suggested that it would inevitably happen. Fifty of the 250 pages of my PhD thesis are about Sammer. Though almost no one knows about him, he was truly the most important of all the Czechs who worked for Le Corbusier. If I didn't have that plane ticket, I would never have finished writing it. To fetch the copies of my thesis in their

still-warm bindings I waded through freshly fallen snow. This morning in the snowstorm I handed them in at the university.

Outside it is freezing and I, in haste, am throwing tropical gear into my suitcase. It's absurd. I barely made it to the airport on time. I am wearing white trousers, carrying a straw hat in my hand, and through a frosted-over window I am looking at a rabbit hopping in the snow along the runway. I would rather be cross-country skiing. I feel a mixture of curiosity, fear and a sense of unlimited freedom.

We are flying into the sun. From the dark into the dawn. Green hills. Dusty land. Roofs of houses. Unending roofs of houses. Amongst them, tall palms are swaying from side to side. It looks like it's windy. Sammer sailed here aboard a ship. From Japan via Indonesia. He saw Angkor Wat, Sri Lanka and landed right at Pondy. I should have travelled by ship too or by train or even on a bike. The slower the better. Maybe then the shock would not have been so great.

**Golconde, Pondicherry,
6 January 2016**

Outside, inside. Two different worlds separated by an inconspicuous wall. I get out of the taxi with the large silver suitcase, which I also had in Texas. Curious and full of expectations, I knock on the large wooden door which has a carved lotus in the middle. A zone of peace and quiet opens up, I hear the murmuring of water and feel the cool stone under bare feet. A gentle wind plays with the white robes. I am not sure what is the bigger shock. The racket in the streets or the calm in the souls of my hosts.

**Golconde, Pondicherry,
8 January 2016**

I've brought with me a toy by Ladislav Sutnar, a Czech avant-garde designer. A wooden elephant. A gift to Richard in return for his having found the box and inviting me here.

∧ Antonin Raymond, the Golconde dormitory (1937–45). View from the northeast, with an entrance on the right side. Pondicherry, 2016. Photo: Martina Hrabová.

⌄ The author, with the opened box of documents that Sammer left in Pondicherry in 1942, when he enlisted in the British Army. Pondicherry, 2016. Photo: Eda Kriseová.

Martina Hrabová | The Research Diary

∧ The repository of the Sri Aurobindo Ashram Archive (SAAA), a building without climate control, located outside the main ashram grounds. Pondicherry 2016. Photo: Martina Hrabová.

> Golconde, inner garden. Photo on a postcard from Mona Pinto in Pondicherry to František Sammer in Pilsen, on 1 October 1968. Private collection.

There's something else here too. In Pilsen there are letters from Mother, the spiritual leader of the ashram. She and Sammer wrote to each other throughout their lives and both of them died in the same year. I show Richard digital copies of the letters. When he sees the sacred handwriting, he cannot hide the fact that he is moved. He thought that he knew all the preserved documents. You have brought us more than we can give to you. From this moment we shall entrust you with everything that relates to Sammer. We shall do everything to help you find what you need.

Sri Aurobindo Ashram Archives, Pondicherry
9 January 2016

I enter the courtyard of the old colonial building. A Bengal woman is quietly sweeping the floor with a reed broom. I go upstairs, where Mother used to live. On the table is a brick-red paper box: 10112 SAMMER (Golconde's architect) IN BOX 1061 is written on the label.

> The box containing František Sammer's papers in Pondicherry, 2016. SAAA. Photo: Martina Hrabová.

Bay of Bengal, view from the fishing village of Vaithikuppam. Pondicherry, 2016. Photo: Martina Hrabová.

I feel a bit weak in the knees. I decide it's better to go out and get some air, to go for a walk by the Bay of Bengal. A strong wind from the ocean is causing the waves to swell and the palms to bend, the colourful saris to flutter. It took me several days before I could open the box. For a long time I just couldn't do it. That's when Eda Kriseová came in, while visiting Pondicherry during her trip around India. Her father worked with Sammer in Pilsen after the war. He was his closest friend in Czechoslovakia. Eda has been fond of Sammer since her childhood, when he used to tell her his views on life and his memories, especially those of Japan and India. A journalist and novelist, she was an active dissident during the later years of the Communist regime. After the fall of the regime in 1989, she became an adviser to Václav Havel, the new president. Today, she is constantly asking about that box. Have you seen it yet? What's in it? When will you show it to me? The box, the box, a pox on the box!

> Cigar box from Madras (today, Chennai), in which Sammer kept his photograph collection. SAAA. Photo: Martina Hrabová.
> Letters from Sammer's father, deposited for decades in the SAAA. Photo: Martina Hrabová.

**Pondicherry,
13 January 2016**

Eda is lying on the sofa and slowly nibbling a biscuit. She's exhausted. Emotionally. It's that box. It contains letters. Photos. Documents. Sammer's father was strange. He writes like a psychopath. Did you know that Sammer and Agnes were expecting a child? She had a miscarriage, probably while still in Russia. Martina, how do you deal with this? Badly. I told you already that for several days I couldn't even open it.

In Pilsen there are mainly things that Sammer sent home. What they sent him from home was kept in Pondicherry. In the damp cabinets by the Bay of Bengal for more than 70 years, there were family photos from Pilsen, girls in a canoe on the River Radbuza, photos from ski trips in the Giant Mountains in north Bohemia and letters as well. The other side of the story. Another piece of the mosaic.

If I hadn't come here, I wouldn't have seen the chaotic handwriting of Sammer's father or the sweet notes of his younger brother, Jenda (Jan). I wouldn't have found the missing pieces in the mosaic of the places or segments of the timeline in Sammer's life between the two world wars. I wouldn't have known the way he or Agnes or almost anyone whom I knew from the Pilsen letters actually looked. If I hadn't come here, I would never have been handed the cigar box from Madras. A box

Martina Hrabová | The Research Diary

^ Matrimandir, spiritual centre of Auroville, an experimental township near Pondicherry, founded in 1968. Auroville, 2016. Photo: Martina Hrabová.
> Family photos from Czechoslovakia: the family in the grass, swimming, and a skier. The inscription on the back of the last photo reads: '27 March 1931. At the peak of Javor. If the lady [Agnes] understands skiing, then she must immediately see from this photo that [our friend] Olda is a champ'. All photographs, 7.9 × 5.4 cm. SAAA.

in a box. Containing envelopes and other boxes. With photos in them. Hundreds of miniature photos. People, places, glimmers of atmosphere, hard to say from where exactly and why. Sammer travelled to many countries, knew lots of people, photographed randomly, casually, as if he weren't really taking photographs. Can it even be that an architect travels the whole world and hardly takes a photograph of a single building? What sort of shots are they and who actually took them? Was he even there, or did somebody else send these photos by post? How am I supposed to understand the contents of these boxes within boxes? Isn't this a set-up for some kind of joke?

**Auroville,
February 2016**

I am travelling through villages and towns without end, one blends into the other, with no distinguishable boundary. Dusty red soil. There was previously nothing here but parched earth everywhere. Until Mother founded Auroville. A city on the plan of a galaxy. Everyone is equal and they have come from every corner of the world. Utopia in practice. Boullée, Ledoux and even Buckminster Fuller would be amazed.

A golden globe in the very centre forced its way out of the parched earth, clad in gold leaf. Matrimandir. Only the initiated can enter. I was taken there by Vilas. A happy coincidence, I said. No coincidence, she replied. That's how it was meant to be. A solemn approach, entering, moving in a spiral and a breath-taking core. People from everywhere come here to experience silence around a common centre. Much more than silence.

**Pondicherry,
3 February 2016**

My departure day is approaching. Most of my stay I spent in bed with dengue fever and now I have a suspicious stomach ache. Apparently, illness did not occur to Ray-

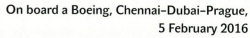

mond when he designed Golconde without a perimeter wall that would seal it off from the surrounding world. The building stands by the municipal sewers and the walls are made of moveable jalousies. Marvellous ventilation, natural air-conditioning, but one really cannot put netting there to keep out insects. The toilets and bathrooms are slap bang in the middle. Right where the long wings of the longitudinal building meet. In a magnificent room at the end of one of the residential wings I experience true harmony of proportions. But feeling ill here is not a good idea. That has been whispered in the town since time immemorial and I did not want to give it a try.

**On board a Boeing, Chennai–Dubai–Prague,
5 February 2016**

I got on board thanks to Eda. And thanks to a letter from Dr Pandey, who persuaded the employees of the airport that I was fit to fly. And also thanks to Yogi. He had never seen me before, but he took time off work to get me safely to the airport. Three hours in a late-night taxi, glimmers of shacks, little groups of people, palms and animals in the flames of fires lit on the dusty road.

In my pocket I have a small envelope with a concealed blessing from Mother and, in a fever, I see the silver suitcase vanishing on the check-in conveyor. Now the smiling team of Emirates airline employees will no longer be able to get rid of me. I count the minutes of the unending flight. Eda bravely passes the time with stories of India, Czech dissidents from Communist times and other jungles. Václav Havel Airport, Prague. I wrap myself up in my winter coat. For the first time in my life, I experience a feeling of the happiness of returning to my native land.

**The Czech Republic,
Summer 2016**

Ever since I have been assembling the Sammer mosaic, I have seen a book. First it was a novel. But now there are photos. A story in pictures. I am always being asked: *What do the photos look like? What is their nature?*

Well, it's hard to say… Actually, they aren't even very nice. They are not art nor do they make a documentary… Often, it's impossible to say what's on them…

What did he take them with? What period is the camera from?

Some cheap camera from the 1930s, though possibly he had two… a better one in reserve, for better shots. He took photographs on film and made contact sheets himself, on the move, during his travels, as it was done in those days.

What is interesting about them?

They form a picture. At once a personal diary and a portrait of the times. Sammer travelled where his friends from Le Corbusier's atelier travelled. He photographed the same things they photographed. Those photographs contain the nodes of a mutually linked people. The nodes of the widespread network of the avant-garde from the times between the two world wars, which link all the continents.

**Hranice na Moravě,
15 August 2016**

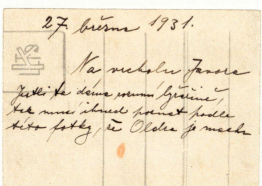

For half a day my relatives and I have been trying to place the bases of the columns. They are the only part of the church that Sammer recorded. The banister on which kids slide down, and the bases. It is St Petersburg. Shapes, openings, and the glazing of windows, the utility poles, cars, ships, trains, buses, streets, shop windows, the marketplace, paving, clothing, interiors, and ambience. We clutch at anything that could indicate the time and place of the photographs. Hundreds of photographs.

It is like an addictive game. Each photograph surely must have a sign that makes identification possible. We project enlargements on the wall and at the same time search for anything similar on the web. Phones, tablets, computers at the ready. My cousin Jurriën van Duijkeren and his wife Inara Nevskaya are architects and according to them this game is a favourite in their profession. The more concealed the identifying features, the greater the triumph when the architect is able to figure out the building, time or place.

That's amazing! Sammer is in Moscow. He's standing on Pushkin Square. To his left is the Izvestia Building, in front of him is a Russian Orthodox church, a Pushkin monument and an unknown boy in knee socks. Would somebody please explain to me how an architect could photograph a boy in knee socks instead of the Izvestia Building?

Jurriën is angry. He can't understand it. Just as he can't understand the fish in the water, an empty meadow beside a Japanese temple and the pile of blurry coast photographed from a ship. Surely an architect doesn't travel to be able to bring this back as a souvenir.

And what if he does?

What if he had bought a postcard of the Izvestia Building, or already had it in photographs in magazines and books? If it interested him, he could sketch it. Like any artist who thinks and even observes the world around him with his hands in a certain way. Le Corbusier did it the same way.

**Architekturzentrum Wien,
14 October 2016**

I'm looking around the bookshop. So many new books, as ever. They have a table and chairs here; I can sit down and leaf through publications. I take a five-kilogram book, one of the four volumes of Charlotte Perriand's collected works. I look through the chapter about the life of this designer in the 1930s and I see a man covered in sand. Pierre Jeanneret on the beach, photographed by Charlotte Perriand. I know this photo. I saw it in the box!

I continue leafing through the book. Charlotte's studio at Montparnasse. A bedroom, pictures on the wall, a fur on the bed, a shirt and a hat in a partly opened cupboard, the *fauteuil grand confort*, just sink into it. A model of a hotel in the mountains, tunas in a barge, Charlotte cooking in the kitchen. All of that is in the box. With the one difference – in India these photos were preserved with captions for Sammer.

À mon ami Sammer – Les lavages de la cuisine, tu te rappelles?
To my friend Sammer – Cleaning the kitchen, do you remember?

What other photographs from the box were taken by Charlotte? Which ones were taken by Pierre Jeanneret and which ones by other friends? Is there anything even by Le Corbusier? Which ones in the box are originals and which ones are copies? What did Sammer photograph and what was sent to him by friends? How can I tell who actually stood behind the camera, who pressed the shutter release?

**Café Beaubourg, Paris,
23 November 2016**

Tim Benton is sitting upstairs. We are meeting before the conference. Le Corbusier and politics, a jack-in-the-box, sealed up for a long time. Let's discuss something else. You found what in India?

Photos that no one has seen yet. With the exception, that is, of those who know them from elsewhere. For instance, the ones Charlotte Perriand used to send to

Sammer. He wanted her to work with him in Moscow. Or that they would at least go on holiday together. They wrote letters to each other, advising each other about work and about life.

Pêches, raisins, bon petit bain dans les vagues [...] Ça ne te dis rien? Au pieds, avec tant et toutes les autres choses sur le dos. –
Peaches, grapes, a bit of nice swimming in the waves [...] Does it remind you of something? On foot, with so many things and everything on our backs.

Sammer was the first of them to go to Japan. *Everything here has its own inner life and it is nature where everything takes place [...] Remember, it's something to be alive for!*
He wrote to Paris, without an inkling of what Japan would later mean to Charlotte.

Follow the technical traces on the photographs, Tim advises. The damage to the shot in places where the negative was held in the camera. Notice the optics, the focus, the shutter speed. Charlotte also took photographs. Pierre and Le Corbusier too. In this way, they explored shapes, objects and nature, mainly in the 1930s. The photographs were studies, material to build on. This is different. A personal diary, a network, an image of a social network. The recording of memories before they escape. A trace of time, which is always flying.

Archives Charlotte Perriand, 15 rue Las Cases, Paris, 30 November 2016

A sunny morning. Coffee ran out and there wasn't time get some more. What can we do for you? I know about someone who was close to Charlotte. They fought together for the same cause; they used to see each other in the 1930s and corresponded by post. Paris–Moscow–Tokyo, that is what interested them both. It was like a family bonded by shared ideas. People connected forever, despite distances and regimes. I am looking for photos. I need to find out which ones are by Charlotte, by Pierre or by Le Corbusier. I need to put together the mosaic, to find the nodes of the network, to see the links between people who at that time were fighting for a new world.

It is like a detective novel, a story of a search, one full of suspense. An ashram in India. A forgotten box containing traces of great figures of history. From all corners of the world, they met in one cigar box from Madras. From the time they were left there, they remained in a musty cupboard. It could have been devoured by mould, swept away by a tsunami, torn to shreds by a gale. Both stories have to be heard. The research and the history. The box as a book. Yes, it is a book. Now it just needs to be read.

| František Sammer, 1930s. Contact print, 6 × 8.5 cm. SAAA.

The Le Corbusier Galaxy

The Le Corbusier Galaxy

'We're still old friends – Le Corbusier, Jeanneret, Charlotte Perriand, Sert and his wife and many others, including Sakakura and Adam. Paris is still beautiful and exciting; we are gradually encountering all the beauty we knew before'.[1] These words were written in 1937 by the architect František Sammer (1907–73) in a letter to his parents in his native Czechoslovakia. At that time he had already been working for four years in the Soviet Union, and he would soon depart for an architectural office in Tokyo. In 1937 he went to Paris to see a building site at the Exposition internationale des arts et des techniques dans la vie moderne, to join in the atelier's work and to meet with people who had been close to him from the start of his career. His contact address was, as always, Charlotte Perriand's studio in Montparnasse or 'at the well-known address Le Corbusier–Jeanneret, 35 rue de Sèvres, Paris 6e'.[2]

Almost continuously from 1924 to 1965, this was the address of the atelier[3] led by Le Corbusier (1887–1965), who perceived his projects as laboratory experiments and saw creating as the process of a 'patient search'. Le Corbusier however, was not alone in this search; he was continuously looking for inspiration and would not have managed without his closest colleagues. From almost the very beginning, between the two world wars, the atelier was in fact run by him and his cousin, Pierre Jeanneret (1896–1967),[4] or 'Pierre le silencieux', as he was later called by the critic-historian Sigfried Giedion.[5] Charlotte Perriand (1903–99) soon joined the small team, and was in charge of interiors.[6] The operation of the atelier in the period between the two world wars is inextricably linked with these figures. One of the aims of this book is to contribute to our knowledge of the atelier. After the Second World War, the organization of work at 35 rue de Sèvres changed significantly, but, just as in its early years, the atelier still needed the work of dozens of young volunteer assistants from around the world.

Perhaps it was also because Le Corbusier himself had come to Paris from another country, Switzerland, that he welcomed new arrivals of all nationalities. He thus created a base for the emergence of an international community, whose members were linked not only by their approach to the profession, but also by their view of the world and ideas about how to live life. Le Corbusier later described the atelier as a 'meeting place, through which passed, over the years, almost 200 young architects from the four corners of the world'.[7] Young architects worked there, mostly without salary, having come from France, Switzerland, Czechoslovakia, Yugoslavia, Hungary, Japan, the Netherlands, Belgium, Greece, Germany, Scandinavia, North and South America. A complete list, with commentary, of all Le Corbusier's assistants has yet

> Snapshot from the Le Corbusier–Jeanneret atelier, c.1929. From the left: Ernest Weissmann, Le Corbusier, Nikolai Kolli, Albert Frey, an unidentified man, Charlotte Perriand, Pierre Jeanneret. Archives Charlotte Perriand, Paris (AChP).

---

1 | Archiv města Plzně (City of Pilsen Archives – AMP), František Sammer Papers, letter to his parents, 30 January 1937. Among the friends Sammer mentions are Le Corbusier, Pierre Jeanneret, Charlotte Perriand, Josep Lluís Sert, Muncha Sert, Junzo Sakakura and Alex Adam.
2 | Ibid. The address in the letter, 35 rue de Sèvres, sometimes abbreviated to '35S', became synonymous with the Le Corbusier atelier.
3 | Le Corbusier usually called the place where he worked his *atelier* in the sense used by a sculptor, painter or group of artisans led by a master, and that is the reason why I use the word throughout this book instead of architectural practice or the more common names office or studio. For more on the term *atelier* in connection with Le Corbusier's practice, see Marc Bédarida, 'Une journée au 35S', in Roger Aujame et al., *Le Corbusier, Moments biographiques: XIVe Rencontres de la Fondation Le Corbusier*, Paris: La Villette, 2008, p. 28.
4 | Pierre Jeanneret, Le Corbusier's right hand man, helped to run the atelier at 35 rue de Sèvres from 1924 to 1940. A book providing a comprehensive picture of Jeanneret and his work has yet to be written. What we do know about him comes from a variety of sources, for instance, posthumous contributions published in *L'Architecture d'Aujourd'hui*, no. 136, February–March 1968, pp. V-XII, and 'Hommage à Pierre Jeanneret', *Werk: Schweizer Monatsschrift für Architektur, Kunst und künstlerisches Gewerbe* VI, 1968, pp. 377-96. See also Hélène Bauchet-Cauquil and Françoise-Claire Prodhon, *Le Corbusier, Pierre Jeanneret: Chandigarh, India 1951-66*, Paris: Galerie Patrick Seguin, 1987 or Hélène Cauquil, 'Pierre, l'autre Jeanneret', in Hélène Cauquil and Marc Bédarida (eds), *Le Corbusier: l'atelier 35 rue de Sèvres. Bulletin d'Informations Architecturales*, Paris: Institut français d'architecture, 1987, pp. 4-8; and Catherine Courtiau, 'Jeanneret (Pierre)', in Jacques Lucan (ed.), *Le Corbusier, une encyclopédie*, Paris: Centre Georges Pompidou, 1987, p. 213. The architectural historian Maristella Casciato has long made the life and work of Pierre Jeanneret a subject of her research, and her new book *Le Corbusier Album Punjab, 1951*, Zurich: Lars Müller, 2024, includes numerous photographs by Jeanneret.
5 | Sigfried Giedion, 'Hommage à Pierre Jeanneret', p. V.
6 | Charlotte Perriand worked in the Le Corbusier–Jeanneret atelier from 1927 to 1937, where, in particular, she was in charge of designing interiors. For a good, though not always reliable, source of information, see her autobiography, *Une vie de création*, Paris: Odile Jacob, 1998. For scholarly works, see Mary McLeod (ed.), *Charlotte Perriand: An Art of Living*, New York: H. N. Abrams in association with the Architectural League of New York, 2003, or the later four volumes of Jacques Barsac, *Charlotte Perriand: L'Œuvre Complète*, 4 vols, Paris: Éditions Norma, Archives Charlotte Pérriand, 2014-19.
7 | 'Mon atelier de la rue de Sèvres s'est trouvé être le centre de ralliement, au cours des années, de près de deux cents jeunes architectes venus des quatre horizons de la planète'. Le Corbusier, 'Entretien avec les étudiants des écoles d'Architecture', in Le Corbusier, *La Charte d'Athènes*, Paris: Éditions de Minuit, 1957, p. 183.

to be made, but the names of many of the people involved, including the approximate times they worked there and identifying information, is available at the Fondation Le Corbusier in the 'Répertoire des collaborateurs' (List of assistants).[8] Some of them only stayed at 35 rue de Sèvres for a short while and were not so involved in the work there. Others gave the atelier their all and became fully-fledged members of the creative team.[9]

Perriand once described the milieu of the atelier as the 'galaxie Le Corbusier'.[10] If we look at the basic definition of the term in astronomy, we see that a galaxy is a gravitationally-bound system of stars and other components that orbits a common core. The individual parts are in motion, but always keep in relation to each other and to the core.[11] I suggest comparing the basic principle of a galaxy to the operation of a network of people. In this case, it is the circle of architects and designers joined together by the milieu of the Le Corbusier–Jeanneret atelier.[12] We may see the core as Le Corbusier's charismatic personality, together with the atelier at 35 rue de Sèvres, and the galaxy, the system of stars, as the people who orbited around him, drawn by his powerful gravitational field. Following Perriand's metaphor, I thus take the liberty of calling this social unit the 'Le Corbusier galaxy'. Using the Czech architect František Sammer as my main example, I shall try to show that this galaxy was an exceptionally vibrant unit, which remained functional even after the departure of its individual members from the atelier, regardless of geographical distance, the flow of time and the fundamental twists and turns in the history of the twentieth century.

'Livre noir'

Precious few documents remain that would help us to understand how the Le Corbusier–Jeanneret atelier operated in the years between the two world wars.[13] One valuable source of such information is the so-called 'Livre noir' (Black Book), in which the finished architectural drawings at the atelier were entered.[14] Beginning in February 1929, each drawing was entered with a number, the date, a description of the assignment and the name of the draughtsman. On the basis of the records of the individual working days, one can begin to understand the approach taken on specific projects and the various ways in which these projects were interlinked. The 'Livre noir' helps to understand how various designs came into being together on one drawing board and which draughtsman collaborated on which projects. The historian Tim Benton has compared the conceptual interconnectedness of the sheets of paper in the atelier at 35 rue de Sèvres to the uncovering of archaeological layers.[15] In these layers is concealed the creative process that took place behind Le Corbusier's projects. At the same time, one can begin to detect the traces of the architects who developed the conceptual sketches, step by step, layer by layer, all the way to their actually being carried out.

The involvement of young architects from Czechoslovakia was considerably helped by the atmosphere of the newly-founded republic, the excellent political and cultural relations between France and Czechoslovakia and also the francophone orientation of Czechoslovak intellectuals. Czechoslovaks were amongst the first assistants at the Le Corbusier–Jeanneret atelier and were present there almost continuously until the Communists seized power in Czechoslovakia in early 1948. At the very beginning of the atelier in the mid-1920s, for example, Karel Stráník and Vladimír Karfík, who would later be renowned architects, joined the atelier. Then, a few years later came Eugen (Evžen, Eugene) Rosenberg and Jan Sokol. Of the lesser-known, though no less important, architects I must also mention Josef Danda, Jan Reiner, Vladimír Beneš and the sole Czech woman assistant at 35 rue de Sèvres, Magda Jansová. Shortly after the Second World War, Jaroslav Vaculík and Václav Rajniš began work-

^ Envelope of a letter from Sammer's family in Pilsen addessed to him at the Le Corbusier–Jeanneret atelier, 35 rue de Sèvres. Private archive.

> The 'Livre noir' and a page with the registration of drawings made by Sammer. The abbreviations CR, B, DAL and CU indicate parallel work on the projects for the Cité de refuge (of the Salvation Army), the apartment house at 24 rue Nungesser-et-Coli in Boulogne-Billancourt, an urban plan for Algiers, and the Pavillon Suisse in the Cité internationale universitaire de Paris. FLC S1-(16)1-56.

---

[8] Fondation Le Corbusier, Paris (FLC), 'Répertoire des collaborateurs de Le Corbusier ayant travaillé à l'atelier 35 rue de Sèvres ainsi qu'aux travaux executés à l'étranger'. Hereafter I will refer to the source as to the 'Répertoire des collaborateurs'.
[9] The special ambience of the Paris atelier and the way Le Corbusier worked in the 1920s and 1930s is also discussed in detail in Martina Hrabová, 'Mýtus a realita: čeští asistenti Le Corbusiera 1924-1937', PhD diss., Charles University, Prague, 2016. For further literature, see n. 13.
[10] Perriand, Une vie de création (n. 6), p. 36: 'Je ne pus plus m'impliquer totalement, trop absorbée par la galaxie Le Corbusier'. Perriand writes this in connection with the initiatives of the Union des artistes modernes, which she participated in, though not intensely, because at the time she was completely absorbed by the 'galaxie Le Corbusier'.
[11] Ian Ridpath (ed.), Oxford Dictionary of Astronomy, Oxford; New York: Oxford University Press, 1997, pp. 180-81. For details about the origin, laws and variability of galaxies, see Paul Murdin (ed.), Encyclopedia of Astronomy and Astrophysics, vol. 1, Bristol; London: Institute of Physics, 2001, pp. 861-908.
[11] Ian Ridpath (ed.), Oxford Dictionary of Astronomy, Oxford, New York: Oxford University Press, 1997, pp. 180-81. For details about the origin, laws, and variability of galaxies, see Paul Murdin (ed.), Encyclopedia of Astronomy and Astrophysics, vol. 1, Bristol and London: Institute of Physics, 2001, pp. 861-908.
[12] I use the term 'the Le Corbusier–Jeanneret atelier' as it is widely used when discussing the atelier that operated between the two world wars.
[13] For the organization and approach to work at 35 rue de Sèvres, see Cauquil - Bédarida (eds), Le Corbusier: l'atelier 35 rue de Sèvres, (n. 4). For his recommendations and providing me with publications, I am indebted to Jean-Louis Cohen. The lack of sources on its inter-war years has been pointed out by the British historian Judi Loach, who has done extensive research on the atelier in the post-war period. See Judi Loach, 'Studio as Laboratory', The Architectural Review, January 1987, pp. 73-77, id., 'L'Atelier Le Corbusier: Un centre européen d'échanges', Monu-

ments historiques, no. 180, 1992, pp. 49-52. For the details of the operation of the atelier, see Jerzy Soltan, 'Working with Le Corbusier', in H. Allen Brooks (ed.), *Le Corbusier*, Princeton: Princeton University Press 1987, pp. 1-16; Gordon Stephenson, 'Chapters of Autobiography I–III', *The Town Planning Review* 62, no. 1, January 1991, pp. 7-36; and, most recently, Maristella Casciato, '35 rue de Sèvres: At Work in the Atelier', in Jean-Louis Cohen (ed.), *Le Corbusier: An Atlas of Modern Landscapes* (exh. cat.), New York: The Museum of Modern Art, 2013, pp. 240-46. For the approach to work at the Le Corbusier-Jeanneret atelier in the period between the wars, see also Hrabová, 'Mýtus a realita' (n. 9).

14| FLC, 'Livre noir'. This is sometimes cited as the 'Cahier noir' or the 'Black Book' or even the 'Log Book'. For her having brought my attention to the importance of this source and for her other help in my research, I am indebted to Mary McLeod.

15| Tim Benton, 'Drawings and Clients: Le Corbusier's Atelier Methodology in the 1920s', *AA Files*, no. 3, January 1983, pp. 42-50. For the application of this methodology, see Benton's pioneering book, *The Villas of Le Corbusier and Pierre Jeanneret, 1920–1930*, 2nd edn., (1987) Basel; Boston; Berlin: Birkhäuser, 2007.

16| Karel Stráník (1899-1987) and Vladimír Karfík (1901-96) worked at 35 rue de Sèvres in 1925 and 1926, Evžen (Eugen, Eugene) Rosenberg (1907-90) and Jan Sokol (1904-87) in 1929, Josef Danda (1906-99) in 1932, Jan Reiner (1909-2010) from 1932 to 1935, Vladimír Beneš (1903-71) from 1936 to 1937. After the war, Václav Rajniš (1907-after 1985) worked there from 1945 to 1946 and Jaroslav Vaculík (1921-95) from 1949 to 1950. For details, see Hrabová, 'Mýtus a realita' (n. 9). For the encounters of Le Corbusier and Czechoslovakia see Martina Hrabová, 'The Many Faces of the Master: Le Corbusier and Czechoslovakia', in Irena Lehkoživová and Joan Oackman (eds.), *Book for Mary: Sixty on Seventy*, Prague; New York: Quatro Print, 2020, pp. 174-87.

17| For a detailed discussion of architects from Czechoslovakia at the Le Corbusier-Jeanneret atelier between the wars and their subsequent professional development, see Hrabová, 'Mýtus a realita' (n. 9).

ing for Le Corbusier.[16] By 1948, when the free movement of Czechoslovak citizens was fundamentally limited by the coming to power of the Communist regime, at least 15 architects from Czechoslovakia had passed through the atelier.[17]

After the Communist takeover, a number of these people faced persecution from the new regime, some of them emigrated and some were able to function in the state-controlled architectural profession for the next few decades. Experience gained in the inter-war Paris atelier was not, from the point of view of the Communist Czechoslovak regime, the most attractive item on one's CV. Few architects could openly discuss their involvement in the avant-garde atelier in Paris without risking their ability to make a living in the profession. All the more valuable, then, is the picture provided by the period records directly documenting events and jobs at 35 rue de Sèvres.

The information in the 'Livre noir' can act as a critical mirror held up to those who have left behind embellished recollections of their professional connection to Le

∧ A number of small-format and uncatalogued photos from Sammer's collection. SAAA. Photo: Martina Hrabová.

> František Sammer, early 1930s. Contact print, 3.2 × 4.5 cm, front and back. SAAA.

Corbusier. Conversely, however, it reveals the importance of assistants we may never have heard of. Amongst the Czech daughtsmen entered in the 'Livre noir' the name, or rather abbreviation, SAM truly stands out. It was used by the Czech architect František Sammer, appearing in the 'Livre noir' next to the biggest projects at the beginning of the 1930s. It features several dozen times, in contrast to those of his compatriots, who were responsible for only a few drawings, if any. Back in his native land after the war, Sammer became established as the architect of one of the first Czech housing estates in the socialist realist style and as an urban planner for the City of Pilsen. For political reasons, however, he could not talk much about his experience of the pre-war years.[18] Sammer's importance in the operation of the Le Corbusier–Jeanneret atelier is confirmed by those entries in the 'Livre noir' and by other documents in the Le Corbusier archive in Paris.[19] Further evidence is found in Sammer's remarkably voluminous, still unpublished, correspondence in archives and collections held in various places around the world. Thanks to a series of happy coincidences, a great number of documents have been preserved, with detailed records about Sammer's inter-war career. They constitute a unique source about the life of this Czech architect and at the same time provide a valuable report on how the international avant-garde operated. Sammer's newly found collection of photographs, preserved deep inside the ashram in Pondicherry, adds considerably to this mosaic of information.[20] The great number of small-format photos, mostly contact prints, breathes life into the historical and occasionally tedious information in written sources, and provides accompanying period illustrations.

[18] For Sammer's international importance, see Martina Hrabová, 'Between Ideal and Ideology: The Parallel Worlds of František Sammer', *Umění* 64, no. 2, 2016, pp. 137–66.

[19] Comprising many thousands of items, the Le Corbusier archive is among the largest collections of personal papers in the history of architecture. Almost all Le Corbusier's personal papers, as well as the archive of the atelier at 35 rue de Sèvres, are in the care of the FLC (Paris).

[20] Sri Aurobindo Ashram Archives, Pondicherry (SAAA), František Sammer Papers. I began analyzing and identifying the photos in the collection in January 2016 when I discovered it during my research stay in Pondicherry, India.

[21] I continue to identify and analyze the photographs in Sammer's collection in my further research.

[22] Sammer attended the Czech State Technical School in Pilsen and two semesters at the Faculty of Architecture and Civil Engineering of the Czech Technical University in Prague (ČVUT). Details of his architectural studies are deposited in the archive of the school: 'Nacionále studentů školy architektury, Archiv ČVUT', Prague. For other biographical information, see the 'Timeline' part of this publication.

[23] In his correspondence Sammer uses different names for Le Corbusier (including Corbu and Corbusiér) and I have preserved these in the quotations.

[24] AMP, František Sammer Papers, Sammer to his parents, 29 April 1931.

[25] The architect Čestmír Rypl (1902–75) is mainly known as a teacher at the Czech State Technical School in Pilsen. There is no trace of him in the records deposited at the FLC; however, his work at the Le Cor-

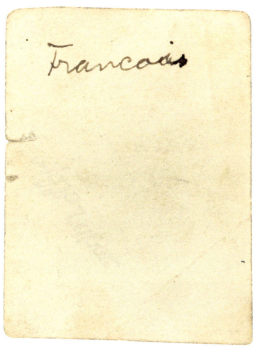

busier–Jeanneret atelier is confirmed by an officially-certified copy of a confirmation of Rypl's practice issued by Le Corbusier and Pierre Jeanneret, held in the private archive in the Czech Republic. According to the Certificat from 10 December 1928, Rypl worked at the 35S from 15 September to 10 December 1928, and assisted on a project of a house in Poissy (Villa Savoye) and some housing projects – 'Il s'est occupé particulièrement des plans pour une maison à Poissy, de ceux pour des immeubles-locatifs à bon marché etc.'. For sharing this information, I am indepted to Petr Klíma.
As Sammer's father remarks in letters, it was Rypl who recommended Sammer to Le Corbusier. SAAA, František Sammer Papers, letters to Sammer from Pilsen, 17 December 1934 and 17 January 1936.
26| AMP, František Sammer Papers, of 27 October 1931.
27| Ibid., Sammer to his aunt (whom he called Auntie Schwarzová, hereafter simply 'Auntie'), 7 January 1931.

Sammer's photograph collection

The collection, comprising about 500 photos taken around the world, is of a completely different nature from that of the written reports in the letters. The photos from Sammer's collection were taken in many countries and contain historically valuable information. However, they can only be properly understood with the help of other documents, especially primary sources. For the scholar they initially represent mysterious ciphers, inciting one to search for the reasons, the when, where, with whom and why these photos were taken. The photos are often difficult to read – sometimes they even seem clumsy and tend to conceal their messages – but as soon as they have been identified, they bring to life a new message and evoke the atmosphere of moments that passed long ago.

The unifying feature of the collection is the fact that Sammer intentionally saved these photos, whether he took them or someone close to him did. They were taken in a limited period of time, from 1931 to 1939. The architect parted with them in 1942, when he enlisted in the British Army in India and left his collection in the safekeeping of the ashram in Pondicherry. This book is neither a technical nor an aesthetic analysis of the discovered photos. Rather it is an attempt to answer some particular questions. Under what circumstances and why was a certain photograph taken? What or who is depicted in the photograph? Who actually pressed the shutter release? But the process of searching and uncovering the layers of content hardly ends here.[21] The current state of knowledge provides especially unusual insight into the dynamic world of the inter-war avant-garde and the network of people connected to the Le Corbusier–Jeanneret atelier in Paris.

35 rue de Sèvres, Paris, 1931

Sammer arrived at the door of the Le Corbusier–Jeanneret atelier in April 1931. He had left Czechoslovakia for Paris without having completed a degree in architecture at the Czech Technical University in Prague,[22] with only rudimentary knowledge of French and no connection to avant-garde art or other intellectual circles. He was chiefly interested in the practice of architecture. In search of new opportunities, people and ideas, he set out straight for the crucible of the international avant-garde, where he began to build a network of friends and future colleagues. 'Today I went to see Corbusier;[23] tomorrow I am going there again. He has to talk about it with Jeanneret',[24] Sammer wrote home immediately after arriving in Paris. Shortly thereafter, he joined the atelier.

He came to 35 rue de Sèvres with a recommendation from Čestmír Rypl, a Pilsen architect who had worked there a few years earlier.[25] Rypl's activity does not appear at all in the records of the atelier, but his introduction of Sammer to Le Corbusier fundamentally influenced the career of his young compatriot. Sammer wanted to get as much experience as possible, to explore the world and, ideally, to find employment abroad. 'I am not going back to Czechoslovakia under any circumstances',[26] he wrote home, not concealing the distaste he felt at the idea of finding a career in his native country. In his reflections about his future, he aimed further, even beyond the borders of France. 'Once I have travelled the whole world, maybe I will choose a better place for life. God knows where that will be. What do you think, Auntie?',[27] Sammer wrote home to Pilsen.

In the Le Corbusier–Jeanneret atelier, the world opened up to Sammer. Instead of staying for several months as he originally planned, he worked there for a full two years, until spring 1933. He eagerly joined the wide range of activities and embraced the efforts to create new types and forms of modern architecture. Along with that, he became part of the community of people who wanted to build a better society by means of this initiative.

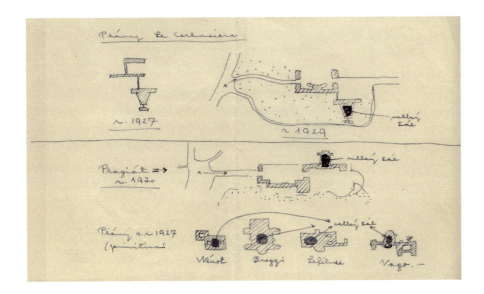

< Drawing showing the development of the designs for the competition for the Palais de la Société des Nations in Geneva, in a letter from Sammer to his parents in Pilsen, 18 July 1931 (see n. 36). AMP.

In the early 1930s the atelier was in its heyday. It had finally succeeded in getting commissions for large projects and Le Corbusier was also conquering the world, travelling and lecturing on every continent.[28] Because of the variety of his activity he spent little time in the atelier and the work there was mainly carried out by his assistants under the supervision of his closest colleagues.

Sammer was 24 years old when he came to the atelier, and already during his first month there he figured out the basic approaches to work, quickly gaining the trust of his 'bosses'. The atelier was busy with a wide variety of tasks that went beyond the usual architectural practice. 'The activity of the individual workers is not precisely specified here, so everybody who wants, has the chance to do everything',[29] Sammer wrote in one of his first letters home. While working on projects and on construction sites, the attention in the atelier was also paid to editorial work, communication with the public and the promotion of Le Corbusier's ideas. Apart from drawing, Sammer helped with the graphic design of the plans and photographs intended for reproduction. He participated in the preparation of the *Plans* periodical, whose production was based in the atelier, and he wrote: 'It is an avant-garde magazine, but very sensible. Le Corbusier is on the editorial staff, too, and we are all a bit flattered that we are at the epicentre and get news first-hand. We make the drawings for it, and the whole office[30] is mad about *Plans*. Of course we have an opportunity to see and hear all the contributors, because in part of our office (which is very long, high and therefore airy and very loosely divided into a reception part and a working part) is the *monde*, where *les plans* for *Plans* are hatched'.[31]

Le Corbusier took part in the publishing of *Plans* from 1931 to 1933 and this periodical, like the earlier *L'Esprit Nouveau*, became the main platform for disseminating his cultural, political and economic views.[32]

Surprisingly early on Le Corbusier began to entrust Sammer with working up his conceptual sketches into drawings. 'I advanced again a bit with Corbusiér. I now make sketches first-hand. It goes like this: I pay attention to Corbus. when he tries to draw his idea freehand on paper. He talks and indicates more than he draws. From that imperfect sketch and lots of notes, I then try to draw the thing without impinging on the idea and so that it can be built. It sometimes entails a lot of reflection, but is very interesting'.[33]

Sammer was given the opportunity to work directly with primary ideas in the form of Le Corbusier's sketches. It is a testimony of the master's trust in his young assistant and a confirmation of his abilities.[34] Sammer's active involvement in the many diverse problems being addressed in the atelier is also demonstrated by his complex orien-

28| See Tim Benton, *Le Corbusier conférencier*, Paris: Moniteur, 2007.
29| AMP, František Sammer Papers, letter to his parents, 26 May 1931.
30| Probably out of habit and in the spirit of common architectural usage Sammer sometimes in Czech calls the atelier at 35 rue de Sèvres 'the office' (*kancelář*). For Le Corbusier's use of the term atelier, see n. 3.
31| AMP, František Sammer Papers, letter to his parents, 30 June 1931.
32| The importance of the *Plans* periodical and its content is discussed by McLeod in the chapter 'Architecture and Revolution: Regional Syndicalism and the Plan' in Mary McLeod, 'Urbanism and Utopia: Le Corbusier from Regional Syndicalism to Vichy', PhD diss., Princeton University, 1985, particularly pp. 108–41. For a thorough overview of authors and topics of the individual issues, see Mary McLeod, 'Plans: Bibliography', in Kenneth Frampton (ed.), 'Le Corbusier 1933–1960', *Oppositions*, nos. 19/20 (Winter/Spring 1980), Cambridge, MA: MIT Press, 1980. More recently, see Mary McLeod, 'Le Corbusier, planification et syndicalisme régionale', in Rémi Baudouï (ed.), *Le Corbusier 1930-2020: Polémiques, histoire et mémoire*, Paris: Tallandier, 2020, pp. 203–23.
33| AMP, František Sammer Papers, letter to his parents, 13 June 1931.
34| For the importance of Le Corbusier's entrusting the drawing of his originally sketched-out ideas to his assistants, discussed in the context of the post-war operation of the atelier, see Loach, 'Studio as Laboratory' (n. 13), p. 74; Marc Bédarida, 'Rue de Sèvres 35: L'Envers du décor', in Lucan (ed.), *Le Corbusier, une Encyclopédie* (n. 4), p. 355. The design process in the inter-war years is examined in depth in Benton, 'Drawings and Clients' (n. 15). Using research on the Czech assistants at rue de Sèvres 35, I discuss in detail the organization of work there in Hrabová, 'Mýtus a realita' (n. 9).
35| Personally examining the terrain in Geneva and the project for the Palais de la Société des Nations served Le Corbusier in 1928 as the

> An interview with Le Corbusier, published in the Prager Presse (see n. 37). Standing in for his boss in Le Corbusier's absence, Sammer replied to the questions asked by the journalist Zdenka Watterson.

starting point for work on the Mundaneum project, a central part of which is known as the Cité Mondiale. In 1929, the Mundaneum became the subject of Le Corbusier's public debate with the Czech avant-garde theorist Karel Teige. For the context of this dispute, see George Baird, 'Introduction to Karel Teige's Mundaneum' (1929) and Le Corbusier's 'In Defense of Architecture' (1933), in *Oppositions 4*, 1974, pp. 80–81; Jean-Louis Cohen, 'Introduction', in Karel Teige, *Modern Architecture in Czechoslovakia and Other Writings*, introduction by Jean-Louis Cohen, translated from Czech by Irena Žantovská Murray and David Britt, Los Angeles, CA: Getty Research Institute, 2000, pp. 1–55; Rostislav Švácha, 'Before and after the Mundaneum: Karel Teige as Theoretician of the Architectural Avant-Garde', in Eric Dluhosch and Rostislav Švácha (eds.), *Karel Teige 1900-1951: L'Enfant Terrible of the Czech Modernist Avant-Garde*, introduction by Kenneth Frampton, Cambridge; London: MIT Press, 1999, pp. 107–39.

36| AMP, František Sammer Papers, letter to his parents, 18 July 1931.

37| Zdenka Watterson (Paris), 'Ein Besuch bei Le Corbusier', *Prager Presse*, 29 May 1932, p. 3. I am most grateful to Irena Lehkoživová for having found this interview and providing it to me. Zdena (Zdenka) Foustková Watterson (1890–80) was one of the few Czech women journalists who made a mark in the inter-war years. An editor of the women's section of the *Prager Presse*, she deserves credit for expanding the range of topics it covered well beyond fashion, seeking contributions on the fine arts, architecture and lifestyle. For more on her and other pre-World War II Czech women journalists, see Lenka Penkalová, 'Rubriky pro ženy v denním tisku 20. let 20. století a jejich autorky: Olga Fastrová, Marie Fantová, Milena Jesenská, Staša Jílovská a Zdena Wattersonová', PhD diss., Charles University, Prague, 2011. I thank Irena Žantovská Murray for bringing the importance of Zdenka Watterson to my attention.

tation in the continuing struggle over the lost competition for the Palais de la Société des Nations in Geneva. Le Corbusier had already developed the project in 1927 and, to the general indignation of the community of modern architects, he did not receive the international commission. The failure of his first competition for a large public building came as a great disappointment to Le Corbusier and he would continue to fight for it in the years to come.[35] In summer 1931 he again appealed against the results and drew up a statement summarizing the whole process. An illustration comparing the entries was made at that time by Sammer, who then described the whole affair in a letter to his parents, in which he reproduced his sketches.[36]

The confidence Le Corbusier had in Sammer is also confirmed by the recent discovery that Le Corbusier later had him answer questions on his behalf in a long interview for the Prague German-language daily, the *Prager Presse*. Under the title 'Ein Besuch bei Le Corbusier', it was published in the Sunday edition, on 29 May 1932. In the almost full-page interview, conducted by the journalist Zdenka Watterson, the Paris architect (through his mouthpiece Sammer) describes in detail his past and present projects and presents his visions for the future.[37] His Czech assistant had adopted his boss's rhetoric to such a degree that Le Corbusier did not have to concern himself with the interview at all. Sammer later amusedly reported to his parents in Pilsen: 'I read this interview by Mrs Watterson and noticed that despite the fact that I had dictated the various things to her precisely, she botched it from a professional standpoint. It was actually me who gave the interview, because Corbu did not have time. I hope that you didn't notice any of the mistakes the lady made'.[38]

The family from the atelier

At 35 rue de Sèvres it was, however, not only a matter of teamwork on assignments of all kinds. Just as giving it one's all at work was extremely important, so too was free time, which in those years people from the atelier often spent together.[39] 'It is [...] the office of Le Corbusier and P. Jeanneret, where I work and have fun, where I have also found good friends with whom I spend all my free time',[40] Sammer wrote home at the end of 1931.

An important role in bringing the members of the atelier closer together was played by their involvement in the project for the Palace of the Soviets competition in Moscow. They were intensively occupied with this assignment from October to December 1931 and the work required joining forces, which in turn resulted in a great many spontaneous events.

'In our atelier certain moments were particularly intense, when, for example, completing the plans for the Palace of the Soviets, for the City of Antwerp and for the City of Algiers. The fatigue is crushing but we are moving ahead as a team'.[41]
Le Corbusier recalled the competition in the *Œuvre complète*, referring to it as an example of important teamwork and the mutual exchange of inspiration between him and his young assistants. That is also confirmed by reports that Sammer sent in his letters home in the period when work on it was under way at 35 rue de Sèvres:

< Le Corbusier and Pierre Jeanneret with a model of the Palais des Soviets. Photo: Walter Limot.

[38] AMP, František Sammer Papers, letter to his parents, 1 July 1932.
[39] This fact, which might otherwise be easily considered banal or not worthy of scholarly consideration, has been repeatedly pointed out by Tim Benton, a leading expert on the life and work of Le Corbusier. Of his recent works, see Tim Benton and Bruno Hubert, *Le Corbusier, mes années sauvages sur le bassin 1926–1936*, Le Petit Piquey: Tim Benton & Bruno Hubert, 2015.
[40] AMP, František Sammer Papers, letter to his aunt, 22 December 1931.
[41] 'Il fut certains moments tout particulièrement intenses dans notre atelier: lorsque, par exemple, se terminaient les plans pour le Palais des Soviets, ou les plans pour la Ville d'Anvers, ou ceux pour la Ville d'Alger. La fatigue est écrasante, mais on avance en bloc, en équipe'. Le Corbusier, 'Preface', in Willy Boesiger (ed.), *Le Corbusier et Pierre Jeanne-*

'It is a project for the Palace of the Soviets which is keeping me busy long into the night. [...] It is exhilarating work, hand in hand with the two captains, Corb. and Jean[neret]. [...] They are both fond of me, and when all of us who are working closely together have dinner hurriedly, chatting in haste, so that we can get back soon, we are friends par excellence'.[42] From the same period comes Sammer's report of a dinner at Perriand's, where noodles cooked with Le Corbusier's favourite recipe were served.[43]

From the human aspect, this period of the atelier was exceptional and the sense of belonging felt by the closest colleagues resembled that in a family. That was how Perriand saw the milieu at 35 rue de Sèvres, too,[44] and Sammer wrote of it in a similar way: 'I could not find better company anywhere in the whole wide world than what I have here. [...] It is always very jolly and we thus have a first-rate family in which we get along superbly, exchange opinions and all of us feel fine'.[45]

In their free time they used to go on excursions to the environs of Paris and also visited works built by Le Corbusier: 'Today is Sunday. We are going to Garches to look at Corbusiér villas'.[46] The correspondence and photos from this time provide insight into the intimacy and atmosphere, into stories, experiences and relationships. These were like lines of force in the background of the big events and provided a source of energy for efforts at the professional level.

> A page of a letter from Sammer to his parents in Pilsen, 22 December 1931, in which he provides the recipe for 'Noodles à la Corbusier'. AMP.

'Once I have gained the experience of a lifetime, once I have a family and am incapable of the enthusiasm of a 24-year-old [...], I swear that I will very gladly recall how [...] I made noodles with cheese and butter and ate steak {(Corbusier, one evening, when we were having dinner and talking about food [not in some fancy restaurant but at Charlotte Perriand's and we had made it ourselves, and Pierre Jeanneret in a blue apron was being the waiter] said that when impoverished it is better to eat noodles with cheese and butter, that he had once got sick from eggs and that it was noodles that saved his life.) (Make 'Noodles à la Corbusier' one day: cook noodles, then drain them (but don't rinse them in cold water!) and mix the drained noodles in a bowl with a knob of butter (not melted) and grated parmesan cheese. Mix it all together (the cheese becomes sort of threadlike) and you have to add a bit of pepper!)} and eat the steak. –'

---

ret, *Œuvre complète 1929–1934*, vol. 2, 18th edn (1934) Basel: Birkhäuser, 2013, p. 11.

42| AMP, František Sammer Papers, letter to his parents, 27 October 1931.

43| In late 1931 Perriand was still living in her first studio on Place Saint-Sulpice. In 1932, she moved to Montparnasse, close to Fernand Léger's studio. Her colleagues from Le Corbusier's circle, including Sammer, were well acquainted with Perriand's studio, where she often hosted her friends.

44| See Perriand, *Une vie de création* (n. 6), p. 27.

45| AMP, František Sammer Papers, letter to his parents, 11 October 1932.

46| Ibid., letter to his parents, 13 June 1931.

< Snapshot from the street.
Contact print, 4.5 × 3 cm. SAAA.

'But you mustn't think that Paris is somehow glittery. It is all somehow nonchalant, sometimes even excessively so'.

From one of Sammer's early Paris letters to his family in Pilsen, 11 May 1931. AMP.

< Paris, 1930s. Contact prints, front and back, 4 × 2.6 cm. SAAA.

050

Architect-photographer

Sammer used a camera from the very start of his explorations. In letters home he first mentions the photos in connection with Le Corbusier's Villa Savoye: 'The day before yesterday we were in Poissy to look at the new villa that was recently built. [...] You might later find a picture of this villa in a magazine. But here it is first-hand. The pictures are not the best because it was almost evening and I had to use longer exposures, and the camera was shaking a little'.[47] In the same letter he also refers to photos from Paris: 'The last photographs are, I think, typical of Paris. It is an abbot, who with exemplary eagerness has burrowed like a mole into the books laid out in front of a shop in rue Saint-Pierre [sic]'.[48]

But we will only be able to imagine these photos. Most of the photographs Sammer sent home were lost, most likely destroyed during the persecutions that Sammer faced in Czechoslovakia after the Second World War.[49] The written descriptions of the photos, preserved in the correspondence, in which the young architect tries to communicate his main impressions to his relatives in Pilsen, are, however, highly valuable. Like the photos that we can examine in this book, they tell us at what moments Sammer picked up the camera and considered suitable for taking a shot.

When taking photos Sammer paid the same attention to monuments or the recently-built Villa Savoye as he did in his snapshots in the streets of Paris, and of the latter he saved only a few of the city and its environs. In the photograph collection that Sammer deposited in Pondicherry, they remain as fleeting memories of well-known places and moments experienced that cannot be repeated.

The quantity of photos that were taken and saved was also influenced by the fact that photography cost money, of which, particularly at first, Sammer had little: 'I am sending you a photo from Chartres. It has been in the camera for a year. For a year I didn't take any photos. Money!',[50] he explained after his first year in Paris.

Despite his humble means, he did not miss any opportunity to become acquainted with his environment. 'Please believe that it is easier for me not to eat than not to go to see an opera',[51] he confided in a letter to Pilsen, and already during his first year at 35 rue de Sèvres he was looking for a way to explore the world beyond Paris.

Summer 1931

Summertime, particularly the month of August, meant holiday travel and with the regularity of a Swiss clock Le Corbusier and Pierre Jeanneret also set out on theirs. In the summer of 1931, they left on what would become the renowned car trip around Spain, and then travelled to Morocco and Algeria. As we shall see, this journey inspired Sammer, too. But he spent his first summer mainly in the atelier, completing, with a few other colleagues, work that had already been started. In mid-August, however, he managed to arrange a trip of his own. 'Corbusier is on holiday until the end of August and tomorrow we are going to finish all the work at the office, [...] so we are going too'.[52] With two Swiss colleagues from 35 rue de Sèvres, Edwin Bosshardt and Edmond Wanner,[53] Sammer set out for Great Britain. It was his first journey off the continent; in fact, the Channel crossing from Dieppe to Newhaven was his first time at sea and the first time he saw the Atlantic. The trip made a deep impression on him: 'Imagine, I arrive in a foreign country and everything I see meets my expectations'.[54]

We get a vivid picture of this journey thanks not only to the letters Sammer wrote to his family in Pilsen, but also to the photos found in Pondicherry. He travelled in search of knowledge and new experiences, and with the aim of looking for paid work. He met with the distinguished architects John Murray Easton, Louis de Soissons and Edward Prioleau Warren, who gave him freely of their time, offered him much advice and took him on excursions to places outside London.[55] When later

---

47| Sammer describes the visit to the Villa Savoye in a letter to his parents. Ibid., 5 May 1931.
48| Ibid.
49| This is my assumption, based on what eye-witnesses have stated and it is supported by a search carried out by the Security Services Archive of the Czech Republic (Archiv bezpečnostních složek České republiky – ABSCR), see ABS, archive report of the Pilsen Regional Department of the Ministry of the Interior, operative files, archive record no. 790 PL. Sammer was repeatedly invited to interrogations by the state police which sometimes took place overnight; due to the increased control of the state, he cut off his contacts with foreign countries and his chances for international collaboration were completely blocked. For more see p. 140 and n. 428.
50| AMP, František Sammer Papers, letter to his parents, 1 July 1932.
51| Ibid., letter of 26 May 1931.
52| Ibid., 13 August 1931.
53| The 'Répertoire des collaborateurs' contains the information that the two Swiss men worked in the atelier in 1931. The Hungarian architect János Wanner (1906-87) worked there too, in 1931 and 1932, which may be confusing when reading some sources.
54| AMP, František Sammer Papers, a letter to his parents, 28 August 1931.
55| For details, see 'Excursus 1', p. 157 and n. 7.

< Pavillon Suisse (in the Cité internationale universitaire de Paris) under construction, summer 1932. FLC L2(8)13. Photo: Albin Salaün.

> A page from Sammer's letter to Pilsen, 24 February 1933. AMP.
Le Corbusier refused to send his autograph to Sammer's younger brother, Jenda, in Pilsen. Instead, Junzo Sakakura contributed to the boy's autograph collection, and promised that one day he would be famous:
'Kind regards from a Japanese architect, a good friend of your brother François's. Yours faithfully, J. Sakakura'

Jenda replied to his brother:
*'Dear Franti,
The letter from Sakakura made me very happy. Let's hope he is famous as soon as possible! There's no hurry at all with the Corbusier [autograph]'.*
From Jenda Sammer's letter to František in Paris, 28 February 1933. AMP.

>> A photograph of Junzo Sakakura, inscribed on the back: 'To dear Sammer, with the best memories, Paris, January 1937, Sakakura'. SAAA.

writing home about his time in Great Britain, he emphasizes in one of his letters: 'I would add to this preface that we were furnished with recommendations from Corbusier'.[56]

In the gravitational field of the galaxy

After his first visit in 1931, Sammer returned to Great Britain several times and remained in regular touch with British friends. Similarly, he remained in touch with the French milieu after leaving Paris. Precise identification of the photos from these countries is difficult and the dates I provide of individual photos are only approximate. It's also unclear who took some of the photos. The photographs circulated among friends and Sammer's collection contains photos by other, still unidentified persons. From Pilsen, Sammer was receiving mail that included photographs from his friends and relatives. He would then send his pictures of the wider world to Pilsen. A few remarks in the correspondence confirm that some of the photos were taken by Sammer's friends from Le Corbusier's circle. 'Auntie, I am sending you one photo so that you see roughly how I look. It is from February and was taken in the Alps, where we were on a trip for a few days',[57] wrote Sammer to his aunt in Pilsen. The date of the photograph – February 1932 – corresponds to the time when Sammer and Perriand were hiking together in the mountains, and the photo was probably taken by one of the people on the trip.[58] Elsewhere he writes: 'I am attaching a photo Sakakura took on the roof of the Cité Universitaire ([it is of] the Pavillon Suisse)'.[59] Thanks to the photographs preserved in Pondicherry, we now know what Sammer and his friends looked like in their Paris years.

The Japanese architect Junzo Sakakura (1901–69) came to the atelier at 35 rue de Sèvres in 1931, like František Sammer, and he worked there until 1936. He was part of the innermost circle of Le Corbusier's colleagues, and spent a great deal of time with Perriand and Sammer. The diminutive, hardworking Japanese man was an easy butt of friendly jokes. Sakakura's professional qualities were, however, undeniable and Sammer, too, greatly respected him. Evidence of that is a letter Sammer wrote to his brother, Jenda, who longed for autographs of famous architects at the atelier:

56| AMP, František Sammer Papers, letter to his sister, Miloslava (Milča, Milána) Gschwindová, 25 August 1931.
57| Ibid., letter to his aunt, 15 April 1932. For a complete translation of the letter, see 'Excursus 1'.
58| Perriand recalled Sammer taking part in trips to the mountains: 'Bien souvent, les fins des semaines, je débauchais les amoureux du ski de l'atelier: Sammer, Wanner, Sakakura. Nous partions le vendredi soir pour le Jura, les Alpes... Nous revenions à l'atelier le lundi matin, pas toujours en bon état, mais heureux'. Perriand, *Une vie de création* (n. 6), p. 58.
59| AMP, František Sammer Papers, letter to his parents, 20 September 1932.

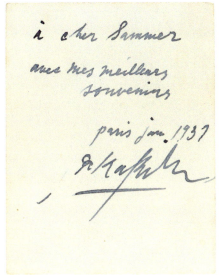

> Charlotte Perriand shared František Sammer's love of mountains and mountain climbing. Here she is in a photo with an inscription on the back: 'January 1933 – To my friend Sammer'.
Photograph, 5.3 × 6.8 cm. SAAA.

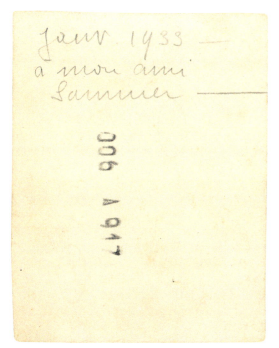

'Very often, at the end of the week, I would poach ski-lovers from the atelier: Sammer, Wanner, Sakakura. On Friday evenings we would leave for the Jura Mountains, or the Alps… We returned to the atelier on Monday mornings, not always in good shape, but happy'.

Perriand, *Une vie de création* (see n. 58).

'Well, I have spoken to Le Corbusier regarding what you asked about [...] You know, he grudgingly gives autographs. [...] I also know a Japanese man, whom I will ask to write something to you. [...] He too will be a famous architect'.[60]
Sakakura did indeed become one of the founders of modern Japanese architecture and played an essential role as an intermediary between East and West. His sense of humour and self-irony are evident in his message to the young boy Jenda from Pilsen: 'Kind regards from a Japanese architect, a good friend of your brother François's [sic]. Yours faithfully, J. Sakakura'.[61]
For Sammer, his contact with Perriand was uniquely important. 'With Mme Perriand it will be friendship par excellence. Partly because we see each other often, and have many of the same interests outside the office, too. For me it is really new and rare, terribly lovely. [...] It is the kind that tends to encourage activity, because it is a relationship between two architects, two people of the same profession, and that almost always has vitality as a consequence'.[62] These words, which Sammer wrote shortly after making Perriand's acquaintance, were confirmed in the following years. They were united not only by their profession, but also by a love for the mountains and the sea and the ability to enjoy life. Apart from the written sources, this is confirmed by photographs from Sammer's collection. The photo of Perriand at the top of a mountain in winter, with the dedication 'to my friend Sammer'[63] from January 1933, evokes the atmosphere of their now legendary trips to the French Alps. Perriand had set out on the trip with 'lovers of skiing from the atelier'[64] and in this connection she later mentions Sammer in her memoirs.[65]
From the beginning of his work at 35 rue de Sèvres, Sammer assisted Perriand with designing interiors,[66] and he also discussed with her the possibility of collaborating outside the office.[67] In September 1931, he invited her to accompany him on one of his visits to Meudon-Val-Fleury where he used to travel to take a rest from 'French Paris'.[68] A villa there, designed by the Dutch artist, theorist and architect Theo van Doesburg, used to be the meeting place of a diverse international society. Sammer was first brought there by Abraham Elzas, the Dutch architect who co-designed the villa, to whom Sammer had been introduced by André Lurçat.[69] In the inter-war years, Lurçat was a leading figure of French modern architecture[70] and a competitor of Le Corbusier, to whom Sammer had introduced Elzas.[71] That is attested to not only by Sammer's correspondence, but also by an October 1931 entry in the 'Livre noir'.[72] Shortly after these two architects were introduced, Elzas signed one drawing at 35 rue de Sèvres during the work on the Pavillon Suisse (Fondation Suisse or Pavillon Le Corbusier) in the Cité internationale universitaire de Paris. Comparing Charlotte Perriand to the lady of the house, Nelly van Doesburg, Sammer describes Perriand as 'young and somewhat choleric, with an alto voice and quick gestures like a boy'.[73] Shortly after the visit to Meudon, Sammer went with Perriand, Edmond Wanner and Sakakura to Cologne, to prepare an installation at an exhibition of modern interior design.

This exhibition, the Internationale Raumausstellung (IRA),[74] took place in Cologne from 20 October to 20 December 1931. Simultaneously with the presentation of the 35 rue de Sèvres atelier, it also exhibited works, for example, by Adolf Loos, Bruno Paul and Victor Bourgeois. The Paris delegation installed a backlit wall with a model photograph of the radical project for the redevelopment of Paris called the 'Plan Voisin',[75] as well as tubular steel furniture and the now-famous Chaise longue.[76] The exhibit included a multi-coloured synthetic carpet made of 12 tourist rugs with lions and leopards on them, bought on the terrace in front of the café Les Deux Magots. It was provocatively, and contrary to the German programme of Neue Sachlichkeit, placed under the designer chair.[77]

> Le Corbusier, Pierre Jeanneret and Charlotte Perriand, interior installed at the Internationale Raumausstellung (International Interior Design Exhibition – IRA) in Cologne, in 1931. AChP.

60| Ibid., letter to his brother, 24 February 1933.
61| Ibid. with a note from Junzo Sakakura in Japanese and German: 'Viele herzliche Grüsse von einem japanischen Architekten, einer der guten Freunden Ihres Bruders François. Ihr getreuer J. Sakakura'.
62| AMP, František Sammer Papers, letter to his parents, 4 October 1931.
63| 'Janv 1933 – à mon ami Sammer'.
64| See Perriand, Une vie de création (n. 6), p. 58. Perriand and her love of mountains is the topic of Pernette Perriand-Barsac (ed.), Charlotte Perriand: Carnet de montagne, Albertville: Maison des Jeux olympiques d'hiver, 2013.
65| Ibid.
66| AMP, František Sammer Papers, letter to his parents, 26 May 1931.
67| Ibid., 28 August 1931. 'I hope to get a job at Mme Perriand. I keep hoping but it is not possible now in that case to do anything, because Mme P. is on vacation'.
68| Ibid., 23 September 1931.
69| Ibid.
70| For basic information about Lurçat, see Jean-Louis Cohen, André Lurçat, 1894-1970: L'Autocritique d'un moderne, Liège: Mardaga, 1995. Disagreements between Lurçat and Le Corbusier about architecture, and also, indeed mainly, about politics, were expressed at the Congrès Internationaux d'Architecture Moderne (CIAM), of which both men were members. In no time, the conflict led to a public debate, mainly in the Soviet Union, where Lurçat was working from 1934 to 1937. An active member of the CIAM, Lurçat was advocating 'rational architecture', prefabrication and work with the modular system, with which he strongly influenced the development of architecture after the Second World War.
71| AMP, František Sammer Papers, letter to his parents, 23 September 1931.
72| Drawing no. 2773, C. U. plan de situation, 6 October 1931, FLC, 'Livre noir'.
73| AMP, František Sammer Papers, letter to his parents, 23 September 1931.
74| For a contemporary report on the exhibition, see Ruth Hildegard Geyer-Raack, '"IRA" Internationale Raumausstellung Gebr. Schürmann, Köln', Moderne Bauformen 30, 1931, pp. 607-16, quoted in Arthur Rüegg, Le Corbusier: Furniture and Interiors 1905-1965, Zurich: Schei-

degger & Spiess, 2012, pp. 126 and 297. For the exhibition in the context of interior design at the Le Corbusier–Jeanneret atelier, see also Arthur Rüegg, 'Equipement', in Lucan (ed.), *Le Corbusier, une Encyclopédie* (n. 4), p. 132.

75| The 'Plan Voisin' was first presented by Le Corbusier at the Pavillon de l'Esprit Nouveau in 1925. The design comes from his project 'Ville Contemporaine de Trois Millions d'Habitants', which gained him a great deal of attention at the Salon d'Automne in Paris in 1922 and whose main principles he continued to develop in his urbanist visions.

76| 'Chaise Longue' (1928) is one of the main prototypes of furniture developed in the Le Corbusier–Jeanneret atelier. These are essentially linked with the arrival of Perriand in 1927.

77| For the exhibition in the context of Perriand's work, see Mary McLeod, 'Charlotte Perriand: Her First Decade as a Designer', *AAFiles*, no. 15 (summer 1987), p. 10. McLeod also discusses it, compared and contrasted with the German milieu, in the introductory essay to the first comprehensive publication about Perriand's work as a designer in McLeod (ed.), *Charlotte Perriand: An Art of Living* (n. 6), p. 13. For a description by Perriand see Perriand, *Une vie de création* (n. 6), pp. 73-74.

78| AMP, František Sammer Papers, letter to his parents, 18 October 1931.

79| Perriand, *Une vie de création* (n. 6), p. 74: 'mon luxe à moi, c'était d'inviter Sammer, Wanner, Sakakura, mes gardes du corps et mes "grouillots" à descendre le Rhin jusqu'à Lorelei'.

80| AMP, František Sammer Papers, letter to his parents, 18 October 1931.

81| See n. 53.

82| According to the 'Répertoire des collaborateurs', the Hungarian architect Károly Dávid (1903-73) worked in the atelier from 1931 to 1932, like his cousin, the Hungarian architect János (later, Hans) Wanner. For a background of Hungarian architects in general and the connection between the experience of the Le Corbusier–Jeanneret atelier and inter-war Hungarian architecture, see János Bonta, 'Functionalism in Hungarian Architecture', in Wojciech Leśnikowski (ed.), *East European Modernism: Architecture in Czechoslovakia, Hungary, and Poland between the Wars, 1919-1939*, with an introduction and essays by Wojciech Leśnikowski, New York: Rizzoli, 1996, pp. 125-77.

83| AMP, František Sammer Papers, letter to his parents, 18 October 1931.

In a letter home, Sammer describes the improvised last-minute preparations for the exhibition: 'On Saturday night, when we finished work, M. Jeanneret came to me and confidentially told me that if I wanted to go to Cologne to arrange the exhibition with Mme Perriand, he would very gladly contribute money. Wanner and Sakakura joined us, and after three hours of sleep we set out'.[78] Despite other experiences from those years in the Le Corbusier–Jeanneret atelier, it is the Cologne exhibition that stood out in Perriand's memory. In her autobiography, she recalled a night swim in the rapid currents of the Rhein with her companions. 'It was a luxury for me to invite Sammer, Wanner and Sakakura, my bodyguards and "errand boys" on a journey down the Rhein all the way to the Lorelei'.[79] The event was described similarly by Sammer upon his return to Paris: 'The exhibition of furniture did not require much work (we exhibited an interior and the Plan Voisin, a utopian vision of a future Paris), so we had lots of time to go on excursions outside the city, along the Rhein, and so on. It was very lovely. We were like madmen and we returned content, merry, and rested, with bottle of good wine for the two good lads Corbusier and Jeanneret. Of course we drank it together with many other people in our intimate circle and thus spent an unforgettable evening'.[80]

Though Jeanneret sent him to Cologne with the promise of remuneration, Sammer wrote home in no time that he was completely broke: 'I have no money because I spent a bit in Cologne, but I am not hungry: Wanner[81] and Sakakura take turns feeding me, sometimes so too do M. David[82] and Mme David, who find it amusing that I eat with such gusto'.[83]

The Depression as a bonding agent

Most of the people at the Le Corbusier–Jeanneret atelier found themselves similarly destitute. The long Depression made their lives more difficult of course, yet it acted as an intense driving force as well. For individual members of the atelier, the understanding of architecture and its social role was changing. At the same time, the sense of belonging and the joint efforts to find a way out of the poverty had imprinted themselves on the regime at 35 rue de Sèvres. In that respect, Le Corbusier was sympathetic – though he took advantage of the voluntary work of his assistants, he was also well aware of their difficulties, and sometimes actively helped them in the search for paid employment outside the atelier.

Those who worked full-time at Le Corbusier's naturally inquired occasionally into the possibility of remuneration. After some time spent in the atelier, Sammer wrote home: 'I talked to Corbusier a few times about employment, but the position he takes is that he helps with advice and connections, but cannot compromise this principle. That is, he cannot make an exception and pay me, because he would then have to pay everyone. He is very concerned to help, and asks, recommends, but for the time being all in vain'.[84]

On all his travels, Sammer set out generously furnished with relevant contacts from 35 rue de Sèvres. At one point Le Corbusier was trying to negotiate employment for him in Casablanca,[85] and also significantly pushed to get him employed in the Soviet Union, where Sammer did, in fact, later go for work after the atelier. Likewise, Sammer looked for employment for others: 'McClellan[86] is running out of money and Corbusier has been looking for a place for him in Moscow',[87] Sammer wrote in a letter to his parents. McClellan was eventually helped by Sammer himself in getting work in the Prague office of the Czech architect František Albert Libra.[88]
Nevertheless, Sammer had no desire to go back to his homeland. He kept abreast of the news from Czechoslovakia and received reports about architecture from his brother-in-law, the architect Otakar Gschwind.[89] In his collection of photographs he even kept four shots of works of Czech modern architecture and at one time was corresponding with the Baťa company about employment opportunities.[90] However, he deliberately wrote to the company's head office in French and then reported home that he saw working for Baťa only as a transitional phase before finding employment abroad,[91] ideally in the Soviet Union.
While searching for a paid position, Sammer met with a number of well-known designers in France. Right at the start of his Paris sojourn he made the acquaintance of Frantz Jourdain, 'a revivalist architect, who built *La Samaritaine*, the first building with an iron structure'.[92] Thanks to him, Sammer became acquainted also with Auguste Perret,[93] who 'received him very, very kindly',[94] though he did not offer him a paying job. Sammer probably sought employment from André Lurçat, too.[95] Interestingly, Sammer later clashed with Lurçat, particularly in the Soviet Union,[96] when, in a number of public debates, he joined those championing Le Corbusier.[97] Among the interesting architects Sammer met was Paul Nelson,[98] whom he encountered by accident. In summer 1932, he bumped into him at the English Channel with his whole office: 'By chance I met friends there, who work for the architect Nelson, who has moved his whole practice there for the summer. Now the lads are swimming more than working. Not bad, eh?'[99]
Considering that it comes from the depths of the worldwide economic crisis, Sammer's report may seem startling. But the 'joie de vivre', sport and an ability to use one's free time actively were among the basic values of the modern movement, and had little in common with prosperity. 'We are a society of jobseekers',[100] Sammer wrote to his parents, and described the staff of the Le Corbusier–Jeanneret atelier as an illustration of the Great Depression: 'Bad news about the whole world. You know, at our office it is like at an international laundry and everyone is complaining. Especially America and central Europe. Czechoslovakia is always being talked about, how it is hanging on. Hungary is moaning. Greece the same. England is rejoicing that the value of sterling is going up, but a representative of that nation [at our office] is suffering with holes in his shoes and he is sorry that he changed pounds into gold at an exchange rate of 80 francs. "We make the economy" – all of us'.[101]
Sammer gradually participated in architectural competitions and projects for private investors, working on them with colleagues from the atelier. With their help, he kept

> Karel Řepa, a row of commercial-industrial pavilions at the Exhibition of Physical Training and Sport in Pardubice, Czechoslovakia, 1931. Photographs, 7.3 × 4.5 cm. SAAA.

The City of Zlín, Czechoslovakia, view of architecture built by the company of the shoe manufacturer Tomáš Baťa (1876–1932) and, after his death, of his half-brother Jan Antonín Baťa (1898–1965).

[84] Ibid., January 1932, the original is antedated 11 January 1931.
[85] Ibid., 30 January 1932: 'Corbusier has talked about me with the president of the Société des grands travaux hydrauliques, M. François de Pierrefeu, with whom I then talked and was promised a position in Casablanca, Morocco'.
[86] Hugh Derby McClellan (1908–2002), an American architect, worked at 35 rue de Sèvres for three months, from late March to the end of July 1931, most often at the side of František Sammer and Edwin Bosshardt. In Paris he enrolled at the École des Beaux-Arts, and visited a number of countries in Europe, including Italy, Germany, Belgium, England and Czechoslovakia. Beginning in 1935, he worked as an architect in the United States. *The AIA Historical Directory of American Architects*, Membership File, Hugh Derby McClellan (ahd1029171), New York, Washington, DC: The American Institute of Architects Archives. For further information, see Mardges Bacon, *Le Corbusier in America: Travels in the Land of the Timid*, Cambridge (MA); London: MIT Press, 2001, pp. 5 and 323. For the opportunity to consult them and their help in finding sources, I thank Mary McLeod and Mardges Bacon.
[87] AMP, František Sammer Papers, a letter to his parents, 13 June 1931.
[88] Ibid., 30 June 1931. 'With my help, McClellan got a job in Prague and it makes me really happy, as much as it does him. He's going to Prague the day after tomorrow'. McClellan worked for Libra for less than a year, from July 1931 to March 1932. After he was sacked, he returned to Paris. AIA Historical Directory (n. 86) and AMP, František Sammer Papers, letters to his parents and aunt, 9 March 1932.
[89] The Pilsen architect Otakar Gschwind (1890–1968) was the husband of Sammer's sister Miloslava (Milča). Together they had three sons: Otakar (b. 1928), Allan (b. 1928) and Kamil (b. 1931). Gschwind worked as an architect and builder in Pilsen, where he became known especially for his modernist building of the Municipal Columbarium II (1932–33). For her help in searching for information about Gschwind, I thank Štěpánka Pflegerová of the Pilsen City Archives.
[90] AMP, František Sammer Papers, letters to his father from early 1932.
[91] Ibid., letter to his father, 21 January 1932; the manuscript is antedated 1931
[92] Ibid., letter to his father, 30 January 1932. Frantz Jourdain (1847–1935) was a Belgian architect and theorist. Although his design for this Paris department store (built between 1905 and 1910) is not the first building with an iron structure, as stated by Sammer, it is a landmark example of a steel-frame construction in a public building. He was a father of the painter, interior designer and Art Nouveau pioneer Francis Jourdain (1876–1958), whose left-wing activity in Paris was important for Sammer's future decisions.
[93] Ibid., letter to his parents in Pilsen, 12 September 1931: 'I hope that you know his name – he is a great architect. [...] a nineteenth-century figure, also very elegant'.

> View of family homes in Nad Ovčírnou, a district of Zlín.
>> Miroslav Lorenc and Vladimír Karfík, Společenský dům (Communal House; later, hotel Moskva; today, Interhotel Zlín), 1931–33.
All photographs, 7.3 × 4.5 cm. SAAA.

94| Ibid.
95| See Cohen, *André Lurçat* (n. 70).
96| For details about the debate, see Jean-Louis Cohen, *Le Corbusier et la mystique de l'URSS: Théories et projets pour Moscou 1928-1936*, Brussels: Mardaga, 1987, pp. 263-65.
97| For details about the development of Sammer's ideological positions while in the Soviet Union, see Hrabová, 'Between Ideal and Ideology' (n. 18).
98| Paul Daniel Nelson (1895-1970), a French architect of American origin, had his own practice in Paris beginning in 1928. He was friends, for example, with Le Corbusier, Auguste Perret and the painter Fernand Léger, and he was an important intermediary between the United States and France.
99| AMP, František Sammer Papers, letter to his father, 17 August 1932.
100| Ibid., letter to his parents, 12 September 1931.
101| Ibid., letter to his aunt, 9 March 1932.
102| Ibid., letter to his parents, 12 September 1931.
103| Ibid., 30 January 1932. For the precise dates and purpose of Perriand's first trip to the Soviet Union, see Hrabová, 'Between Ideal and Ideology' (n. 18), pp. 139 and 155. See below, pp. 84-85 and n. 203.
104| AMP, František Sammer Papers, letter to his parents, 1 March 1932.
105| Ibid., 9 March 1932.

an eye out for job opportunities elsewhere. Edwin Bosshardt, a former assistant at the atelier thus acted as his 'spy in Switzerland'[102] and it was also in search of work that Charlotte Perriand set out 'on reconnaissance missions' in the Soviet Union at the beginning of 1932.[103]

A professional in a crew of amateurs, 1932

Things became markedly worse in the spring of 1932, when the Depression hit hard in France. The assistants left 35 rue de Sèvres en masse, and in mid-March Sammer too decided to leave. Surprisingly, Pierre Jeanneret, in reaction to Sammer's announcement, offered him a monthly salary of 1,000 francs. In a letter home, Sammer described how things stood now: 'The financial crisis at the Office (by that I mean my fellow employees) is threatening to empty the place of people and thus hurt the firm, and hence the famous twelfth hour. When the time came, the choice was made'.[104] Shortly afterwards, he wrote: 'The office is still full, but after Easter it will be almost empty. It seems that of twelve we now number three – [from] England, America, Czechoslovakia, perhaps also Japan. It is questionable whether we can count on reinforcements'.[105]

Le Corbusier and Jeanneret therefore finally made an exception, and Sammer became one of the few people paid in the atelier at that time. 'In the fabulous amateur

< František Sammer, a perspective drawing of the Pavillon Suisse at the Cité internationale universitaire de Paris, 3 August 1931. FLC 15334.

> Sammer's drawing reproduced in Boesiger (ed.), *Le Corbusier et Pierre Jeanneret, Œuvre complète 1929–1934*, vol. 2, p. 75 (see n. 41).

crew of the office, I am the first to become a professional',[106] he wrote home. The offered remuneration hardly meant a decent living, but it did enable Sammer to remain in Paris for another full year.

Though he had achieved a better position in the atelier, Sammer did not stop looking for a better paying job and for opportunities to work on his own projects. Much as he had done before with Alfred Altherr, a Swiss colleague, when preparing an entry to a competition for a school in Zurich,[107] Sammer also helped Károly Dávid with the plans for Dávid's own house in Budapest.[108] The ideal time for this was summer, when operations at the atelier slowed down and the remaining staff in Paris could use it for their own jobs as well. When Sammer failed to meet the deadline for the competition for a sanatorium in the Tatra Mountains of Slovakia, he was twice as sorry because 'Corbu and Jeanneret are going on holiday together in mid-July and we were guaranteed time and room to work'.[109]

While in the summer of 1932 Le Corbusier and Jeanneret spent their time collecting natural objects on the beach and in the area of Le Piquey,[110] Sammer took full charge of the atelier. He oversaw the building site of the Pavillon Suisse at the Cité internationale universitaire de Paris, the Cité de Refuge for the Salvation Army and even Le Corbusier's Immeuble Porte Molitor, 24 rue Nungesser-et-Coli on the outskirts of Paris: 'We are now alone in the Office and I have three building sites. Jeanneret and Corbu have gone on holiday, so I am running around like a headless chicken'.[111] Sammer was well acquainted with these projects. While at 35 rue de Sèvres he made dozens of drawings ranging from technical details to working drawings to perspective views and urban plans.[112] His drawings were also chosen by Le Corbusier to illustrate his projects in publications at the time and a number of them are included in the *Œuvre complète*.[113]

Among Sammer's first assignments at the atelier was making drawings for the Pavillon Suisse. He joined in the project during its final stage and his first work registered in the 'Livre noir', a perspective drawing of the building, was eventually reproduced

106 Ibid., 1 March 1932. Few assistants achieved this position in the inter-war period, and Sammer was probably the first and only one to receive a salary in this period. As far as we know, the pay was modest; for example, the Swiss architect Alfred Roth, who worked in the atelier from 1927 to 1929, earned 900 francs per month, and the Yugoslav Ernest Weissmann, who worked in the atelier from 1928 to 1930, had most of his living expenses covered by his family. For Roth see Témoignages in Cauquil and Bédarida, *Bulletin d'Informations* (n. 13), p. 9, and Tamara Bjažić Klarin, *Ernest Weissmann: Društveno angažirana arhitektura, 1926–1939/Socially Engaged Architecture, 1926–1939*, Zagreb: Architectonica, Hrvatska akademija znanosti i umjetnosti/Croatian Academy of Sciences and Art, 2015, p. 33.

107 According to the 'Répertoire des collaborateurs', Alfred Altherr (1911–72) worked in the atelier in 1931 and 1932. He later made his mark as an architect and designer in Switzerland. See Joan Billing et al., *Alfred Altherr Junior: Protagonist der Schweizer Wohnkultur* (exh. cat.), Baden: Design+Design, 2013. He worked with Sammer on the plans for the school in Zurich in January 1932. AMP, František Sammer Papers, letters to his parents from early 1932.

108 AMP, František Sammer Papers, letter to his parents, 1 May 1932: 'I am also working a bit for Dávid, who is making plans for his own single-family house in Budapest'. The building, in Sómloi street, was completed by the architect Károly Dávid in 1933. It clearly reflects Le Corbusier's single-family houses of the 1920s and provides evidence of Dávid's knowledge of these projects.

109 AMP, František Sammer Papers, letter home, 1 July 1932.

110 From 1926 to 1936, Le Corbusier spent most summers on the Atlantic coast of France, in the village of Le Piquey at the Bassin d'Arcachon (Arcachon Bay). In addition to relaxation, he found inspiration here in the local environment and in objects that he discovered along the coast. See Niklas Maak, *Le Corbusier: The Architect on the Beach*, Munich: Hirmer, 2011, and Tim Benton, 'Atlantic Coast: Nature and Inspiration', in Cohen (ed.), *An Atlas* (n. 13), pp. 163–67, or the small publication that accompanied the exhibition, Benton and Hubert, *Le Corbusier, mes années sauvages sur le bassin 1926–1936* (n. 39).

111 AMP, František Sammer Papers, letter to his parents, 2 August 1932.

112 FLC, 'Livre noir'.

113 Boesiger (ed.), *Le Corbusier et Pierre Jeanneret, Œuvre complète* (n. 41). For example the perspective drawing of the Pavillon Suisse (FLC 15334) on p. 75, the section (FLC 2789c) on p. 86, and the drawings of the foundations of the building (CU 2900 and 2901) on pp. 88 and 89; the acoustic study of the ceiling of the Palace of Soviets (FLC 27239) on p. 134; the variant drawing of the facade of the apartment building at 24 rue Nungesser-et-Coli (FLC 13351) on p. 144; the drawings for the residential district for the Domaine de Badjara, Oued Ouchaïa, near Alger, for example the perspective of the whole complex (FLC 31508)

Projet du Pavillon

on p. 161, the section (FLC 13973a, b) on p. 163, the perspective of the interior of the building unit (FLC 13966) on p. 165 and a section of the boulevard (FLC 13976) on p. 168.

114| Ivan Žaknić, *Le Corbusier: Pavillon Suisse: The Biography of a Building*, Basel: Birkhäuser, 2004, p. 162, about Sammer's drawing, no. FLC 15334. For an analysis of the building, see William J. R. Curtis, 'Ideas of Structure and the Structure of Ideas: Le Corbusier's Pavillon Suisse, 1930–1931', *Journal of the Society of Architectural Historians* 40, no. 4 (December 1981), pp. 295–310.

115| For details about the project, see Jacques Sbriglio, *Immeuble 24 N. C. et Appartement Le Corbusier/Apartment Block 24 N.C. and Le Corbusier's Home*, Basel: Birkhäuser, 1996, and Marie-Jeanne Dumont, 'Immeuble de la Porte Molitor' & 'Appartement de Le Corbusier', 24 rue Nungesser-et-Coli', in *Le Corbusier: Plans*, Paris, Tokyo: Codex Images International. Certain Czech scholars have suggested that the architect Eugen (Evžen, Eugene) Rosenberg may have participated in this project (see Vladimír Šlapeta and Václav Jandáček, *Český funkcionalismus – Stavební kniha*, Brno: Expo Data, 2004, p. 79, and Petr Vorlík, *Meziválečné garáže v Čechách*, Prague: VCPD ČVUT, 2011, p. 47, quoting Petr Pelčák, Vladimír Šlapeta and Ivan Wahl, *Elly Oehler/Olárová – Oskar Oehler/Olár, Architektonické dílo/Architectural Work* (exh. cat.), Brno, Olomouc: Spolek Obecni dum Brno, Muzeum umeni Olomouc, 2007, p. 81), but this conjecture is inaccurate. When Le Corbusier was given the commission for 24 rue Nungesser-et-Coli in 1931, Rosenberg had not worked at 35 rue de Sèvres for a year and a half. For details, see Hrabová, *Mýtus a realita* (n. 9).

116| Archives Charlotte Perriand (AChP), Sammer to Perriand, 8 September 1934: 'Tu ne sais pas combien je pense à tout energie que vous perdez là bas pour les petites emmerdements d'ordre Boulogne etc. – Ici il s'agit du travail'.

117| Ibid., 19 January 1935. 'Et nous ici – on fait travail des bâtisseurs des pyramides'.

in the *Œuvre complète*. The author of a detailed book on the building, Ivan Žaknić, calls the drawing 'the most attractive image of the whole complex'.[114]

When Sammer began working on the Cité de Refuge building, alterations were being made to the approved project at the atelier; these were being carried out during the course of construction, which had begun in the summer of 1930. Sammer was elaborating supplementary technical drawings at the drawing board and he was chiefly enrolled on the building supervision at the construction site.

Sammer's role in the design of Le Corbusier's apartment building at 24 rue Nungesser-et-Coli in Boulogne was different from that in the Cité de Refuge. He was involved in the design from the beginning, and from summer 1931 to autumn 1932 he worked on the project closely with Perriand and Jeanneret, who were largely responsible for construction and interior planning whenever Le Corbusier was travelling or had commitments beyond those at the atelier. Sammer contributed with plans and drawings for the whole building and eventually with those for Le Corbusier's own apartment on the top two floors.[115]

It is the building that Sammer later liked to bring up while working in the Soviet Union. In comparison with the big projects in Moscow, for him it embodied the pointless refinements and 'annoyances of the Boulogne type',[116] which were being dealt with in Paris. He compared the tasks of Soviet architects, by contrast, to those of the 'builders of the pyramids'.[117] The atmosphere of the Depression and the left-wing leanings of artist circles, however, had formed Sammer's view of the world already during his Paris sojourn. His interest in left-wing ideals and the Soviet Union also grew in contrast to the outlook of his father, who was a businessman, though also a member of the National Democratic Party. Sammer's political thinking was thus becoming extreme, which even Le Corbusier poked fun at. Evidence of that is found in a story about a carpet, which Sammer mentions in a letter, during the final work on the apartment building at 24 rue Nungesser-et-Coli. [See the illustration on p. 61]

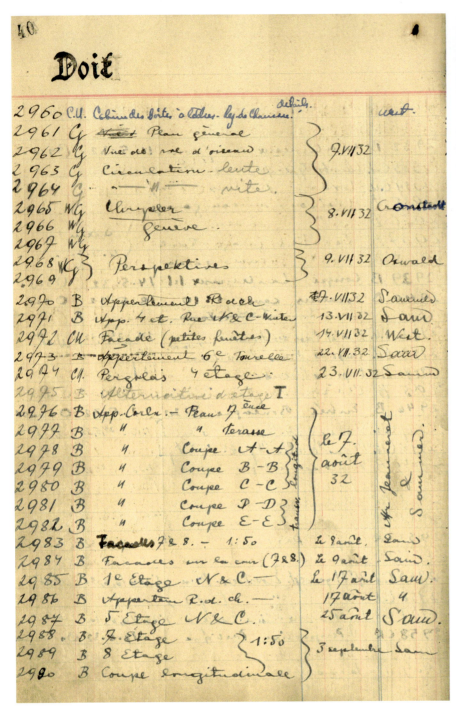

The female element

It is widely known that Le Corbusier did not actively seek collaboration with women. He even turned down Perriand initially, saying that 'we do not embroider cushions' in the atelier.[118] He was married though,[119] and repeatedly teased Sammer for being single, which he linked with Sammer's political views. For Sammer, however, women were important both personally and professionally. At 35 rue de Sèvres he was close to both Charlotte Perriand and Jane West (1907–2003). West seems to have been the first woman architect who arrived at the Le Corbusier–Jeanneret atelier from the United States, and at that time was also the only trained woman architect there. She came to 35 rue de Sèvres at the beginning of 1932 and stayed for less than a year.[120] She collaborated with Sammer on a number of projects at the atelier,[121] and they often spent their free time together in the company of other American artists living

118| When she recalled her start at 35 rue de Sèvres, Perriand liked to quote Le Corbusier's words 'on ne brode des coussins ici'. See the interview in Cauquil and Bédarida (eds.) *Le Corbusier: l'atelier 35 rue de Sèvres*, (n. 13), p. 11, and Perriand, *Une vie de création* (n. 6), p. 25.

119| Yvonne Gallis (1892-1957) made the acquaintance of Le Corbusier in 1922, and was married to him from 1930 until her death.

120| For West's arrival at the atelier, see AMP, František Sammer Papers, letter to his parents, 11 January 1932. 'Miss West, an American, who has been in the office for a few days, has been talking about the great poverty and unemployment in America'. According to the 'Livre noir', West worked at 35 rue de Sèvres from January to the summer of 1932, and the last entered drawing she signed is dated 14 July. See Avigail Sachs, 'Jane West Clauss', online at Mary McLeod and Victoria Rosner (eds.), *Pioneering Women of American Architecture*, https://pioneeringwomen.bwaf.org/jane-west-clauss/ Accessed 4 August 2023. Jane West's life and work, particularly her links with Europe, has been a subject of my continuing research. For providing me with valuable information and their remarks, and for making a number of sources available to me, I am indebted to Mary McLeod and Carin Clauss.

121| FLC, 'Livre noir'. Like Sammer and other members of the atelier, West joined in the work that was under way on plans for the three large buildings of the Pavillon Suisse for the Cité internationale universitaire de Paris, the Cité de refuge (for the Salvation Army), and the Molitor apartment house at 24 rue Nungesser-et-Coli.

122| AMP, František Sammer Papers, letter home, 1 May 1932. Thanks to Jane West, architects from the circle of Le Corbusier made the acquaintance, for example, of the sculptress Agnes Larsen (1910-2002) and the painter Anne Heyneman (1909-68). Information from Sammer's correspondence is also confirmed in Gordon Stephenson, 'Chapters of Autobiography I–III', *The Town Planning Review* 62, no. 1 (January 1991), p. 18, and Gordon Stephenson, *On a Human Scale: A Life in City Design*, ed. by Christina DeMarco, Fremantle, Western Australia: Fremantle Arts Centre Press, 1992, p. 27. I am indebted to Carin Clauss for drawing my attention to Stephenson's autobiographical publication. For details, see also Agnessa [*sic*] Larsen, *Graffiti on My Heart: An Autobiography*, Seattle, WA: Peanut Butter Publishing, 1994. For having brought Larsen's autobiography to my attention, and for having made it available to me, I am indebted to Carin Clauss.

> Interior of Le Corbusier's apartment at 24 rue Nungesser-et-Coli, including the cow-hide carpet. FLC L2(10)85. Photo: Albin Salaün.

'We are all anticipating a revolution here and Le Corbusier has taken away from Germany a beautiful Persian carpet with black-and-white cows, which was at the exhibition there, on the assumption that it [the revolution] will come later in France than in Germany. But he says it in jest. He also said to me: – Well, I wanted to cut off a cow for you when you marry (the carpet is seven metres long and has nine cows), but in this case you won't get anything, because Communists don't marry. – You can imagine how sad I was. But the cows are really very beautiful. When we were doing the apartment for Corbu (on the roof of an apartment building in Boulogne) his only worry was whether he would be able to roll out the carpet. It was then decided that it would probably be necessary to cut off a cow, which was supposed to be mine. – So much for that'.

Sammer's description of the cow-hide carpet known from the Le Corbusier apartment, in a letter home to Pilsen, 11 October 1932. AMP.

<< A page from the 'Livre noir', where drawings for the apartment house at 24 rue Nungesser-et-Coli are registered under the initial B. The entry from 7 August 1932 states that this is Pierre Jeanneret and František Sammer's work for Le Corbusier's own apartment on the top floor of the building. FLC S1-(16)1-55.

< František Sammer, a variant drawing of the street façade of Le Corbusier's apartment house at 24 rue Nungesser-et-Coli in Paris, of 28 September 1931. FLC 13351.

˅ Anne Heyneman. Private archive.

> Jane West in Glacier National Park, Montana, USA, 1933. Photograph, 11.6 × 8.7 cm. SAAA.

in Paris: 'Recently lots of work in the Office and free time spent on walks and all kinds of conversations. [...] Otherwise, with nice girls, all of them American [...] Apart from a woman architect with us in the office, they are a sculptress, Agnes, and a painter, Anne'.[122]

It was in this group of friends that Sammer met the partner with whom he would travel and get to know the world. Agnes Larsen (1910–2002), an American with Norwegian roots, had attended a private school for girls, the Anna Head School, in Berkeley, California, where she was greatly influenced by Galka Scheyer, a citizen of the

<< Agnes Larsen, 1930s.
Contact prints, 2.5 × 3.8 cm. SAAA.

world and a driving force in circles promoting modern art.[123] Larsen came to Paris in autumn 1931, in order to study art, particularly sculpture. She used to go to the studio of the Russian-born sculptor Ossip Zadkine and, under his supervision, sculpted a stone *Head*, which was exhibited at the 1932 Salon d'Automne.[124] Agnes was at Sammer's side not only in Paris, but also in the Soviet Union and India. She often travelled to other places for her own work as a sculptor or visited her family in Honolulu. A number of the photos in Sammer's collection were taken together with her. Most of the inscriptions on the backs of the photographs that have them are by Larsen and she even had some of the negatives that are preserved in Sammer's collection developed while she was in Honolulu.

When high-quality photographs were needed to document the artwork she was making in Paris, Larsen was given a helping hand by her friends in Le Corbusier's circle. For example: 'There's another American working at Corbus's. His name is Andreas, son of a famous German painter – Feininger',[125] Sammer mentioned to Larsen one day after coming home from 35 rue de Sèvres. Shortly afterwards, Larsen reported to her mentor, Scheyer: 'Andreas obviously likes photography better than architecture. He is going to take pictures of my sculpture'.[126] At the beginning of his career, therefore, someone who would later become one of the most celebrated photographers of the twentieth century took photos of Larsen's sculptures.[127] Some of these shots have been preserved in Sammer's collection in Pondicherry.

Sammer talked about his relationship with Larsen as a marriage that had begun in 1932,[128] regardless of the lack of a formal, administrative confirmation. Not only did

[123] Galka Scheyer (1889–1945), an artist, collector and art dealer, came to the United States from Germany in 1924. With the approval of the Bauhaus, she represented a group of European modern artists, which she had founded and called the Blue Four. The members of the group were Lyonel Feininger, Paul Klee, Wassily Kandinsky and Alexej von Jawlensky, and it was thanks to Scheyer that the American public found out about their work. See Victoria Dailey, Natalie Shivers and Michael Dawson, *LA's Early Moderns: Art, Architecture, Photography*, introduction by William Deverall, Los Angeles, CA: Balcony Press, 2003, particularly pp. 42 and 43, and Peg Weiss, *Galka Scheyer and the Blue Four: A Dialogue with America*, Berkeley, CA: University of California Press, 1986.

[124] Larsen, *Graffiti* (n. 122), pp. 179–80, 187.

[125] Ibid., p. 196: Andreas Feininger, the son of a famous Bauhaus painter, Lyonel Feininger, found his way to Le Corbusier thanks to a family friend, Walter Gropius. He went to the atelier at 35 rue de Sèvres for nine months, from autumn 1932 to July 1933, and also pursued photography. Most of the negatives from his Paris sojourn, however, have not been preserved. See Thomas Buchsteiner and Ursula Zeller (eds.), *Andreas Feininger: Ein Fotografenleben/A Photographer's Life 1906–1999*, Ostfildern: Hatje Cantz, 2010, and Joel Smith, *Andreas*

∧ Agnes Larsen in a sculpture studio, Paris, 1930s.
Photograph, 2.9 × 3.6 cm. SAAA.
> Agnes Larsen, *Head*, stone. The work was shown at the Salon d'automne, Paris, in 1932.
Photograph, 8 × 11 cm. Photo: Andreas Feininger. SAAA.

Feininger, Poughkeepsie, NY: Vassar College, 2003, p. 12.
126| Larsen, *Graffiti* (n. 122), p. 197.
127| Ibid., pp. 194, 195, 208 and 209.
128| AMP, František Sammer Papers, letter to his father, 12 May 1935.
129| Larsen's works were awarded prizes both at the All-Russian Academy of Art in Moscow and in Honolulu, where her family lived. In December 1933 she won first prize at the Moscow academy for a bust of Karl Marx, which was intended for mass production. In spring 1935 she received the Grand Prize of the Honolulu Academy of Arts for her sculpture *Torso*. Considering the date of the quoted letter, it is likely that Sammer is referring to the prize received in Honolulu. Larsen, *Graffiti* (n. 122), pp. 274, 277, 306 and 311.
130| AMP, František Sammer Papers, letter to his father, 12 May 1935.

Le Corbusier comment on that sarcastically, but so too, did Sammer's conservative father. That's why in a letter to his father, Sammer later tried to describe the nature of his and Larsen's personal life:

On marriage

'Dad, you know, I feel like quite a happy person. [...] As you perhaps know, I am in love with my girlfriend, Agnes [...] She is a sculptress and received first prize at the exhibition of the Academy of Fine Arts.[129] [...] I don't know what you would think about the life we lead. It is quite different from what you know and have led. She and I both work. We understand each other very well. And we love each other. She is the best friend I have now. I respect her work and she respects mine. We have roughly the same view of things and also about life in its chief outlines. Where we differ in our views, we try to figure out objectively what is correct in the circumstances and we educate each other. Agnes is really merry, good, and beautiful [...] I am 28 years old and Agnes is probably 24. – That's it. – That would be our biography.'[130]

In reply, Sammer's father shared his views of the institution of marriage:
'You know that I have experience with marriage and you were witness to it too. So, I think that in most cases out of a hundred the life of lovers is much happier in our country before the wedding than afterwards. In both my cases after the wedding, the woman – I don't recognize equality, because my wives were not working to earn money for the family – changed from who she had been before. She was protected because there were children here. [...] In your world, you have what is known as

the emancipation of women. [...] Here in Czechoslovakia, marriage is a lifelong problem. It can make one's whole life beautiful, but it can ruin it, too. Where you live now, it will probably be better. [...] Your life cannot be compared with mine. I therefore cannot judge how I would have acted at your age, had I lived in your circumstances. [...] I think like this for your happiness and for the happiness of us all. There is, then, a bit of selfishness in my words when I say that I wish you happiness also in marriage.'[131]

The institution of marriage and especially its impact on the role of woman in society occupied the thoughts not only of modern women, who were able to withstand the test in the competitive milieu of Paris art circles, but also of the architects of Le Corbusier's circle. The topics of keeping one's maiden name, wearing one's hair short, freedom of speech and of movement and the careers of women were actively debated by them. Valuable testimony to that has been left by Larsen in her autobiography, in which we read that the most immediate example for these young men was Perriand, whom they encountered daily and also worked directly with. Sammer, too appreciated her: 'Take Le Corbusier's interior designer Madame Perriand. She doesn't lose her femininity just because she's efficient and talented in the office. And, by the way, she's kept her maiden name'.[132] The architect Gordon Stephenson remarked: 'It's obvious that even without the vote, women like her influence politics and have secured lots of freedoms other women only dream of'.[133] The architect Alex Adam, in the company of Jane West, Agnes Larsen and Anne Heyneman, said: 'Let's drink to the new woman!'[134]

Despite the conscious efforts for emancipation, the free professional development of these three women artists could not be taken for granted.[135] They still await a fitting appreciation and their place in the history of the twentieth century. Anne Heyneman left Paris and returned to California, where she would work as an illustrator.[136] Agnes Larsen worked between the wars as an artist in various countries around Europe and later enjoyed success with her sculptures in Honolulu and the Soviet Union. After returning to the United States, Jane West soon joined professional

< Agnes Larsen and František Sammer in a car, 1930s. Contact print, 3 × 4 cm. SAAA.

^ Photos of Sammer's parents from his collection in Pondicherry. The photo of his father is inscribed 'Dad' on the back and the photo of his mother and father together is inscribed on the back: 'Whit Monday, 10 June 1935, Dad and Mum, in Česká Kubice'. Photographs, 5.6 × 5.6 cm. SAAA.

131| SAAA, František Sammer Papers, a letter to Sammer from his father, 22 May 1935.
132| Larsen, *Graffiti* (n. 122), p. 91.
133| Ibid. Larsen quoting Stephenson. I discuss Stephenson below.
134| Ibid. p. 89. Larsen quoting Adam. I write about Adam in some detail below.
135| This group of women who supported one another on their trips and sojourns in Europe are a subject of my continuing research.
136| For this information, I am indebted to Carin Clauss.

'Yesterday, I began a new piece of sculpture – a bust of Karl Marx –, about eight inches high – for a competition. Portraits are easy for me because I like doing them. I try to probe the inner person'.

Agnes Larsen in a letter to her family in Hawaii, 2 November 1933, quoted in Larsen, *Graffiti*, p. 265 (see n. 122).

∧ Agnes Larsen, *Karl Marx*. In December 1933, the bust, intended for mass production, was awarded First Prize at the All-Russian Academy of Arts in Moscow. Contact prints, 3 × 4 cm. SAAA.

› Agnes Larsen, *Head of a Crying Child*. Moscow, January 1936. Contact prints, 3 × 4 cm and 2.7 × 3.8 cm (detail). SAAA.

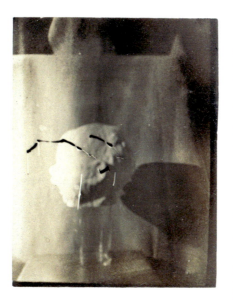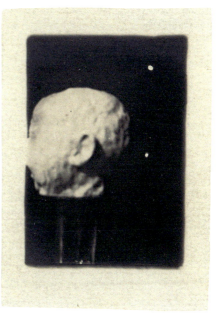

'I called on Carol, who has a three-month-old baby. The child was crying when I arrived, and wouldn't stop. Carol said, 'She's not hungry, wet or tired, so I let her cry'. Well, I took out my plasticene and, in a half an hour, modeled her bawling head, life-size. It came out well'.

Agnes Larsen in a letter to her family in Honolulu, 10 January 1936. Quoted in Larsen, *Graffiti*, p. 342 (see n. 122).

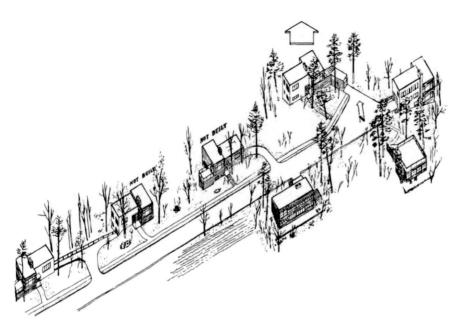

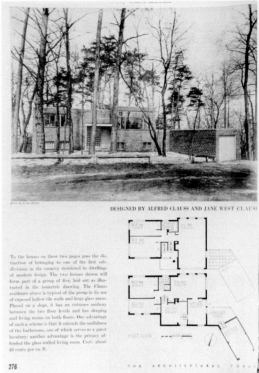

forces with her husband Alfred Clauss,[137] and, together with him, now adding his surname to her own, she devoted herself to modernist projects, which were, in this environment, strikingly innovative. From 1934 to 1945 they designed and built a complex of seven family houses, called 'Little Switzerland', in Knoxville, Tennessee.[138] Here, they also built their own house, whose interior makes no secret of Clauss's having found inspiration in the works of Mies van der Rohe[139] or West's experience of the Le Corbusier–Jeanneret atelier.[140] Sammer's collection includes four photographs of the interior of their home, which are published here for the first time. Eventually the Clausses joined in the regional development work of the Tennessee Valley Authority (TVA), which had also interested Le Corbusier and his circle.[141]

Urban Planning

In addition to his continuing work on large buildings at the beginning of the 1930s, Sammer drew the auditoriums for the Palace of the Soviets and perspective drawings for the whole complex. He was also responsible for some additional drawings for the already-completed project of the Villa de Madame Hélène de Mandrot and of the Wanner house.[142] In spring 1932, he began working on several projects for Algeria as well. He joined in one of the early phases of Le Corbusier's 'Plan Obus' for Algiers.[143] 'I am still working at Le Corbusier's, where I am beginning an urban plan for the city of Algiers',[144] Sammer wrote to his parents in early 1932, and in December of that year he wrote: 'The whole thing is now being re-worked and supplemented with economic information. We have won over an interested party, for whom we are now planning the development of properties near Algiers'.[145]

The private investor was a businessman, now known only by his surname, Durand, who had hired Le Corbusier to plan a residential district for the Domaine de Badjara, Oued Ouchaïa, near Algiers. Sammer's involvement in the project is confirmed not only by entries in the 'Livre noir' and specific drawings he made, but also by a photo of the model of one of the apartment buildings, which Sammer kept until the moment he left his photograph collection in Pondicherry in 1942.

Sammer had encountered urban-planning ideas as soon as he began working at 35 rue de Sèvres. In the *Plans* periodical, whose publishing Sammer assisted in, Le

< Alfred Clauss and Jane West Clauss, a residential community called Little Switzerland, in Knoxville, Tennessee, built from 1934 to 1945. Reproduced from Wodehouse, 'Houses by Alfred and Jane Clauss in Knoxville, Tennessee' (see n. 138).

∧ The Clauss Residence I (aka Hollow Tile House) in Little Switzerland, Knoxville, Tennessee. Exterior and floor plans, The Architectural Forum, April 1940, p. 276 (see n. 138).

137| Alfred Clauss (1906-98) was from Munich and worked in the United States beginning in the early 1930s, which is also where he met Jane West. Insight into their collaboration is provided, for example, by A. H. Alexander, 'Blueprint for Happiness: Teamwork in Marriage', *The Philadephia Inquirer*, 19 February 1950, p. 18. A source of biographical information about Clauss is the obituary by Bill Price, 'Alfred Clauss, 91, Retired Designer of Many Buildings', *The Philadephia Inquirer*, 11 June 1998, p. 116. For her advice on this topic and for providing me with these sources, I am again grateful to Mary McLeod..

138| Executed projects by Alfred and Jane West Clauss in Knoxville were publicized in leading architectural periodicals of the day. See 'House Portfolio', in *Architectural Forum*, April 1940, pp. 276-78, and 'In Knoxville, Tennessee... Designed by Alfred Clauss and Jane West Clauss', *Pencil Points: Progressive Architecture* 26, February 1945, pp. 60-62. In particular, see 'Alfred e Jane West Clauss, un villaggio in cooperativa', *Domus: La casa dell'uomo* 210, 1946, pp. 4-8, and Lawrence Wodehouse, 'Houses by Alfred and Jane Clauss in Knoxville Tennessee', *ARRIS*, vol. 1, 1989, pp. 50-61. For her research and providing me with these sources, I am indebted to Irena Žantovská Murray.

139| Wodehouse puts emphasis on this aspect of the career of Alfred Clauss, who gained practical experience at the office of Mies van der Rohe before his departure for the United States. Wodehouse, 'Houses by Alfred and Jane Clauss in Knoxville Tennessee' (n. 138)

> Interior of the Clauss Residence, Knoxville, Tennessee, and a photograph of the Clausses's son Peter Otto at the age of six weeks. On the back of one of the photos is written: 'Our House'. Photographs, 5.8 × 3.8 cm, developed and printed in Knoxville, Tennessee, on 8 December 1936. SAAA.

140| In this connection, Mardges Bacon discusses the houses in Knoxville from the perspective of Jane West. See Bacon, *Le Corbusier in America* (n. 86), pp. 5, 6, 292, 293 and 389.

141| For the connection between the TVA and Le Corbusier, see Mardges Bacon, 'Le Corbusier and Postwar America: The TVA and Béton Brut', *Journal of the Society of Architectural Historians* 74, no. 1 (March 2015), pp. 13-40.

142| FLC, 'Livre noir'.

143| In the very heart of Algiers, in the Quartier de la Marine, Le Corbusier planned to build a business center connected with residential neighbourhoods in the Quartier Fort l'Empereur by motorway ramps. Part of the project is for a great residential viaduct alongside the coast. For more on the project, see Jean-Pierre Giordani, 'Urbanisme, projets A, B, C, H, Alger, Algérie 1930', in *Le Corbusier: Plans* DVD, Paris, Tokyo: Codex Images International, 2005-06. For an analysis of the projects and Le Corbusier's fascination with Algiers, see Mary McLeod, 'Le Corbusier and Algiers', in Frampton (ed.), *Le Corbusier 1933-1960*, special issue of *Oppositions* (n. 32), pp. 54-85.

144| AMP, František Sammer Papers, letter to his parents, January 1932; the original is antedated 11 January 1931.

145| AMP, František Sammer Papers, letter to his parents, 20 December 1932.

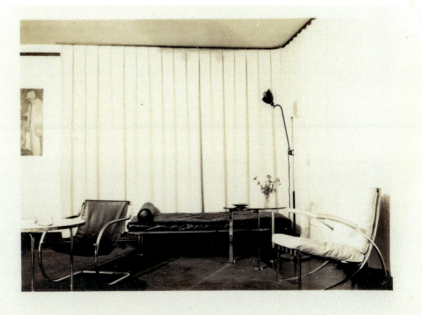

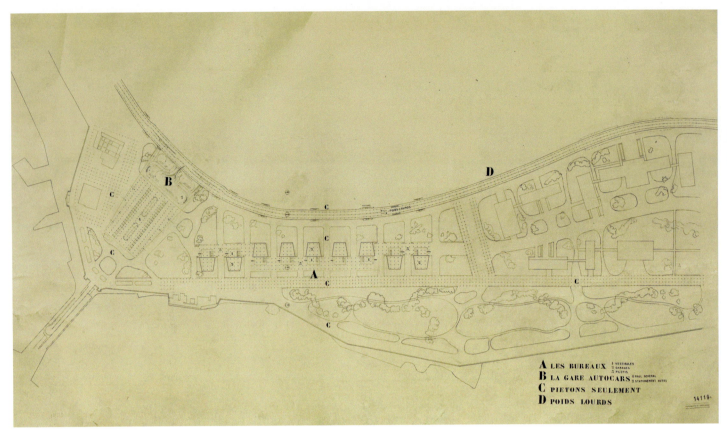

Corbusier first presented his radical concept called the 'Ville Radieuse', with all its political, economic and social justifications. The project of a decentralized city divided into zones according to function was developed by Le Corbusier as a reply to a questionnaire about the urban planning of Moscow that the town council of which had sent him in 1930. He then developed the design created for the Soviet capital into a universal solution for other cities around the world, for example, in urban plans for Geneva, Antwerp and Stockholm.[146] Even the big commissions for buildings from the beginning of the 1930s, which Sammer had worked on in Paris, were not perceived by Le Corbusier as merely independent projects. For him they were laboratories, testing grounds for ideas, which he wanted to implement further on a much larger scale: in urban planning.[147]

Sammer's colleagues in the atelier, Stephenson and Adam,[148] who would become his lifelong friends, were involved in urban planning as well. Already in the summer of 1932, Sammer began working with Adam on a competition entry for an urban plan of Stockholm.[149] Later, they were supposed to be joined by Stephenson, who at the time was trying to establish himself in Great Britain.

Alex Adam (1905–after 1969), born Alek Kertész, came from Budapest. He arrived in Paris in the late 1920s to study architecture and later worked in Great Britain.[150] Gordon Stephenson (1908–97), a graduate of the Liverpool School of Architecture, and later a close colleague of the distinguished British urban planner William Holford,[151] came to Paris in 1930 on a two-year postgraduate scholarship. In the evenings he attended the Institut d'urbanisme at the Université de Paris, and from November 1931 to April 1932 he worked at 35 rue de Sèvres during the day, sharing a drawing board with Sammer.[152] Stephenson was the first architect in the Le Corbusier–Jeanneret atelier who came from Great Britain.[153] In the international community that Le Corbusier formed with his assistants at 35 rue de Sèvres, Stephenson was usually called 'Robert', since he represented the country of the writer Robert Louis Stevenson, whose adventure stories were known around the world.[154]

^ František Sammer, a drawing for the Plan Obus (Shrapnel Plan), 21 March 1932, a drawing of part of the ground level of the business district of the city of Algiers, located below the elevated motorway. FLC 14119.

> František Sammer, a drawing of the first variant of the project for a residential quarter of an entrepreneur by the name of Durand, for the Domaine de Badjara, Oued Ouchaïa, Algeria. A general plan, from 11 October 1932. FLC 13951A.

>> Sammer's drawing of the residential quarter of the entrepreneur Durand, Oued Ouchaïa, Algeria. Reproduced in Boesiger (ed.), Le Corbusier et Pierre Jeanneret: Œuvre complète 1929–1934, vol. 2, p. 161 (see n. 41).

> Le Corbusier, a residential block with receding floors, designed for a residential district to be developed by the entrepreneur Durand, Oued Ouchaïa, Algeria. Model. Photograph, 11.6 × 12.2 cm. SAAA. (A copy is held also at the Fondation Le Corbusier, FLC L1(1)8.)

146| It was then published in full as Le Corbusier, La Ville Radieuse, Boulogne-sur-Seine: Éditions de l'Architecture d'Aujourd'hui, 1935. For the political background of the project and the development of published versions of Le Corbusier's 'La Ville radieuse' in contemporary periodicals from 1930 onwards, see McLeod, 'Urbanism and Utopia' (n. 32).

147| Le Corbusier in Boesiger (ed.), Le Corbusier et Pierre Jeanneret, Œuvre complète (n. 41), vol. 2, p. 11: 'Qu'avons-nous donc fait pendant ces années 1929–1934? Quelques bâtiments d'abord, puis beaucoup de grandes études d'urbanisme. Ces bâtiments ont joué le rôle de laboratoires. Nous avons voulu que chaque élément construit pendant ces années-là fut la preuve expérimentale qui permettrait de prendre en toute sécurité les initiatives indispensables en urbanisme'.

148| According to the 'Répertoire des collaborateurs' Adam worked in

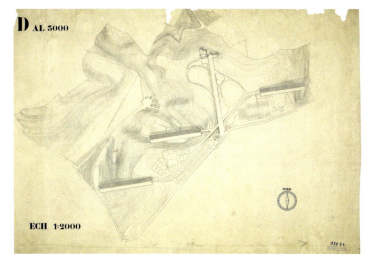

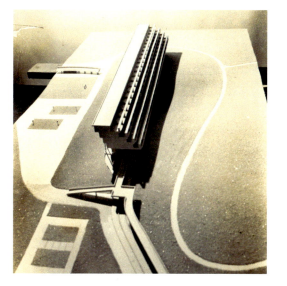

the atelier in 1932, and Stephenson in 1931 and 1932. Although Adam entered 35S sooner than Stephenson, he first signed a drawing listed in the 'Livre noir' on 26 October 1932 and Stephenson first signed one much earlier, on 15 December 1931. These are great examples of the nature of the data entered in the 'Répertoire des collaborateurs' and the 'Livre noir' only being indicative. The exact dates of the stay and tasks of the architects at the 35S are to be searched optimally with help of other period sources.

149| AMP, František Sammer Papers, letter to his parents, 5 August 1932.

150| Regarding Adam's Hungarian origin, see Larsen, *Graffiti* (n. 122), p. 90. See also Gordon E. Cherry and Leith Penny, *Holford: A Study in Architecture, Planning and Civic Design*, London: Routledge, Taylor & Francis e-Library, 2005, p. 47. I discuss Adam in my other research.

151| William Holford (1907–75), a British architect, established himself in the field of urban planning and was involved in the reconstruction of British towns after the devastation caused by German bombing during the Second World War. As a teacher he will be forever linked with the Liverpool School of Architecture. He also served as president of the Royal Town Planning Institute (1953-54) and of the Royal Institute of British Architects (1960-62), and his works had an international impact, including projects built in Australia and South Africa. For details, see Cherry and Penny, *Holford* (n. 150).

152| Gordon Stephenson, 'Chapters of Autobiography I–III', *The Town Planning Review* 62, no. 1 (January 1991), p. 23. For more, see his recollections in Stephenson, *On a Human Scale* (n. 122).

153| Stephenson, *On a Human Scale* (n. 122), p. 29. Le Corbusier 'was also interested because nobody from Britain had worked with him and he was a great admirer of British watercolourists', Stephenson wrote, recalling his start with Le Corbusier.

154| Ibid., p. 41. The popularity of the Scottish writer Robert Louis Stevenson (1850–94) and the association of his name with Great Britain at that time is also clear from Sammer's reports of his first visit to the country, See 'Excursus 1'. p. 156.

155| AMP, František Sammer Papers, letter home, 2 May 1932.

156| Ibid., 20 September 1932.

157| Ibid., 20 December 1932.

From the entries in the 'Livre noir' it is clear that Sammer and Stephenson collaborated on several assignments at the Le Corbusier–Jeanneret atelier. These were not, however, only tasks for the atelier. Sammer helped Stephenson with projects for his school, and in one letter home he mentions that he was 'doing a bit of work for [...] Stephenson, who is busy with a small town-planning project for the Institut d'urbanisme'.[155] Together, they also mulled over their own plans for the future. Winning an architectural competition, which would offer them employment in Europe, would, for a while at least, help the young architects out of destitution. 'My friends Adam and Stephenson are jobless [...] Stephenson is in England [...]. Then, of course, he will come here straightaway, so that all three of us can work on a project for Stockholm. We are still hoping for an employment opportunity here in Paris',[156] Sammer wrote home in autumn 1932.

Another possible solution to unemployment was leaving the group of architects at 35 rue de Sèvres to work in the Soviet Union. They constantly debated this possibility, discussing options with other interested people from Le Corbusier's circle. 'After the Christmas holidays, Stephenson will come [...] and we are putting our hopes in establishing a programme for Russia. We are also putting our hopes in an alliance with our friend Adam, who has been hard hit by the Depression, but, you know, we all look after one another and so get by',[157] Sammer wrote in a letter home at the end of that year.

< Gordon Stephenson and Alex Adam, 1936. On the back: 'Tour de l'an 1936 – Trip of the year, 1936'. Photograph, 12 × 8.7 cm. SAAA.

Leaving 35 rue de Sèvres, Spring 1933

Sammer eventually became involved in the competition project for an urban plan for Stockholm, probably only as part of an assignment at the Le Corbusier–Jeanneret atelier. That is confirmed by a remark in a letter of February 1933: 'We have finished the project for Algiers and are now working on a project for Stockholm'.[158] Nevertheless, in this same period, he already knew that he wanted to leave 35 rue de Sèvres and to try his luck as an independent, professional architect. To that end, he joined forces with his friends and together they entered a competition for an urban plan for the City of Antwerp. In the first half of 1933 the Le Corbusier–Jeanneret atelier was also working on plans to submit.[159] Stephenson, Adam and Sammer, together with Holford,[160] had, however, decided to come up with an alternative design. For this task, they spent a few weeks of intensive work at the home of Stephenson's parents in West Kirby, near Liverpool: 'We have formed a group of four friends to embark on this [...] In England I'll be a guest of Gordon Stephenson'.[161]

Sammer left Paris at the beginning of March 1933 and until the last moment did not know what direction his career would take him. Though he had decided to quit his salaried job at 35 rue de Sèvres, he knew that he could return any time. 'If I return from Russia (if I return), I will definitely again get work at Corbusier's, if I want it',[162] he replied to the apprehensive questions of his father, and by way of explanation added: 'If I keep my cozy job at Corbík's, I will not know more than I know now. If I am unemployed in Czechoslovakia, it will be worse'.[163] Sammer remained in regular touch with Le Corbusier, Jeanneret and the others from the atelier, and before he took on more work, he set out on a great journey to know the world.

Sammer's itinerary for that trip in 1933 included several places connected to people associated with the Le Corbusier–Jeanneret atelier. Inspired by Perriand's travels, Sammer first planned a trip to the 'Balearic Islands, which seem like paradise'.[164] Ultimately, he chose the Iberian Peninsula and the Maghreb, where in previous years his bosses Le Corbusier and Pierre Jeanneret had travelled. They had already driven through Spain by car in 1930, together with the painter Fernand Léger. A year later, shortly after Sammer's arrival at 35 rue de Sèvres, they returned to Spain and included the Maghreb, particularly Tétouan in Morocco and towns in the Algerian interior.[165] Here they found inspiration for future projects on which Sammer would also work with them,[166] and they came to know places that he too, on their recommendation, would later visit.

158| Ibid., 16 February 1933.

159| The international competition for the urban plan of the left bank of the River Scheldt at Antwerp was announced in 1932 and was closed the following year without having selected a winner. Of the 95 projects, four (in a Neoclassical spirit) were given awards, but none was ever chosen to be built. Architectural periodicals of the day, however, were dominated by Le Corbusier's design, which was made in collaboration with the Belgian architects Huib Hoste and Félix Loquet, and, like a number of other entrants, was disqualified from the competition for not having met the technical requirements. Despite its failure, this design became a source of inspiration and Le Corbusier devoted himself to the project in the following years as well. See Patrick Burniat, 'Urbanisme de la rive gauche de l'Éscaut, 1933, Antwerp, Belgium', *Le Corbusier Plans Online*, Echelle 1 Internationale-Fondation Le Corbusier, and *Le Corbusier et le mouvement moderne en Belgique 1920-1940* (exh. cat.), Liège: s.n., 1988, pp. 66–73. For a detailed contemporary account of the competition, including criticism of the technical requirements, see Victor Bourgeois, 'Le Concours International pour l'Urbanisation de la Rive gauche de l'Escaut, à Anvers', *La Cité* 11, no. 8 (July-August 1933), pp. 145–68.

160| The architects agreed to collaborate during Holford's Paris visit in January 1933. Stephenson, *On a Human Scale* (n. 122), p. 45. See also Cherry and Penny, *Holford* (n. 150), p. 47.

161| AMP, František Sammer Papers, letter home, 16 February 1933.

162| Ibid., 24 February 1933.

163| Ibid.

164| Ibid., letter to his parents, 2 August 1932. The Balearic Islands, and especially the simplicity of the vernacular Mediterranean architecture on Ibiza, provided the mainstay and inspiration for the basic ideas of the modern movement. Of the architects from Le Corbusier's circle, Josep Lluís Sert developed this connection for the rest of his career. See Antonio Pizza (ed.), *J. Ll. Sert y el mediterráneo/J. Ll. Sert and Mediterranean Culture*, [Barcelona]: Colegio de Arquitectos de Catalunya, [1997], pp. 65–71. For Perriand's photographs of the Balearic Islands in 1932, see Barsac (ed.), *Charlotte Perriand* (n. 6), vol. 1, pp. 296 and 297, and id., *Charlotte Perriand et la photographie: l'œil en éventail*, Paris, Milan: 5 Continents, 2011, pp. 216–20.

165| For Le Corbusier's trips to Spain and the Maghreb, see Juan José Lahuerta, 'Spain: Travelling to See the Already Seen', in Cohen (ed.), *An Atlas* (n. 13), pp. 140–45, or the chapter 'Algeria' in Tim Benton, *LC FOTO: Le Corbusier Secret Photographer*, Zurich: Lars Müller, 2013, pp. 370–85. For details about Le Corbusier and Spain, see Juan José Lahuerta (ed.), *Le Corbusier y España*, Barcelona: Centre de Cultura Contemporània, 1997.

166| See McLeod, 'Le Corbusier and Algiers' (n. 143) and pp. 66–69 above about Sammer's collaboration on Le Corbusier's projects for Algiers.

167| The Port Vell Aerial Tramway, built on the occasion of the 1929 Barcelona International Exposition, offers a scenic route above the town between the hill called Montjuïc and La Barceloneta, originally a fishing village.

168| AMP, František Sammer Papers, letter home, 15 March 1933. Larsen, *Graffiti* (n. 122), p. 216. Sert's name is spelled variously in the literature: in Spanish, José Luis Sert, and in Catalan, Josep Lluís Sert. I have chosen the latter for this publication.

Spain and the Maghreb

Throughout his Paris sojourn Sammer was short of money for photographic material. However, on his travels, he frequently used a camera, having found sufficient resources to take photographs. He travelled with two cameras, for formats of 3 × 4 cm and 6 × 9 cm negatives. Most of the photos have been preserved as contact prints made on the then-popular Velox photographic paper. Some of the shots he even took with both cameras, as is evident, for example, from the bird's-eye-view of the Port of Barcelona. The photos from the aerial tramway between the hill called Montjuïc and the beaches at Barceloneta[167] differ from one another only by a tiny shift in perspective, which was caused by the movement of the cable car. The photos could have been taken by Sammer, Larsen, who was travelling with him, or indeed any friend who was present.

In Barcelona, Sammer and Larsen were guests of Josep Lluís Sert (1902–83),[168] who would become a leading figure of modern architecture in Spain. They knew one

> A double-decker bus in Barcelona and the Casa Milà by Antoni Gaudí, from 1906–12. Contact prints, 3 × 4 and 2.6 × 4 cm. SAAA.

∨ A view of the station of the Port Vell Aerial Tramway on Montjuïc. The cable car was built on the occasion of the 1929 Barcelona International Exposition. Contact print, 5.7 × 8.8 cm. SAAA.

∨ 'Barcelona – a view from the small cabin of the cable car'. Photo with an inscription by František Sammer on the back. Contact print, 2.6 × 4 cm. SAAA.

'And then Barcelona: functioning disorder and filthy splendour. – A warm reception by my friend Sert, trips to the surrounding area, and, fish and crabs and wine and oranges for lunch – the best things I have ever eaten in my whole life. –'

Sammer in a letter to his parents in Pilsen, 15 March 1933 (see n. 168). AMP.

 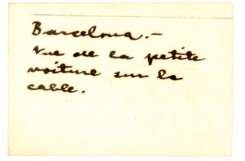

another from the Le Corbusier–Jeanneret atelier and met repeatedly in future years.[169] One of the recollections of the meeting with Sert in Spain has been preserved by Sammer in a photo casually taken on the street. Sert and his wife are shown here in lively conversation with a man standing with his back to the camera as other people pass by. The photograph gives equal attention to the anonymous pedestrians, in fact it is the moment in the shot that has greater value than the legibility of the figures of Sammer's friends. Nor was Sammer interested in an objective record of architectural works; the view of Sert's recently built Casa Bloc in Calle de Muntaner is one of the few photographs of modern architecture in Sammer's collection. Of the vast housing block, however, we see only part of a corner. The Barcelona street with the original buildings occupies the same space as the new, modern building. More than a document of a future monument to modern architecture, the photo offers a hint of a once-experienced atmosphere, a little window into a situation in which there remains room for mystery and personal communication. The contrast between Sammer's photo and most architectural photography is striking: note for example a photo of the same building, which the Italian architect Alberto Sartoris kept in his collection of photographs.[170]

With his own way of seeing the world, Sammer, together with Larsen, continued his travels. From Barcelona they headed south, through Valencia, Madrid, Toledo, Córdoba, Seville and Granada, all the way to Algeciras in the Strait of Gibraltar [see Excursus 2]. From there, they boarded a boat to Morocco, especially 'to see Tétouan, which according to Pierre Jeanneret is apparently something one must do'.[171] The villages and towns hidden in the Moroccan steppes and hills largely had traditional Arab and Berber inhabitants. The unique urban scenery, views of market places, streets and crowds of people bundled up in traditional costumes were captured by

< Josep Lluís Sert and his wife, Muncha Sert, in a Barcelona street. Photograph, 3 × 3.9 cm. SAAA.

∧ Calle de Muntaner, Barcelona, with an apartment building Casa Bloc on the corner, designed by Josep Lluís Sert. Contact print, 3 × 4 cm. SAAA.

169| Ibid. (n. 1), letter to his parents, 30 January 1937, and the text below on pp. 120, 124, and 125
170| Antoine Baudin (ed.), *Photography, Modern Architecture and Design. The Alberto Sartoris Collection: Objects from the Vitra Design Museum*, Lausanne: EPFL Press and the Vitra Design Museum, 2005, p. 122.
171| AMP, František Sammer Papers, letter to his parents, 15 March 1933.

^ A view of the Moll de Barcelona (Barcelona Dock) in the Port of Barcelona from the cable car. Contact prints, 5.7 × 8.8 cm and 3 × 4 cm. SAAA. A third photo is deposited in the AMP, František Sammer Papers, LP 1796, inv. no. 311.

v Josep Lluís Sert, apartment house in Calle de Muntaner, 1929. Photo: Oriol. Arxiu Històric del COAC.

> 'Spain between Barcelona and Algeciras'. Photograph, 2.6 × 4 cm. SAAA.

'A colleague of François's, who works with Corbu and also has his own studio here, drove us about in his tiny car and gave us helpful suggestions for our itineraries. He is José Sert, one of the best city planners in Europe, though he's only about thirty'.

Agnes Larsen in a letter sent from Barcelona to Honolulu, 9 March 1933. Quoted in Larsen, *Graffiti*, p. 216 (see n. 122).

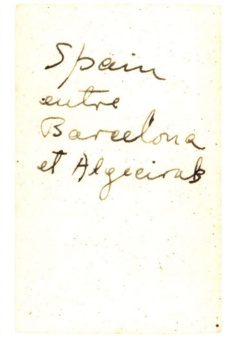

^ Agnes Larsen at the kasbah (fortress) in Chefchaouen, Morocco. Photograph, 8.1 × 5.2 cm. SAAA.

Sammer in a series of photos taken on 6 × 9 cm negatives. Most of the photos were taken in Tétouan and the mountain city of Chefchaouen, its fortifications, streets and the surrounding hills.

These places were difficult to access. Sammer and Larsen could only reach some of them on horseback. But Sammer's collection does not include touristy shots. The series of photographs from Morocco seem to have been taken clandestinely, often in motion, in an attempt to capture the hubbub of local life. The photographer aimed his camera at a moment in time rather than at static buildings or figures posing for a portrait. The only piece of pictorial evidence we have that Sammer was not travelling through Morocco alone is in the left-hand side of a shot of the fortress in Chefchaouen, where a laughing Larsen has appeared by chance. The photo is blurry, not to mention that Larsen, who has been caught in motion, is hardly recognizable. Yet Sammer was not only content with making his own contact print of this negative; he chose to have this photograph printed by a professional.

In her autobiography Larsen mentions the range of colours and the intensity of light in Africa, which encouraged her and Sammer to document the trip in drawings and watercolours.[172] Sammer wrote home: 'I have taken quite a lot of photographs and when I have developed them all I'll send you pictures'.[173]

The series of photographs from the Maghreb show that Sammer used the camera to capture sequences of motion and time. In this respect, his photographs are strikingly similar to records Le Corbusier made later, when, in 1938, he travelled around Algeria with a movie camera.[174] Le Corbusier's picture sequences, particularly from the market places in the cities of Beni-Isguen and Ghardaïa, are captured with the same approach as Sammer's when photographing the tangle of little streets of traditional villages and towns in Morocco.

172| Larsen, *Graffiti* (n. 122), pp. 220 and 221. 'Excursus 2', p. 169. Unfortunately, none of this work has survived.
173| AMP, František Sammer Papers, letter to his sister Miloslava (Milča), 26 March 1933.
174| For a thorough analysis of Le Corbusier's work with a still camera and movie camera, see Benton, *LC FOTO* (n. 165). Le Corbusier began to use the movie camera in 1936; see ibid., pp. 168–87. For Le Corbusier's films and photos from Northwest Africa, see ibid., pp. 370–85.
175| AMP, František Sammer Papers, postcard to his brother Jan (Jenda), 6 April 1933. See the plate on p. 76.
176| Miloslava (Milča, Milána) Gschwindová, née Sammerová (1904–42), officially a housewife, was a volunteer nurse in the Red Cross and a member of the Communist resistance during the German occupation. Highly involved in the printing and dissemination of anti-Nazi leaflets, she was imprisoned in 1940 and executed by guillotine in Berlin on 4 September 1942. 'Dokumentace popravených Čechoslováků za druhé světové války v Berlíně – Plötzensee', Institute for the Study of Totalitarian Regimes, Prague, https://www.ustrcr.cz/uvod/popraveni-plotzensee/ Accessed 4 August 2023. See also AMP, František Sammer Papers: Jindra Nezbedová, 'Těžko se vrátím...', newspaper cutting from the column 'Ženy, které bychom měli znát', 6 September 1969, call number LP 1790, and 'Miroslava Gschwidnová', Gedenkstätte Plötzensee website: https://www.gedenkstaette-ploetzensee.de/totenbuch/recherche/person/gschwindova-miloslava Accessed 18 May 2023.
177| AMP, František Sammer Papers, letter to his sister, Milča, 26 March 1933.

⇞ > North Morocco in Sammer's photographs.
Contact prints, 5.7 × 8.8 cm. SAAA.

∧ > Stills from Le Corbusier's film shot in Algeria, 1938.
FLC 6148, 6334 and 6242.

Using a similarly cinematographic approach, Sammer also recorded moments of travelling by boat. A captured scene from a quickly moving sailing boat evokes the experience of moving swiftly across the water. From various stages of voyages on vessels of all kinds come photographs of the surface of the water, moving away from the coast and the mainland towards the horizon. Similarly, there is a preserved sequence of photos of the departure from Gibraltar, where, on 6 April 1933, Sammer and Larsen boarded the *Dempo*, a Dutch passenger and cargo ship, for Southampton.[175] Two printed photos of an approaching ship are supplemented by a contact print of man with a small suitcase walking along a wharf towards the ship at anchor. The ship in these photographs from Sammer's collection can be identified thanks to a postcard with a mention of the *Dempo*, which Sammer sent from Gibraltar to his younger brother, Jenda, in Pilsen. He also described the whole trip in detail in a letter to his sister Milča, at the end of March 1933:[176] 'Our holidays are wonderful, but we are already talking about Liverpool and looking forward to our friends and work'.[177] In the letter, Sammer already gave his contact address as 'F. S. c/o Gordon Stephenson, Liverpool School of Architecture, Liverpool'. From Africa they headed via Lisbon straight to Great Britain, where they met with the team that was assembled to work on a competition entry for the Antwerp urban plan.

'What we saw from up front resembled an abstract painting'.

A recollection of Agnes Larsen, in Larsen, *Graffiti*, p. 220 (see n. 122).

< A view from a fast-moving sailing boat, the Maghreb. Photograph, 8.1 × 5.2 cm. SAAA.

ʌ Contact prints, 3 × 4 cm. SAAA.

< Contact print, 2.8 × 3.8 cm (a crop of a 3 × 4 cm negative). SAAA.

v Sammer's postcard for his brother, Jenda, from Gibraltar, 6 April 1933. AMP.

'Honza,
Greetings from Gibraltar!
I remembered you and the stamp from Gibraltar, when I returned yesterday evening to Algeciras. Now it is six o'clock in the morning and in a moment we'll be on board the Dempo, a Dutch ship. On 9 April we'll be in Southampton. Frantík. –'

'François and I leaned against the rail to watch the frothy wake trailing at the stern'.

One of Agnes Larsen's recollections, in Larsen, *Graffiti*, p. 220 (see n. 122).

˄ > A sequence of snapshots from 6 April 1933, when Sammer and Larsen boarded the Dempo, a Dutch ship, in Gibraltar. Two contact prints, 3.8 × 2.8 cm and one 3 × 4 cm. SAAA.

> The Basílica da Estrela, Lisbon, a view from the roof. Contact print, 3 × 3.9 cm. SAAA.

˅ Sammer's postcard for his father, sent from Lisbon, 7 April 1933. AMP.

'We drop anchor in Lisbon. Greetings! The trip and the voyage have been great. We are swimming and sunbathing. Tomorrow we will pass by Cape Finisterre. – With best wishes, Frantík'

West Kirby

'I hope, dear Franti, the "Liverpool" competition results in some big money for you, because it is needed',[178] wrote Sammer's pragmatic father shortly before his son left for Great Britain. Yet, it was not only Sammer and his father who hoped that a possible victory in the Antwerp competition would lead to a better future. Stephenson and Adam were facing a similarly uncertain future, and Holford, because of work, even finished his postgraduate scholarship in Rome early.[179] Except for Adam, the other members of the team did not have much experience with large competitions, and they set about the task with great expectations and ambitions.[180]

During April and May 1933, the whole group lived and worked intensively at the home of Stephenson's parents in West Kirby near Liverpool. Sammer was accompanied by Larsen and Holford was accompanied by the painter Marjorie Brooks, whom he had become close to in Rome. 'This is our third day here', wrote Sammer in a letter home on 15 April. 'All four of us are working on that project. We are set up very nicely here. West Kirby is a small village, roughly like Nová Huť. Except that it is at the seaside'.[181] Glimpses of the ongoing work in the family home have been preserved as contact prints of 3 × 4 cm negatives. In blurry photos of the architects in action and of the makeshift office in the living room of the English home there survives the atmosphere of the commitment to work and of the unique encounter. Despite the miniature dimensions and low technical quality, the photographs evoke certain moments even today. The importance these photos had for the people in them is also confirmed by a recent find I made in a Liverpool archive. Photos identical to ones Sammer had were kept by Stephenson as well. What is more, some of Stephenson's photos complement Sammer's.[182] Thanks to the photos from West Kirby, it is also possible to identify one photograph from Perriand's private archive. By comparing a portrait of Adam in the collections of Sammer and Stephenson, one can identify him in one of the Perriand photographs, at rest, described as 'An unknown friend on a wall'.[183]

For the entry for the Antwerp urban plan competition, three architects joined forces, each of whom had at least a year's experience in the Le Corbusier–Jeanneret atelier.

< Agnes Larsen looking out of a window. František Sammer is looking into the window. West Kirby, England, spring/summer 1933.
Contact prints, 5.7 × 8.5 cm. SAAA.

178| SAAA, František Sammer Papers, letter from Sammer's father, sent from Pilsen, 27 March 1933.
179| Cherry and Penny, *Holford* (n. 150), p. 47.
180| Ibid., p. 53. See also Stephenson, *On a Human Scale* (n. 122), p. 46.
181| AMP, František Sammer Papers, letter to his parents, 15 April 1933. The Nová Huť that Sammer means is most likely the village of that name near Pilsen, located in a bend in the River Klabava.
182| Special Collections and Archives of the University of Liverpool (UoLL), Gordon Stephenson Papers, D307/6/2/275-281. For her assistance and willingness in the search for photographs, I am indebted to Robyn Orr.
183| Barsac, *L'œil en éventail* (n. 164), p. 83, with a reproduction of the photograph *Un ami sur un mur*, c.1936.
184| Cherry and Penny, *Holford* (n. 150), pp. 42-43, 52-56.
185| Ibid., p. 53. The authors quote from a letter Stephenson wrote to Holford, 3 February 1933, about the competition: '[the] vital point of all our theoretical plans. The commencement of real action. [...] Anyway, it would be extraordinarily valuable as an essay in team work which we aim at as we move irresistibly leftwards'.
186| See McLeod, 'Urbanism and Utopia' (n. 146) and p. 68 above, where the 'Ville Radieuse' is explained in connection with the *Plans* periodical.
187| The entries of all 95 participants were exhibited in Antwerp, but

> Taking a break in the back yard of a house in West Kirby. In the first photo, from the left, František Sammer and Gordon Stephenson. In the second photo, Sammer in a chair surrounded by friends. Contact prints, 3 × 4 cm. UoLL (see n. 182).

none of them were awarded first prize (see n. 159). In a letter from 17 August 1933, Agnes Larsen, in Moscow at the time, reported on the results of the competition. Quoted in Larsen, *Graffiti* (n. 122), p. 251. 'P.S. We didn't win the Antwerp competition'.

188 | The competition for the 'entertainment hall' in Bexhill was announced in *The Architects' Journal* on 7 September 1933 with the deadline of 4 December of that year. The competition committee judged 230 entries and announced the results in February 1934. Based on the winning project by the architects Erich Mendelsohn and Serge Chermayeff, one of the most emblematic works of modern architecture in Great Britain was built, also known as the De La Warr Pavilion. See Russell Stevens and Peter Willis, 'Earl De La Warr and the Competition for the Bexhill Pavilion, 1933-34', *Architectural History: Journal of the Society of Architectural Historians of Great Britain* 33, 1990, pp. 135-51. The competition entry by Alex Adam, William Holford and Gordon Stephenson did not place among the winning designs. See Cherry and Penny, *Holford* (n. 150), p. 55.

189 | The competition for the building of the town hall in Slough was announced in *The Architect and Building News* 138 (6 April 1934), pp. 8-9. The results were announced in *The Architect and Building News* 138 (20 July 1934), p. 60 and the winning design was published in *The Architect and Building News* 138 (27 July 1934), pp. 98-102. The project plans on which Stephenson worked for the competition did not place among the winners.

They were joined in the project by Holford, who respected Le Corbusier as a town planner.[184] Stephenson at the time saw the project as the culmination of theoretical plans and the beginning of 'real action', at least in the form of the independent team whose left-wing leanings were becoming increasingly apparent.[185] Their monumental urban plan for a whole area on the left bank of the River Scheldt did not conceal its sources of inspiration in Le Corbusier's radical concept of the Ville Radieuse.[186] Part of the project, however, was a diagram in which the young architects compare their design to Le Corbusier's and to the city fabrics of Paris and Antwerp and the garden city of Butte-Rouge in Châtenay-Malabry. Their design differed from the others mainly in its proposal of lower-density settlement and the vast amount of green space, slightly more even than that proposed by Le Corbusier in the Ville Radieuse.[187]

Sammer was one of the four architects to sign the entry. Moreover, photographs of the project drawings are preserved in his collection. He also kept a photo of the competition entry for an 'entertainment hall' in Bexhill[188] and the design for the competition for a new town hall in Slough.[189] At the time when these two projects were designed, however, Sammer was no longer in Great Britain. The presence of copies of the Bexhill and Slough projects in Sammer's collection can therefore be seen as evidence of the lively circulation of information amongst the architects regardless of where they happened to be at the time. Sammer clearly discussed current projects with his friends from Liverpool while he was working in a completely different environment, separated by a considerable distance.

<< Alex Adam at work on the entry for the Antwerp urban plan competition. West Kirby, spring/ summer 1933. Photograph, 5.4 × 8 cm. SAAA. (Gordon Stephenson kept a print of the same photo, now in the UoLL.) (see n. 182).

< Alex Adam, West Kirby, spring/summer 1933. Contact print, 5.7 × 8.5 cm. SAAA.

< Alex Adam in a photograph from the Archives Charlotte Perriand, where he is called an 'unidentified friend' (see n. 183). AChP.

Architects at work on a competion entry for an urban plan for Antwerp at the home of Stephenson's parents in West Kirby, England, spring/summer 1933.
<<< František Sammer and Gordon Stephenson. (Stephenson kept a print of the same photo, now in the UoLL.) (see n. 182).
<< Clockwise: František Sammer, Alex Adam, William Holford. Contact prints, 3 × 4 cm. SAAA.
< William Holford. Contact print, 5.7 × 8.5 cm. SAAA.

'Except for the kitchen and bathrooms, every part of the house has been converted into a studio. Going from one room to another requires stepping over jars of paint and ink, piles of scrap paper and eraser crumbs, and hurdling drafting boards, T-squares, tea cups and bodies of pooped-out architects'.

Agnes Larsen in a letter sent from West Kirby to Honolulu, 25 May 1933. Quoted in Larsen, *Graffiti*, pp. 226–27 (see n. 122).

'Our ideas stemmed from the garden city, Le Corbusier's Ville Radieuse, Walter Gropius' Siemenstadt [sic] and the new towns in the Soviet Union. We ended up with widely spaced high-rise apartments at the relatively low density of 150 persons per hectare. We showed two tunnels linking the banks of the Scheldt, and between them an extension of the business centre. Along the river's edge, we proposed a promenade with public buildings, restaurants and entertainment facilities'.

Stephenson, *On a Human Scale*, p. 46 (see n. 152).

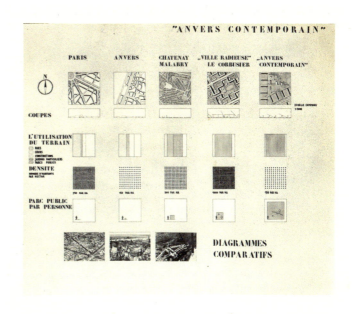

> Alex Adam, William Holford, František Sammer and Gordon Stephenson, urban plan for Antwerp, elaborated in West Kirby, England, summer 1933.

Clockwise: Comparative diagrams, area plan and urban plan for a development on the left bank of the River Scheldt. Photographs, 11.4 × 9.6 cm, 8.6 × 10.4 cm, 10.7 × 10.5 cm. SAAA.

081

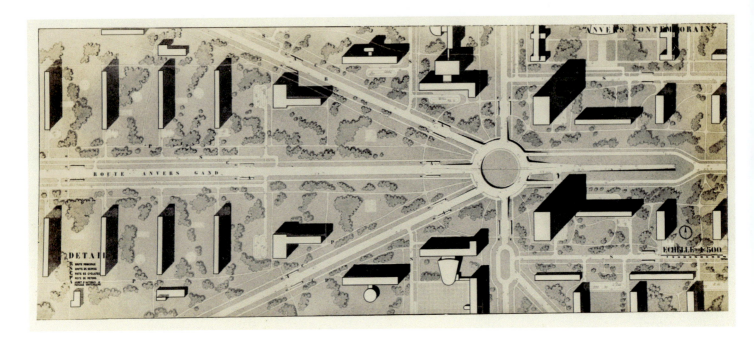

^ Main transport hub of Antwerp with a tunnel entrance. Photograph, 6.1 × 14.2 cm. SAAA.

'At noon on the last day we were still finishing various charts and dodging the photographer who had come to record the documents'.

Agnes Larsen in a letter home, 6 June 1933. Quoted in Larsen, *Graffiti*, p. 227 (see n. 122).

'We're awfully tired, working our heads off all day and much of the night till 2.00 am and less than a week to go. There are number of drawings – charts and perspectives – the largest of which is three meters by three. My job is to sketch in people and vehicles to scale on the streets. […] Bill [William Holford] and Gordon will carry everything to Antwerp and personally set up the exhibit. So far, 250 people have applied for the rules of the competition – fifty of them from the USSR. The winners will be announced in August. First prize is $2,500. There will be two second prizes and four third'.

From a letter Agnes Larsen sent from West Kirby to Honolulu, 25 May 1933. Quoted in Larsen, *Graffiti*, pp. 226–27 (see n. 122).

v Section drawing of the avenues and perspective views of the entrance to Antwerp with the main traffic route. Photographs, 10.8 × 11.8 cm and 10.4 × 12.2 cm. SAAA.

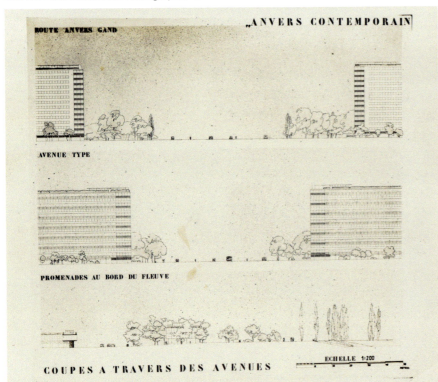

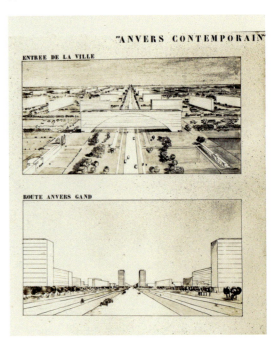

082

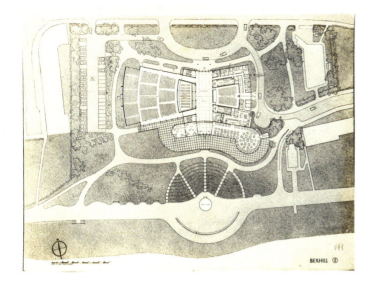 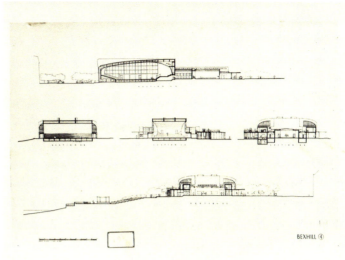

^ Alex Adam, William Holford and Gordon Stephenson, competition entry for an entertainment hall in Bexhill, site plan and section drawings, 1933–34. The auditorium is conceived similarly to Le Corbusier's project for the Palace of the Soviets, which Stephenson and Adam also worked on at 35 rue de Sèvres. Photographs, 14.1 × 10.6 cm and 14 × 10 cm. SAAA.

v Gordon Stephenson, competition entry for the Slough Town Hall, floor plans, elevations, and section drawings, 1934. Photographs, 9.3 × 14.4 cm and 10 × 14.6 cm. SAAA.

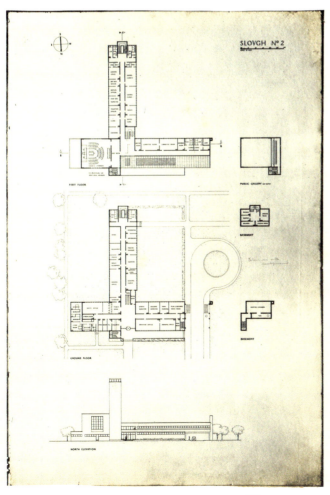 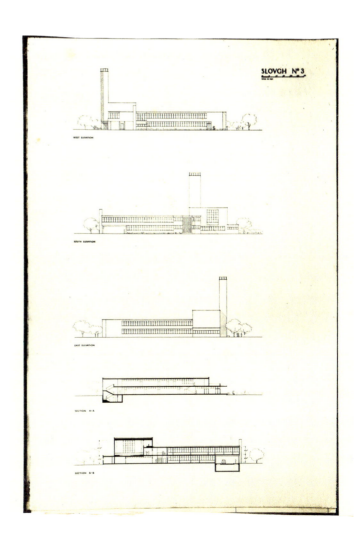

CIAM IV

In spring 1933 and during work on the Antwerp competition, Sammer's future was still wide open. He was negotiating employment in the Soviet Union and impatiently awaiting the fourth international congress of modern architects organized by the Congrès Internationaux d'Architecture Moderne (CIAM).[190] The deliberations were supposed to be held in Moscow, and representatives of the modern movement planned to meet there to discuss contemporary questions of urban planning and what was called the 'functional city'.[191]

At the congress, Sammer registered with a group of architects from the Le Corbusier–Jeanneret atelier.[192] Amongst the names of the delegates from 35 rue de Sèvres naturally we find architects and designers who seriously considered going to the Soviet Union for work. In addition to Sammer, they included Perriand, Stephenson, János Wanner and Weissmann, who hoped to form a group that would join in the ferment of building the new society in the Soviet Union. The original plans for the CIAM congress were supposed to enable some of them to enter the country: 'In Moscow in early June there is a congress of modern architecture. It will be superbly attended and it is the last opportunity for three members of our group, who are having difficulties getting the [Soviet] government to let them in',[193] Sammer wrote in February 1933.

The congress in Moscow was originaly to be held in 1932. The Soviets, however, repeatedly postponed the official invitations and things were made worse by the increasingly difficult political situation. Nor were the plans for a CIAM meeting helped by the affair that emerged after Le Corbusier lost the competition for the Palace of the Soviets, in which he was supported by leading figures of the CIAM. Up until the last moment, the congress was scheduled to open in Moscow in June 1933. Not until late April, however, was the final decision heard – namely, that the congress venue would be changed. Instead of meeting in the Soviet Union, the architects were invited to convene on the deck of a steamship in the Mediterranean. The S.S. *Patris II* was chosen, en route from Marseille to Athens.[194]

'Things have turned out a bit different from what I was expecting', Sammer wrote to his parents in early May. 'I am talking about the congress of modern architecture, which will not be in Moscow, but in Greece. In that case, of course, it will be necessary to decide a bit later about the date of my departure for Russia. I am still waiting for a letter from Mr Teige, the chairman of the Czechoslovak chapter of the CIRPAC.[195] (The congress.) Quite possibly there will be big advantages for congress members. In that case, I would of course participate. That would be in the first half of June'.[196] Not only the venue, however, but also the date of the congress was moved, and on 29 July, when the *Patris II* left Marseille harbour, Sammer had already spent his first few days in the Moscow office of Nikolai Kolli, another former assistant at the Le Corbusier–Jeanneret atelier.

The architects brigade from Paris: 'The Le Corbusier Group'

Sammer and Larsen travelled from Great Britain to the Soviet Union with stops in the Netherlands, Berlin and in Pilsen, where they visited Sammer's family. Sammer brought a camera for his brother Jenda.[197] He did not stay long, however, because he had 'so much work to do, and, after all, when one prepares for something and learns, one sees that one is still missing something to be able to form a picture of the world. Especially now, in these times, which are changing the social orders. The Russians are marvellous'.[198]

Sammer had been interested in working in the Soviet Union from the very beginning of his sojourn abroad. 'Think about Russia constantly', Le Corbusier advised him, 'and work day and night, if necessary, in order to get there'.[199] In his letters home,

190| The Congrès Internationaux d'Architecture Moderne (CIAM) was both a series of congresses on modern architecture and the organization that held these meetings. Le Corbusier was a founding member together with Sigfried Giedion (1888–1968), a Prague-born, Swiss historian of art. At the first congress, held at La Sarraz Castle, Switzerland, in 1928, the foundations were laid, unifying the movement for new architecture and urban planning, understood in a wider social and political context. For details, see Eric Mumford, *The CIAM Discourse on Urbanism, 1928–1960*, Cambridge (MA); London: MIT Press, 2002.
191| The idea of the functional city dominated CIAM discussions beginning with the third congress, which was held in Brussels in 1930. There, Le Corbusier presented his urban plan for Moscow, made the same year (see p. 68), and, together with it, the basic idea of his Ville Radieuse. The CIAM IV became the basis for formulating the urban-planning principles about dividing the city into zones according to function (residential, working, leisure, transportation) in what is known as the Athens Charter, first published during the German occupation of France in 1942 and eventually in an expanded edition as Le Corbusier, *La Charte d'Athènes*, Boulogne-sur-Seine: Éditions de l'Architecture d'Aujourd'hui, 1943.
192| FLC D2-4-445, the list of delegates from 35 rue de Sèvres, which includes not only Sammer's name but also those of his colleague-friends, most of whom appear elsewhere in this book.
193| AMP, František Sammer Papers, letter to his parents, 16 February 1933.
194| For details about the organization of the congress and how it took place, see Mumford, *The CIAM Discourse on Urbanism* (n. 190), pp. 73–91.
195| The Comité Internationale pour la Réalisation des Problèmes d'Architecture Contemporaine (CIRPAC) was the international executive body of the CIAM organization.
196| AMP, František Sammer Papers, letter to his parents, 9 May 1933.
197| SAAA, letter to Sammer in Moscow from his mother, 16 November 1933: 'I must also tell you something about the constant joy Jenda has from the camera you gave him'.
198| AMP, František Sammer Papers, letter to his parents, 9 May 1933.
199| Ibid., 30 January 1932.
200| Ibid., 20 September 1932.
201| Ibid., 21 November 1931.
202| Ibid., 16 March 1932.
203| According to *Une vie de création* (n. 6), p. 40, and other literature, Perriand's first trip to the Soviet Union was in 1931. See Danilo Udovicki-Selb, '"C'était dans l'air du temps": Charlotte Perriand and the Popular Front', in McLeod (ed.), *An Art of Living* (n. 6), n. 4 on p. 273, and

^ László Moholy-Nagy, a snapshot from the CIAM IV, which was held from 29 July to 11 August 1933, on board the *Patris II* and in Greece. A still from his film, the Architects' Congress (05:06).
Moholy-Nagy Foundation & Light Cone.
< A list of members of the atelier at 35 rue de Sèvres, who originally signed up to participate in the CIAM IV congress. FLC D2-4-445.

Jacques Barsac, *Charlotte Perriand: Un art d'habiter 1903-1959*, Paris: Norma, 2005, pp. 112 and 497, or id., *Charlotte Perriand: L'Œuvre Complète* (n. 6), vol. 1, p. 275. A comparison of the information in Sammer's correspondence from this time reveals that that trip was made a year later than has previously been thought. For details, see Hrabová, 'Between Ideal and Ideology' (n. 18), p. 139, notes 43 and 44, and p. 155.
204 | Perriand, *Une vie de création* (n. 6), pp. 47 and 48. Similarly, with information from a personal interview with Perriand in 1997, Udovicky-Selb, '"C'était dans l'air du temps"' (n. 203). See also the more recent Barsac, *Charlotte Perriand* (n. 6), vol. 1, p. 278. For the advice she generously offered me on this topic, I am indebted to Mary McLeod.
205 | AMP, František Sammer Papers, letters to his parents, 16 March 1932 and 2 May 1932.
206 | The Russian architect Nikolai Kolli (1894-1966) played an important role in linking the Paris atelier with the Soviet Union. As a former assistant at 35 rue de Sèvres, he was, after his return to Moscow, entrusted with supervising the construction of Le Corbusier's Centrosoyuz building and he also ran his own office, which made an integral part of the Soviet system of construction work. In his correspondence, Sammer spells Kolli a number of ways (Coly, Colly, Colley), which, when quoting him, I leave as he has spelled them.
207 | In this period, two architects of the same surname worked at 35 rue de Sèvres: Edmond Wanner, a Swiss, and János Wanner, a Hungarian. It becomes clear from other remarks in Sammer's correspondence, that when discussing the trip to Russia, he means János Wanner. 'Repertoire des collaborateurs' (n. 8) and AMP, František Sammer Papers.
208 | Ernest Weissmann (1903-85), a Croatian-born architect, was part of the core of the Le Corbusier–Jeanneret atelier even before Sammer's arrival, and remained in touch with this group for the rest of his career. He repeatedly travelled to Paris and London and worked as a member of the CIAM. He later emigrated to the United States, where he established himself as an architect and also played an important role as an intermediary between America, Europe and the rest of the world. For details, see Klarin, *Ernest Weissmann* (n. 106). For more on Weissmann during the preparations for the CIAM IV and his having considered going to the Soviet Union in search of work, see ibid., pp. 180-84.
209 | AMP, František Sammer Papers, letter to his parents, 2 May 1932.
210 | For more on Francis Jourdain, see n. 92.
211 | AMP, František Sammer Papers, letter to his parents, 1 July 1932.

Sammer then weighed up his other possibilities. In a diagram that he sent to his parents on the matter, he clearly shows how the urgency he felt about this mission was gradually triumphing over doubt, stagnation and uncertainty. He perceived his future as the 'zenith in infinity' [sic],[200] an open field with a hopeful horizon, beyond which he was ultimately one of the few unafraid to risk stepping into the unknown.

In the early 1930s, the Soviet Union witnessed a considerable wave of architects coming from the West to find work and to achieve the vision of left-wing ideals. In 1930, Hannes Meyer, together with a number of other architects from the Bauhaus, as well as Ernst May, Mart Stam and other architects from Frankfurt am Main, went to the Soviet Union. A similar group had formed at the Le Corbusier–Jeanneret atelier around Sammer and Perriand: 'We are going as a working group of four or five architects, with visas issued in France and contracts drawn up there. We are like a sect; we share the same interests'.[201] The journey that Perriand made there in spring 1932 was something like the advance guard: 'Tomorrow Charlotte Perriand is going to Moscow to get work. She will write to us in April and return in May'.[202] Perriand visited the Soviet Union twice, first in 1932 and then in 1934. In her memoirs, she describes her impressions of the first trip, though gives inexact information about the dates and purpose of the journey, antedating it to 1931.[203] She only mentions looking for work in the Soviet Union for the group of architects from the Le Corbusier–Jeanneret atelier during her second visit, in 1934. That same information, based on Perriand's memoirs, circulates in other authors' writing.[204] Sammer's correspondence from that period provides completely new evidence about the purpose of Perriand's first visit to the Soviet Union, and also makes it possible to date her sojourn precisely from 17 March to 2 May 1932.[205]

On 2 May 1932, Sammer had already received fresh reports and instructions from Perriand about how to proceed: 'Charlotte P. has returned [...] Arch. Coly [Kolli][206] personally advised Charlotte, that we should come as a group of at least six, and thus form a working cell. Otherwise, if it is not possible to find six people, our number will be completed by Russians. A third possibility is to come individually and be assigned either to another cell or to work in the office as a clerk. [...] We reckon Ch. P. [Perriand], Stephenson, and me. We await news from Wanner[207] from Hungary and from Weissmann[208] from Yugoslavia, [the latter of whom] knows our intention and has offered his services together with two engineers specialized in concrete constructions. [...] Charlotte was there for almost two months and the whole time stayed only in Moscow to take care of our affairs properly'.[209]
Sammer continued to talk with Hugh McClellan and Alex Adam about participating, and in summer 1932 he wrote home that the matter 'has been shaping up nicely, because the Cercle de la Russie neuve, whose chairman is Francis Jourdain,[210] is establishing contact with young scientists and scholars and people who have gone to Russia from Europe. Apart from that, I have a personal relationship with the arch. Colly and the Vesnin brothers (Russian architects interested in our group, which they call the "Le Corbusier Group"). They promised to do everything for us to get work and be be payed adequately'.[211]

'Holland was full of touristy things to do – a bicycle ride out to Hilversum to see some modern architecture, and a boat ride to Volendam and the Island of Marken in the Zuider Zee. In those two towns the people still wear native costumes every day'.

Agnes Larsen in a letter from the Netherlands to Honolulu, 14 July 1933. Quoted in Larsen, *Graffiti*, p. 229 (see n. 122).

< Raadhuisstraat with the Royal Palace in the background and the Munttoren, Amsterdam. Contact prints, 3 × 3.9 cm. SAAA.

∧ Photos from an outing to Volendam and to Marken, an island near Amsterdam, three contact prints, 3 × 3.9 cm. SAAA.

< Jan Duiker, the Zonnestraal sanatorium, Hilversum, 1926–28. Contact print, 3 × 4 cm. SAAA.

086

^ Berlin. Contact print, 3 × 4 cm. SAAA.

> Agnes Larsen with Milča Gschwindová, Sammer's sister, on Charles Bridge, Prague, during a visit to Czechoslovakia on the way to the Soviet Union, July 1933. Photograph, 5.8 × 7.8 cm. SAAA.

ᵛ Sammer's illustrated explanation of his weighing the pros and cons of leaving Paris to work in the Soviet Union. From a letter to his parents, 20 September 1932. (see n. 200). AMP.

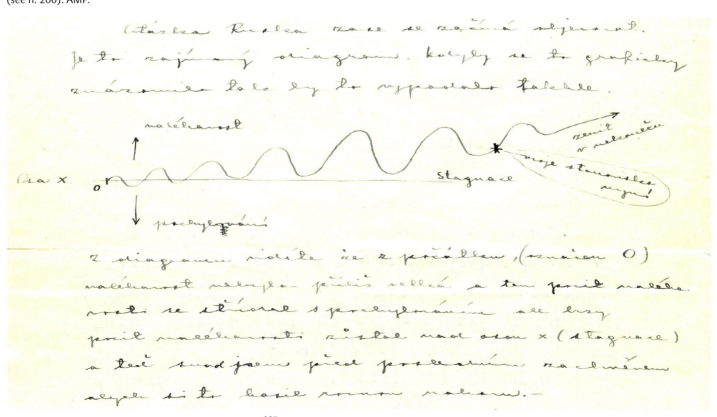

Moscow

The big plans fell through, however, and the 'Le Corbusier Group' ultimately did not join the international brigades of architects in the Soviet Union. Sammer left for Moscow alone and thus seems to have been the only architect from the Le Corbusier–Jeanneret atelier who found work in the Soviet Union amongst the architects who had emigrated from the West.[212] A reason for that may have been the red tape and difficulties in entering the country faced by other members of the group, which the CIAM congress was originally supposed to help resolve. However, leaving for the Soviet Union also meant a journey into discomfort and, in 1933, into an increasingly contentious milieu in politics and architecture. For the unemployed and left-wing young architects, it was a decision that demanded a firm conviction about the meaningfulness of the choice.

Sammer was certainly not lacking in conviction, and he ensured his departure to the Soviet Union from several sides. He was in talks with pro-Russian intellectuals in Paris and also established contact with the movement of left-wing architects in his native Czechoslovakia. To gain the support of the Czechoslovak Levá fronta (Left Front) and its leading figure, Karel Teige, he strategically made use of a recent polemic between Teige and Le Corbusier:[213] 'It is a great shame that Corbu cannot read your book [*Nejmenší byt*[214]]. You know, I pity his intelligence, which is much greater than that of the everyday bourgeois. I hope that he will change a bit once he has carefully read Bukharin's *Materialisme historique*,[215] which Charlotte Perriand and I gave him. Recently, he and a few gentlemen have still been publishing a ridiculous bulletin, *Prelude*[216] (the prelude to action). If you are interested, I will send it to you for a laugh'.[217] In the effort to find favour with him, Sammer offered to keep Teige informed from Paris 'about what is happening around Corbu, around the *Plans* periodical, the Association des Artistes revolutionnaires,[218] La Russie Neuve[219] and so on'.[220] Eventually, Sammer succeeded in receiving confirmation of his participation in the Czechoslovak Association of Socialist Architects (Svaz socialistických architektů) and in arranging contacts with a radical organization of left-wing artists in Paris, the Association des écrivains et artistes révolutionnaires (Association of Revolutionary Writers and Artists – AEAR).[221] The letter of confirmation for Sammer was signed by Karel Teige, Jaromír Krejcar and Josef Špalek on behalf of the Czechoslovak Association. At the time, Krejcar and Špalek were also getting ready to leave in search of work in the Soviet Union.[222]

The document helped Sammer to cut through the red tape of gaining employment in the Soviet Union.[223] He managed on his own to be assigned to the studio of Nikolai Kolli,[224] and found employment thanks to the initiative of Le Corbusier himself, with further assistance from a secretary at the Soviet embassy in Paris, a certain Barkov[225] and Francis Jourdain, one of the pro-Russian intellectuals in the Cercle de la Russie neuve.[226]

In July 1933, Sammer began work at Kolli's studio, to which he had, with the help of all these people, received an invitation from the Soviet Government and the People's Commissariat of Light Industry. With Kolli he worked on a project for a sports stadium,[227] the huge Theatre of the Trade Unions, an apartment building with 74 flats, the Institute of baking, a bridge over the River Moskva and on smaller projects, including a design for a prefab school[228] and a number of 'automatic' petrol stations.[229] Together they won a competition to design the Kirovskaya station of the Moscow Metro, today called Chistye Prudy, which was then built in 1935 by the Metrostroy Department.

Despite the marked change in his way of life and in the conditions of his job, Sammer remained in constant touch with Le Corbusier and with all his friends from 35 rue de Sèvres. With Kolli he also supervised the construction of a building for the Central

---

[212] Of the Western architects who went to the USSR to work, the unique example of František Sammer is also mentioned in Daniel Talesnik, 'The Itinerant Red Bauhaus, or the Third Emigration', PhD diss., Columbia University, New York, 2016, pp. 39 and 41.

[213] For more on Le Corbusier's polemic with Karel Teige, see n. 35.

[214] Karel Teige, *Nejmenší byt*, Prague: Václav Petr, 1932. Published in English as *Minimum Dwelling*, translated by Eric Dluhosch, Cambridge, MA; Chicago, IL: MIT Press and the Graham Foundation for Advanced Studies in the Fine Arts, 2002.

[215] Nicolas Boukharine, *La théorie du matérialisme historique: manuel populaire de sociologie marxiste*, (1921) Paris: Éditions sociales internationales, 1927.

[216] For the political meaning and contextualization of *Prélude* amongst other periodicals whose publication Le Corbusier was involved in, see McLeod, 'Le Corbusier, planification et syndicalisme régional' (n. 32).

[217] Památník národního písemnictví (Museum of Czech Literature – PNP), Karel Teige papers, file 31/A/4, acquisition number 139/62, inv. no. 372, letter from František Sammer, 14 February 1933.

[218] The Association des écrivains et artistes révolutionnaires (AEAR) was founded in France in 1932 as a branch of the International Union of Revolutionary Writers, which was organized in the Soviet Union in 1927 to bring together pro-Soviet and other leftist intellectuals. Among the leading figures of the French organization was Francis Jourdain (n. 92).

[219] By 'La Russie Neuve', Sammer was probably referring to the Cercle de la Russie neuve, a society of left-wing French intellectuals established in 1927 with the support of the Soviet Union and its All-Union Society for Cultural Relations with Foreign Countries (VOKS).

[220] PNP, Sammer's letter to Teige, 14 February 1933 (n. 217).

[221] AMP, František Sammer Papers, letter from the Association of Socialist Architects (Svaz socialistických architektů), 14 August 1933. For more on AEAR, see n. 218.

[222] The involvement of architects from Czechoslovakia is a separate subject of study and one that has yet to be fully considered. For more on this topic, see Hrabová, 'Between Ideal and Ideology', (n. 18), pp. 162-66. In connection with the migration of architects from the Bauhaus to the Soviet Union, Czech architects are mentioned in Talesnik, 'The Itinerant Red Bauhaus' (n. 212). The topic is also discussed, with the use of Russian sources, in Jekaterina Dofková, 'Avantgarda 20.-30. let: Praha–Moskva', PhD diss., Brno University of Technology, 2016.

[223] AMP, František Sammer Papers, letter to his parents, 23 August 1933, in which he mentions the purpose of the confirmation.

[224] Ibid., 24 July 1933. For more on Kolli, see n. 206 and below.

[225] Barkov is also mentioned by Perriand in her memoirs, but it remains difficult to identify him. See Perriand, *Une vie de création* (n. 6), p. 40: 'Je fis la connaissance de Barkof, de l'ambassade'. In a 1971 interview, Sammer mentions Barkov as a secretary of the Russian [*sic*] embassy in Paris. Květa Wiendlová, 'Toulavé boty a cesty domů: Rozhovor s Fran-

> Nikolai Kolli and František Sammer, the Kirovskaya station (today, Chistye Prudy), Moscow Metro, after 5 August 1934. Photograph, 13.1 × 16.9 cm. CCA PH 1998:0030:007.

> Le Corbusier, the Centrosoyuz building, Moscow, 1928–36. Photograph of a model. FLC L3(19)15.

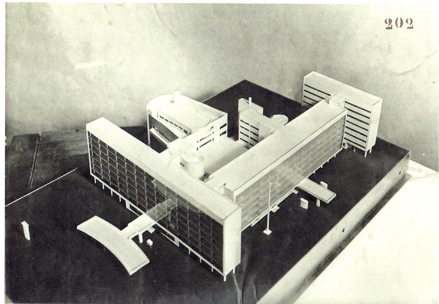

tiskem Sammerem', *Pravda*, příloha (20 February 1971), p. 4.
226| See n. 219.
227| AMP, František Sammer Papers, letters to his parents, 24 July 1933 and 9 April 1934. Work on these projects is also confirmed by Kolli in a letter, written in French, about his collaboration with Sammer in Moscow. SAAA Pondicherry, Kolli to Sammer, 10 July 1937. In the letter, Kolli calls the stadium they were working on together the 'Stade central de URSS à Moscou'.
228| AMP, František Sammer Papers, letter to his parents, 17 February 1935: 'The project of the school and the "Metro" were a lot of work for me'. Sammer mentions the school as the last project he collaborated on with Kolli: ibid., letter to Vítězslav Procházka, 23 April 1970. For the context of Sammer's correspondence with Procházka, see 'The Czechoslovak Architects in the Soviet Union in the 1930s', in Hrabová, 'Between Ideal and Ideology' (n. 18), pp. 162–66.
229| AMP, František Sammer Papers, letter to his parents, 1 January 1936. Sammer mentions these works in a summary of what he did in 1935, which he sent home for the New Year. Kolli too calls these petrol stations 'des Stations de gazolines' [*sic*]. See SAAA Pondicherry, a letter of confirmation from Kolli to Sammer, dated 10 July 1937 (n. 227). After research using Russian sources, Jekaterina Dofková has confirmed the difficulty of making a complete list of the projects that Sammer worked on in the Soviet Union. Dofková, 'Avantgarda 20.–30. let: Praha–Moskva' (n. 222), p. 79.
230| For details about the project, see Jean-Louis Cohen, 'L'epopée du Centrosoyuz', in Cohen, *Le Corbusier et la mystique de l'URSS* (n. 96), pp. 86–137, which also mentions Sammer's participation. See also Fernando Marzá and Josep Quetglas, 'Palais du Centrosoyuz', in *Le Corbusier: Plans*, DVD 3, Paris; Tokyo: Codex Images International, 2005–06. Concerning the development of the construction and the state of the building today, see Jean-Louis Cohen, 'Le Corbusier's Centrosoyuz', *Future Anterior: Journal of Historic Preservation, History, Theory, Criticism*, V, no. 1, (summer 2008), pp. 52–61.
231| Sammer later commented on his involvement in the work on Centrosoyuz in AMP, František Sammer Papers, letter to Vítězslav Procházka, 23 April 1970 (n. 228). Cohen, too, writes about Sammer's participation. See Cohen, 'Le Corbusier' Centrosoyuz' (n. 230), p. 54, and particularly id. *Le Corbusier et la mystique de l'URSS* (n. 96), pp. 122, 128.
232| AChP, Sammer to Perriand, 8 September 1934: 'Beaucoup des saluts à Pierre et Corbu! Que ce que vous faites? ... Dernièrement je pense beaucoup à vous tous. – Venez avec Pierre – Charlotte. – Il faut travailler avec nous ici!!! Vraiment mon vieux. – Tu ne sais pas combien je pense à tout energie que vous perdez là bas pour les petites emmerdements d'ordre Boulogne etc. – Ici il s'agit du travail'. By 'annoyances of the Boulogne type' Sammer was probably thinking about their recent collaboration on the apartment building in Boulogne and Le Corbusier's own apartment there. See above, pp. 59 and 61.
233| AMP, František Sammer Papers, letter to his father, 10 May 1934.

Union of Consumer Cooperatives, known as Centrosoyuz. It was Le Corbusier's first – and only – big Soviet commission. From the very start it was plagued by a number of difficulties.[230] Sammer was thus one of the few people to whom his colleagues at the atelier in Paris could turn with questions related to this building and to current events in the Soviet Union.[231] At the same time, Sammer was continuously urging his allies to stop wasting their energy in Paris and to come and join him: 'Many greetings to Pierre and Corbu! What are you working on? [...] Lately I've been thinking of you all a lot. – Charlotte, come with Pierre. – We need you here to work with us! You have no idea how much I have recently been thinking about all the energy you waste with all those annoyances of the Boulogne type and so forth. Here, we do real work'.[232]

Merging with the masses

With faith in the meaningfulness of the Soviet system, Sammer explained in his letters home the point of his work in the USSR. 'You see the future of humanity in the manner of the good old days and I see it in social revolution and socialism',[233] he wrote to his father. His father had been trying in vain to understand his son's

< František Sammer and Agnes Larsen in the Soviet Union. Contact prints, 2.5 × 3.7 cm. SAAA.

v A street and Red Square, Moscow. Contact prints, 2.5 × 3.7 cm. SAAA.

'Moscow! I first saw her crowded streets from the back seat of a Lincoln touring car, top down. [...] How long before I'd become a part of those crowds, hurrying to or from some important engagement, maybe stopping to chat with someone in fluent Russian? Would it take weeks? Months? [...] Already, in less than twenty-four hours, I was part of the crowd, with private business to attend to. An auspicious beginning'.

Agnes Larsen describing her first hours after arriving in Moscow, in Larsen, *Graffiti*, pp. 240–41 (see n. 122).

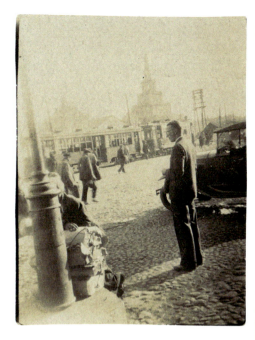  

∧ František Sammer by someone kneeling on Komsomolskaya Square, Moscow; in the background, Kazansky station, 1934. Contact print, 3 × 4 cm. SAAA. (Gordon Stephenson kept a print of the same photo, now in the UoLL.) (see n. 243).

> Celebrations of the anniversary of the October Revolution, Moscow.
Contact prints, 2.5 × 3.7 cm. SAAA.

views and to get insight into events in the Soviet Union despite the censorship and propaganda, which were vigorously filtering the information that was making its way to other countries. 'In short, I have changed a bit; I am interested in other things. I went to Paris as a petit-bourgeois, interested in similar things as [the small town ladies] Sísová, Pehelová and also some of the gentlemen from the hunting club and other societies. [...] Currently, the most important thing is to persuade every one of my colleagues within range that the truth is practised on only one sixth of the globe – in the USSR. [...] Here, a human being is more a human being, especially when there is not much work. For a long time now I haven't ironed my trousers. "My spouse" [Larsen] doesn't care to iron for me either. Thus I am increasingly merging with the masses. Together with my trouser creases, my bourgeois views of life are also vanishing'.[234]

Sammer's photographs taken in Moscow illustrate this desire to blend in with the crowd and the intense pace of life in the country of the first five-year plans. Just as he had in previous years, he recorded the everyday hustle and bustle, random

> Motion sequence taken on the street.
Contact prints, 3 × 4 cm. SAAA.

---

[234] Ibid., letter home, 13 June 1934. It is no coincidence that Sammer calls Larsen his 'spouse'. According to Larsen's recollections, the young couple were married in the Soviet Union on 11 November 1933. They did this particularly for administrative reasons and on the agreement that the union would cease to be valid as soon as they left the country. See Larsen, *Graffiti* (n. 122), pp. 272 and 291.

∧ František Sammer and Agnes Larsen in a street, Moscow. Two pairs of contact prints, 3 × 4 cm. SAAA.

∨ Unidentified monument and Pushkin Square, Moscow; on the upper left-hand side of the second photograph, one can see part of the Izvestia building, designed by Grigory Barkhin, 1925–27.
Pair of contact prints, 3 × 4 cm. SAAA.

∧ Pushkin Square, from Dziga Vertov's film, *Man with a Movie Camera* (1929), (07:06).

pedestrians and children of the street. Sometimes he photographed definite places and events, as in his photos of Red Square and of the celebrations of the anniversary of the October Revolution. By having himself photographed in Soviet settings, he was confirming his presence and active participation in Soviet events.

Some of the contact prints of 3 × 4 cm negatives capture a time sequence from a Moscow street. In the first pair of shots we see a tall woman in a dress, moving smoothly through a mostly empty space and passing by a newspaper stand. Then comes Larsen on a pavement, and only a few moments later Sammer is captured on the same pavement. One can guess the time difference between the two photographs by the probable speed of the pedestrian in the coat and high hat made of fur, who is present in both shots. Sammer and Larsen photographed each other, and in a manner to confirm their presence in a certain place and at a certain time. To be on the safe side, Larsen had herself photographed one more time, a bit further away, then comes a photo of a monument with a lion and then a shot of an unknown boy in knee-socks on Pushkin Square, which is one of the most telling examples of Sammer's photographic eye. The boy in the photo occupies the main space. Behind him we see a monument to the famous writer Alexander Sergejevich Pushkin, as well as a Russian Orthodox church. Only then, in the left-hand margin of the photo, can we make out part of the Constructivist building of the *Izvestia* daily newspaper, which was designed by Grigory Barkhin and erected in 1925–27.[235] Sammer preferred to record the boy, everyday life and the bustling square, rather than this monument of modern architecture.

Sammer's way of seeing reality and of choosing his shots corresponds with Walter Benjamin's understanding of photography at this time. The ordinary person and everyday life were the legitimate subject matter of the photographic picture. This transformation in the subject of interest can be seen in Benjamin in direct connection to the October Revolution and with all the consequences that the revolution had for the development of society.[236] Hand-in-hand with technological developments and the affordability of cameras, photographs no longer had to be taken in a studio, with staged scenes, and photographers could head out into the streets, face-to-face with everyday reality.

A fundamental contribution to the change in the photographic eye was made, according to Benjamin, by Soviet cinematography.[237] In 1929, the Soviet film-maker Dziga Vertov uniquely 'flew through' key moments in a human life and in 120 minutes recorded Soviet reality with a movie camera.[238] The motion sequence in *Man with a Movie Camera* alternates with still shots, pictures framed in the manner of photographs, thus giving them enough space and time to be read. Among the photos from Vertov's spectacular collection of images is one on Pushkin Square in Moscow,[239] set amongst details from streets, photos of new machines, paupers, newborns, poverty and promises of a better future. Sammer composed his photographic collection similarly. A scene from a Russian pub, street children by the water or unknown pedestrians were as important to him as the celebrations of the October Revolution anniversary.

The social and political dimensions are fundamental in the interpretation of the photographs in Sammer's collection. At the same time, it must be borne in mind that most of the photos were taken, and saved, for personal reasons. For his photographs, Sammer carefully selected situations that he could return to, like imprints of his experiences and memories. A typical example is provided by a few photographs of a visit to Leningrad (today, St Petersburg), where Sammer and Larsen set out together with Stephenson during his visit to the Soviet Union in 1934.[240] We barely recognize St Isaac's Cathedral, of which the photographer has recorded only the bases of the giant columns and some children at play. The microcosm of the detail

---

235 | The building of *Izvestia* (one of two official Bolshevik dailies in the Soviet Union) is the only fully constructed work of the architect Grigory Barkhin (1880-1969). The original design was inspired by Walter Gropius and Hannes Meyer's competition entry for a skyscraper for the *Chicago Tribune* in 1922. See Richard Pare, *The Lost Vanguard: Russian Modernist Architecture, 1922-1932*, introduction by Jean-Louis Cohen, New York: Monacelli Press, 2007, p. 56.

236 | For this interpretation, see the Introduction by Esther Leslie to Walter Benjamin, *On Photography*, ed., translated and introduction by Esther Leslie, London: Reaktion Books, 2015, p. 24.

237 | Walter Benjamin, 'Small History of Photography', in ibid., p. 92. Published in 1931, this is among the first essays on the history of the medium. Benjamin presents the same thesis in the now-cult essay published in 1935: 'The Work of Art in the Age of Mechanical Reproduction', published in English as Walter Benjamin, *Illuminations*, ed. with an introduction by Hannah Arendt, preface by Leon Wieseltier, translated by Harry Zohn, New York: Schocken Books, 2007, p. 232.

238 | Dziga Vertov, *Man with a Movie Camera* (1929). This film is key to understanding changes in the modernist point of view. For more on this in connection with Le Corbusier, see Beatriz Colomina, 'Le Corbusier and Photography', *Assemblage* 4, October 1987, pp. 7 and 8.

239 | Ibid., 7':06"

240 | Larsen, *Graffiti* (n. 122), p. 289.

'Gordon [Stephenson] came from England to spend his summer vacation with us. [...] The three of us went to Leningrad for a few days, especially to see the treasures of the Hermitage, but also to experience the grandeur of the city itself'.

Agnes Larsen's description of a visit to Leningrad in 1934, in Larsen, *Graffiti*, p. 289 (see n. 122).

< St Isaac's Cathedral, Leningrad (St Petersburg), view from the portico. Contact print, 3 × 4 cm, 1934. SAAA. (Gordon Stephenson kept a print of the same photograph, now in the UoLL.) (see n. 243).

^ St Isaac's Cathedral, Leningrad (St Petersburg), children playing on the steps of the portico. Contact print, 3 × 4 cm, 1934. SAAA. (Gordon Stephenson kept a print of the same photograph, now in the UoLL.) (see n. 243).

of ordinary life at the portico of the Neoclassical cathedral in the photograph stands in contrast with other photographers' efforts to document the monument and its surroundings. The difference is particularly obvious, for example, in comparison to a shot taken by the Paris-based photographer Pierre-Ambroise Richebourg from shortly after the completion of the cathedral in 1858.[241] Richebourg has captured the portico of the newly-built edifice together with the Admiralty building in the background, thus photographing at once two emblematic works of St Petersburg architecture.[242] In other photos of Sammer's from Leningrad, we see a ship at anchor, which in the composition of the photograph receives the same attention as a little crowd of onlookers on the shore. In other photographs Sammer captured urban scenes or a view from a window onto a street or into a room after a party.

The uninformed viewer might miss the subject matter in these photos but with a bit of imagination is able to enter the atmosphere of the captured moment. That these situations meant something even to people not involved in the scenes is attested to by the fact that Sammer was not the only person who saved them as souvenirs. As we have seen, identical contact prints of some of the photos from the Soviet Union were also saved in Stephenson's collection of photographs.[243]

35 rue de Sèvres outside Paris

Sammer's letters and images of the Soviet Union clearly show that the members of the community that was formed at 35 rue de Sèvres remained in touch even after they had left Paris. Sammer continued to count on his friends and their coming to join him sooner or later. 'We'll see what happens next when my friends from France and England come',[244] he wrote home shortly after arriving in Moscow. Though ultimately no one came to stay permanently, he remained in touch with a number of

[241] Pierre-Ambroise Richebourg (1810–75), *Portico of the St Isaac's Cathedral and the Admiralty*, St Petersburg, Albumen print from wet-collodion glass-plate negative, 32.5 x 31 cm, CCA PH1981:0556:001. Shortly after it was taken, the photo was published in an album with an introduction by Théophile Gautier, *Trésors d'art de la Russie ancienne et moderne*, Paris: Gide, 1859. See Richard Pare (ed.), exh. cat. by Catherine Evans Inbusch and Marjorie Munsterberg, *Photography and Architecture, 1839-1939*, with essays by Phyllis Lambert and Richard Pare, Montréal: Canadian Centre for Architecture, 1982, pl. 59, pp. 238–39.

[242] St Isaac's Cathedral, St Petersburg, built from 1818 to 1858, was designed by the French Neoclassical architect Auguste de Montferrand (1786–1858). The Empire-style building of the Admiralty was designed by Andreyan Zakharov (1761–1811) and built from 1806 to 1823.

[243] UoLL, Gordon Stephenson Papers. The link between Sammer and Stephenson is a subject of my continuing research.

[244] AMP, František Sammer Papers, letter home, 24 July 1933.

∧ Pierre-Ambroise Richebourg (1810–75), portico of the St Isaac's Cathedral, with the Admiralty Building in the background, St Petersburg. Photograph, 32.5 × 31cm, 1859, CCA PH1981:0556:001.
  > Riverside scenery. Contact prints, 3 × 4 cm, 1934. SAAA.
  ∨ View from a window; with the Admiralty Building at the end of the street.
  ∨∨ Weary after a party; the photographer is in the mirror above the sink. Contact prints, 3 × 4 cm, 1934. SAAA. (Gordon Stephenson kept prints of the same photographs, now in the UoLL.) (see n. 243).
     >> František Sammer and Gordon Stephenson on Vasiliyevsky Island, Leningrad (St Petersburg, 1934). Contact print, 3 × 4 cm. SAAA.

095

<< Jane West in Glacier National Park, Montana, USA, 1933. Photograph, 12.2 × 8.8 cm. SAAA.

< The chalet of Jane West Clauss and Alfred Clauss; on the back of the photo: 'Notre Maison–très grande'
(Our very big house). Photograph, 5.5 × 4.2 cm, developed and printed in Chattanooga, Tennessee, March 1935. SAAA.

^ Alfred 'Seppel' Clauss, and Jane West Clauss on a mountain trek, 1935.
Photographs, 4.2 × 5.5 cm. SAAA.

people by means of occasional visits and mostly by correspondence. When few written documents have been preserved, Sammer's collection of photographs reveals a lively exchange of information.

The photos from the United States show that Sammer did not break off contact with his friends overseas either. His parents in Pilsen forwarded letters from America to him in the Soviet Union[245] and Sammer also expected visits from American friends while he was in Moscow.[246] The photographs developed and printed in the United States attest to his being in touch with the architect Jane West.[247] This unique documentation, which shows the refined quality of her work in the United States, is accompanied by a photo of her new-born son, Peter-Otto, in a strikingly modern interior. Besides her professional photographs of her architecture and buildings that she took while travelling around the United States, West shared personal photographs with Sammer. Recalling time spent in Paris years before, she wrote short messages in French on the back of some photos.

Likewise, the photographic documentation of projects in Great Britain attests to Sammer's continued contact with friends in Liverpool. After Sammer had left for the Soviet Union, Holford, Stephenson and, for a while, Adam continued to work on projects together.[248] Holford and Stephenson began their important work at the local school of architecture. Stephenson, however, also visited Sammer a few times in the Soviet Union. 'Gordon will see to things at home and will come here to work [in the future]',[249] writes Sammer in a letter to his parents at a time when Stephenson was visiting him. Stephenson arrived on 30 July 1934[250] and in August he helped Sammer to meet all his deadlines, so that they could set out on a great journey of exploration. On 1 September 1934, Sammer wrote to his family in Pilsen, that he had 'been busy day and night – until yesterday, when vacation began. Last night we left Moscow and are now beginning a month of deserved vacation. [...] We are headed for Constantinople [sic] and Athens. [...] In about an hour we will fly from Moscow (Tushino airport) to Baku and Tiflis [Tbilisi]. There is a bit of fog and we are waiting for it to lift'.[251]

245| Ibid., 20 December 1933: 'I received a letter that you sent from America as well. I didn't even look to see if it had been censored'.
246| AMP, František Sammer Papers, letter home, 9 December 1934: 'Other friends will arrive from America in the spring'.
247| For details, see pp. 60–67 above.
248| Cherry and Penny, *Holford* (n. 150), pp. 55 and 56. For more on the British projects that were being consulted by correspondence, see pp. 79 and 83 above.
249| AMP, František Sammer Papers, letter home, 1 September 1934.
250| AChP, Sammer to Perriand, 8 September 1934. For a photograph of the letter and its translation, see p. 98.
251| AMP, František Sammer Papers, letter home, 1 September 1934.

Hollywood Bowl-
pour les concerts en
plein air à California.

Ici c'est un maison
à Taos. Tres belle comme
composition. n'est-ce pas?

Desous un tour de
radio

> The Hollywood Bowl amphitheatre in Los Angeles, California, 1930s. Written on the back: 'The Hollywood Bowl for open-air concerts in California'. Photograph, 8.2 × 5.2 cm. SAAA.

> A Native American adobe house at the Taos Pueblo, New Mexico. Inscribed on the back: 'Here's a house in Taos. Beautiful composition, don't you think?' Photograph, 8.2 × 5.7 cm. SAAA.

> View from below a radio tower. Written on the back: 'Below a radio tower'. Photograph, 8.3 × 5.3 cm. SAAA.

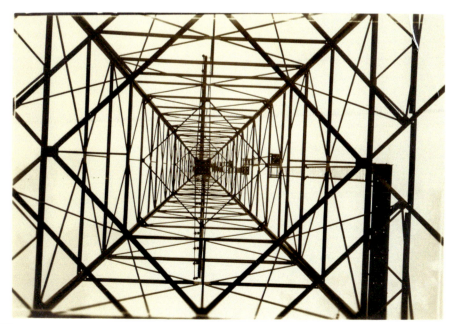

The Grand Tour, Autumn 1934

Though Sammer told Perriand that his trip with Stephenson was like 'un petit tour de cochon',[252] one is justified in calling it a modern version of the traditional Grand Tour of Europe. The two young architects set out on a trip to see ancient traditions and monuments, with a particular interest in the latest achievements of the modern age and a shared professional starting point at the Le Corbusier–Jeanneret atelier. Sammer's father could only marvel at his son's itinerary, writing to him from Pilsen: 'what you do there in Russia is not at all possible here. I mean flying from one continent to another and your vacation trip by airplane'.[253] From the trip Sammer brought back a great number of photographs and postcards and described the details in letters to Perriand. Sammer and Stephenson chose airplanes, trains and ships as their means of transport, and headed across the lands of the Soviet Union, with stops at Tbilisi, Batumi, Sevastopol, the Dnieper Hydroelectric Station (today, DniproHES) and Odesa, then Istanbul before heading to Athens and the surrounding area.

From the dozens of photographs and postcards from Greece in Sammer's collection, we could easily get the impression that he had attended the fourth CIAM congress. If it were not for the correspondence, which clearly documents his early days in Kolli's studio in the period before the opening of the congress,[254] it might well seem

∧ Tbilisi, Georgia. Postcard, 14.8 × 10 cm. SAAA.

∧ The Port of Istanbul. Photo from a postcard series published by Isaac M. Ahitouv, Istanbul. Postcard, 14 × 9.2 cm. SAAA.

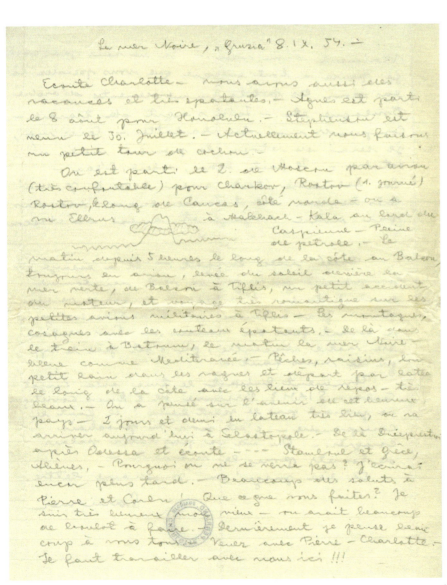

< The first page of a letter from Sammer to Perriand, 8 September 1934. AChP (see n. 250).

'The Black Sea, "Georgia", 8 September 1934. – Look, Charlotte – we are also on vacation and it's amazing. – Agnes left for Honolulu on 8 August. – Stephenson arrived on 30 July. – At the moment we are on a small boys-only trip. – On the second [of September] we flew (very comfortably) from Moscow to Kharkov, Rostov (the first day). From Rostov, along the Caucasus, on the north side – we saw Elbrus [sketch] – to Makhachkala on the coast of the Caspian Sea – full of crude oil. – Beginning at 5 o'clock in the morning along the coast to Baku, still by aeroplane, sun coming up from behind a green sea, from Baku to Tbilisi, a bit of motor trouble and a very romantic journey by small military aircraft to Tbilisi – mountains, cossacks with their marvellous knives. From there by train to Batumi, and the Black Sea in the morning – blue as the Mediterranean. Peaches, grapes, a bit of nice swimming in the waves and departure by ship along the coast with places to stop – very lovely. – We thought about the future of this happy land. – Two and half days aboard the ship, very nice. Today we are to put in at Sevastopol. – From there, the Dnieprestroi [Dnieper Hydroelectric Station], then Odesa, and, imagine - - - Istanbul and Greece, Athens. Why won't we see each other? I'll write you again later. – Many greetings to Pierre and Corbu! What are you working on? I am very happy, dear friend – we have a lot of work to do. – Lately I have been thinking of you all a lot. – Charlotte, come with Pierre. – We need you here to work with us!!!'

'We went up the river Dnepr [sic] to see the great dam which was the biggest in the world at that stage, at Dnepropetrovsk, I think the place was called. We travelled in the yacht of a former grand duke. It was a steam yacht, quite a big ship really, that had been made in Glasgow and was lined with beautiful mahogany panelling. It was rather odd. That's the only expensive yacht I've ever been on'.

Gordon Stephenson, interview from 1991–92, p. 56 (see n. 265).

> Alexander Vesnin, Nikolai Kolli, Georgy Orlov and Sergey Andrievsky, the Dnieprostroi Dam (today, DniproHES) with a power station on the River Dnieper, Zaporizhzhia, Ukraine, 1927–32. Photos from the time of its construction. Postcards, 14.6 × 8.8 cm and 13.9 × 8.7 cm. SAAA..

v Gordon Stephenson aboard a ship, 1934. Photograph, 5.4 × 8.1 cm. SAAA.

---

252 | AChP, Sammer to Perriand, 8 September 1934. He seems to be suggesting something like a boys-only trip.
253 | SAAA, Pondicherry, Sammer's father in Pilsen to Sammer in Moscow, 17 September 1934.
254 | The congress took place from 29 July to 11 August 1933, during which the committee was convened to summarize the conclusions of the whole event. Mumford, *The CIAM Discourse on Urbanism* (n. 190). For details, see p. 84.

that he had visited the same places while attending the official programme of the CIAM IV. Sammer's photographs from the Acropolis correspond to photos that congress delegates took there in 1933.[255] With their visual style, they demonstrate a similar perception of architecture, which served as a source of inspiration even for the most radical modern architects. They also point to his knowledge of the photos that Le Corbusier had taken there earlier in 1911 and in 1933, and Perriand during the congress in 1933.

That is well demonstrated by the photograph of the Parthenon colonnade, which leads the visitor to the edge of the horizon, where a view opens up from the Acropolis hill. The ancient building suggests an axis of tradition, which, rather than being restrictive, enables one to look freely into the future. This view was also recorded by Le Corbusier in 1911, during his first visit to Athens.[256] Perriand, too, on an excursion as part of the CIAM congress in 1933, took a nearly identical photograph.[257] Sammer photographed the same scene a year later, but with the difference that his companion, Stephenson, stands alone looking towards the future from the Acropolis hill.

Sammer's postcards from the Corinth Canal, the Temple of Poseidon in Sounion and the modern dam at Marathon show places that the congress delegates visited as well. During the main trip and on following excursions, many of them took photographs, including the first general secretary of the organization, Sigfried Giedion, who then left a detailed written and photographic report on the whole programme.[258] The fourth CIAM congress was also being documented by the famous photographer, film-maker and former Bauhaus teacher László Moholy-Nagy, using a movie camera.[259] Unlike Moholy-Nagy's lively stills from the congress, Sammer's photographs from Greece are more documentary in nature. His photographic memories of Greece are completely different from his records of other places, which were more like a strip of impressions and associations. This time, he brought back home a series of documentary photographs together with a large number of postcards.

↑↑ László Moholy-Nagy, CIAM IV participants on a excursion to the new dam at Marathon. A still from his film *Architects' Congress* (1933) (19:24). Moholy-Nagy Foundation & Light Cone.
↑ Modern dam at Marathon, Greece, which, beginning in 1931, served as the main Athens water reservoir. Postcard from Sammer's collection, 13.5 × 8.9. SAAA.
<< Sailing through the Corinth Canal, the CIAM IV, 1933. Photograph, FLC L4-7-14.
< The Corinth Canal. A postcard from Sammer's collection, 13.8 × 8.6 cm. SAAA.

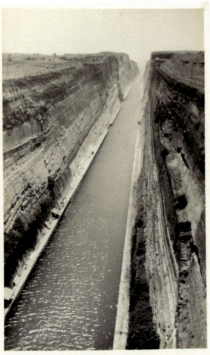

255| I am continuing to research and analyze Sammer's photos from Greece, comparing and contrasting them with the documentation of other CIAM congress participants.

256| FLC L4(19)165. Le Corbusier's photo comes from the great journey known as the 'Voyage d'Orient', which he took in 1911 with his friend Auguste Klipstein (1885–1951), an art historian. For more information about travelling and the friendship it entailed, see Ivan Žaknić, *Klip and Corb on the Road: The Dual Diaries and Legacies of August Klipstein and Le Corbusier on their Eastern Journey, 1911*, Zurich: Scheidegger & Spiess, 2019.

257| See Barsac, *L'œil en éventail* (n. 164), p. 235.

258| Sigfried Giedion, 'CIAM at Sea. The Background of the Fourth (Athens) Congress', *Architect's Year Book* 3, 1949, pp. 36–39. For an analysis of Giedion's photographic documentation of the congress, see Matina Kousidi, 'Through the Lens of Sigfried Giedion: Exploring Modernism and the Greek Vernacular *in situ*', *RIHA Journal* 0136 (15 July 2016), n.p.

259| Unique insight into the course of the congress as photographed and described by László Moholy-Nagy is provided by Chris Blencowe and Judith Levine, *Moholy's Edit. CIAM 1933: The Avant-Garde at Sea, August 1933*, Zurich: Lars Müller, 2019.

Photos of the Parthenon, Acropolis of Athens, visual similarities.
> From Le Corbusier's *Voyage d'Orient*. Photo: Le Corbusier, 1911. FLC L4(19)165.
>> From an excursion during the CIAM IV. Photo: Charlotte Perriand, 1933. AChP.
>>> Gordon Stephenson in the colonnade of the Parthenon, 1934. Photograph, 5.4 × 7.8 cm. Photo: František Sammer. SAAA.

> László Moholy-Nagy, The Temple of Poseidon, Sounion. Photo from an excursion of delegates to the CIAM IV. Sequence from the film *Architects' Congress* (22:10). Moholy-Nagy Foundation & Light Cone.
v The Temple of Poseidon, Sounion. Three postcards from Sammer's collection, 13.8 × 8.5 cm, 13.4 × 8.6 cm, and 13.3 × 8.5 cm. SAAA.

'We had the Acropolis for ourselves, just two relatively young architects, in the days when there were no tourists. [...] We spent the best part of a day there. We caressed it, we stroked it. It was so perfect'.

Gordon Stephenson recalling, almost 60 years later, his first visit to the Acropolis, in an interview from 1991–92 (see n. 265).

< Gordon Stephenson, unidentified man and František Sammer at the Acropolis of Athens. Photograph, 13.2 × 8.2 cm. SAAA.

^ Gordon Stephenson touching the ancient stone, inspecting the fluting and joints of a Doric column of the Parthenon, the Acropolis of Athens. Contact with times gone by. Photograph, 5.5 × 8.3 cm. SAAA.

Sammer and Stephenson together followed the footsteps of their colleagues in the modern movement. It is quite possible that some of their friends joined them during the trip, as is shown in the photograph of Sammer and Stephenson on the Acropolis. The two men travelled with a sound knowledge of Le Corbusier's own impressions, rhetoric and outlook on life. That is confirmed not only by the fact that they treated themselves to travel by airplane, a new but expensive means of transport that fascinated Le Corbusier,[260] but is also demonstrated by parallels in the photographic documentation of the same places. A good example of this is Sammer's photo of the Erechtheion at the Acropolis and a photo that Le Corbusier took in the same place while on his Voyage d'Orient with his friend Klipstein in 1911.[261] One might object that anyone could document the Erechtheion like that. Similarly, it may just be a coincidence that there is a strong likeness between Sammer's postcard with a photograph of a the three-bodied Daemon from the Acropolis museum and a photograph of a detail of the same figure that Le Corbusier took in 1911.[262] However, the identical detail on the corner of the crepidoma of the Parthenon, a photo of which Le Corbusier chose to publish in his well-known *Vers une architecture*,[263] can hardly be considered a coincidence.

We are witnesses to a remarkable phenomenon, in which the radical prophet of the bright new future, and an uncompromising opponent of traditional architectural education, was motivating young architects to study antique monuments. Le Corbusier's fascination with the Parthenon and the foundations of West European civilization was so strong that he passed it on to his assistants in the atelier. This is demonstrated by the fact that Stephenson, an architect with a traditional education at the best schools,[264] could, almost 60 years later, recall his first experience of the Acropolis in connection with Le Corbusier: 'On the whole trip through the USSR, the Black Sea, the Dardanelles, and to Athens, the highlight was the Parthenon on

260 | He even published a book on the subject: Le Corbusier, *Aircraft*, London: The Studio, 1935.

261 | FLC L4(19)79. For the 'Voyage d'Orient', see Žaknić, *Klip and Corb on the Road* (n. 256). See also p. 158 and n. 8 in the 'Excursus' 1.

262 | FLC L4(19)86. The detail of three bearded heads in these photographs belong to the fragment of a three-bodied Daemon, whose lower bodies are intertwined with snakes. The mythological figure comes from the pediment of the Hekatompedon, a forerunner of the Parthenon, and a no longer extant Dorian temple to the goddess Athena, from c.570 BC. The polychromed sculpture is now in the Acropolis Museum, Athens.

263 | Le Corbusier, *Vers une architecture*, Paris: G. Crès, [1923], p. 170, with Frédéric Boissonnas's photograph of the crepidoma of the Parthenon. For the original source, see Maxime Collignon, *Le Parthénon: l'histoire, l'architecture et la sculpture*, photographs Frédéric Boissonnas, Paris: Librarie Centrale D'Art et D'Architecture, Ancienne Maison Morel; C. Eggimann, succr., 1912, pl. 14.

264 | Gordon Stephenson studied architecture at the University of Liverpool from 1925 to 1930. In 1930, he was awarded a Chadwick Fellowship, which enabled him to attend the l'Institut d'Urbanisme de l'université de Paris while gaining practical experience at the Le Corbusier-Jeanneret atelier. From 1936 to 1938, he took his Master's degree in town planning at the Massachusetts Institute of Technology (MIT) in Cambridge, Massachusetts. For more on Stephenson, see p. 68 and n. 148.

∧ Crepidoma of the Parthenon, the Acropolis of Athens (detail). Photo: Frédéric Boissonnas, published in Maxime Collignon, *Le Parthénon* (1912) (see n. 263).

∧ Crepidoma of the Parthenon (detail). Photograph, 8.2 × 5.5 cm. Photo: František Sammer, 1934. SAAA.

> Le Corbusier, *Vers une architecture* (see n. 263), with a reproduction of Boissonnas's photo.

> The Erechtheion. Photo: Le Corbusier, 1911. FLC L4(19)79.
>> The Erechtheion, 1934. Photograph, 8.2 × 5.5 cm. SAAA.
> Heads of the Three-bodied Daemon from the Acropolis museum in Athens (detail). Photo: Le Corbusier, 1911. FLC L4(19)86.
>> Heads of the Three-bodied Daemon in the Acropolis museum in Athens (detail). Postcard from Sammer's collection, 13.6 × 8.6 cm. SAAA.

'You could still see the perfection of the workmanship. You couldn't have inserted a razor blade into the joints [in the marble], even though it was a ruin. [...] For example the stud-like bits in the frieze were originally wooden pegs. The whole thing is really based on timber construction. The capital at the top of a column is to shorten the span of the lintel. Originally it was a much cruder thing'.

Gordon Stephenson describing his experience of the Acropolis, in an interview from 1991–92 (see n. 265).

the Acropolis. We had the Acropolis for ourselves, just two relatively young architects, in the days when there were no tourists. [...]. We spent the best part of a day there. We caressed it, we stroked it. It was so perfect. [...] You could still see the perfection of the workmanship. [...] It took the Greeks, as Le Corbusier said, 500 years to build the Parthenon. [...] What he meant was that the Greeks kept perfecting things [...]'.[265]

The abundant documentation of the Acropolis in Sammer's collection seems like a study in classical art as it might have been made by an architect dutifully trained in Le Corbusier's rhetoric. Nevertheless, the large number of preserved photos of the Acropolis is inversely proportional to the personal view that Sammer later confided to Perriand: 'Greece was good, but I can't say that I was amazed – Delphi moved me. Yes, it was beautiful in Delphi'.[266] From Delphi and its environs, however, Sammer brought back only a few photos, which are, furthermore, over-exposed and the poorest in technical quality of all his photographs from Greece.

Despite the imperfection of the photograph of the amphitheatre in Delphi, one feels its dramatic placement in the surrounding countryside. The remains of the antique theatre turn towards the valley in the hills and, upon closer observation, one notices that, again, a lone observer, Stephenson, is part of the view. Then comes a photo of the ancient stadium in Delphi and two photos of the Greek countryside, a small farmstead and then two locals with a donkey, photographed while resting in the shade. In the places that Sammer was most taken with on the trip, he clearly abandoned any effort at documentation, instead recording his impressions, as he had done in most of his other photographs, as fleeting shots taken almost on the sly.

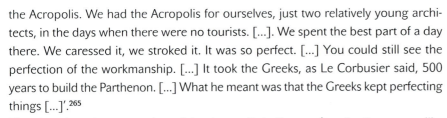

[265] Special Archives and Collections, University of Western Australia (UWA), Perth, 'Oral Interview with Gordon Stephenson', conducted by Criena Fitzgerald, September 1991–February 1992. This document was generously provided to me by Professor David Gordon of Queens University, Kingston, Ontario.

[266] AChP, Sammer to Perriand, 2 December 1934: 'C'était bien la Grèce mais – Je ne peux pas dire que j'étais épaté – Les Delf me touchaient. Oui les Delf vraiment c'était beau'.

A series of photographs from the Acropolis of Athens, each 8.2 × 5.5 cm. SAAA.

'For both of us it was a great emotional experience. It's the only time I've ever looked at something and felt a cold trickle run down my spine'.

Gordon Stephenson interviewed in 1991–92 (see n. 265).

'I can still hear the sound of a shepherd's pipe rising from the valley below'.

Stephenson recalling Delphi. Stephenson, *On a Human Scale*, p. 49 (see n. 152).

< Gordon Stephenson looking into the valley below the amphitheatre of Delphi, Greece, 1934.
Photograph, 8.4 × 5.5 cm. SAAA.

< Amphitheatre of Delphi (detail), 1934.
Photograph, 8.3 × 5.4 cm. SAAA.

'We sat in awe, perched on the slope of Mount Parnassus with the sacred site to ourselves'.

Stephenson, *On a Human Scale*, p. 49 (see n. 152).

∧ Gordon Stephenson on the slope of Mount Parnassus, Delphi, 1934. Photograph, 8.2 × 5.5 cm. UoLL.

\> A view from Delphi into the valley of the River Pleistos, whose source is on Mount Parnassus. Photograph, 8.4 × 5.5 cm. SAAA.

'In 1934, the country was poverty stricken and there were hardly any tourists'.

Stephenson describing Greece in Stephenson, *On a Human Scale*, p. 49 (see n. 152).

\> The Greek countyside; a valley between Delphi and Itea, its port. Photographs, 8.4 × 5.5 cm and 8.2 x 5.5 cm. SAAA.

107

  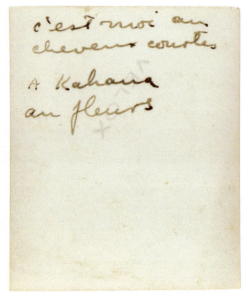

<< Agnes Larsen at a banana tree, Hawaii, January 1935. Photograph, 5.5 × 8 cm. SAAA.
^ Agnes Larsen in Hawaii. Written on the back: 'That's me with short hair, in Kahana, with flowers'. Photographs, 2.9 × 3.8 cm. SAAA.

A life worth living

After Greece, the two architects returned to work, Stephenson to Liverpool and Sammer, via Istanbul, to his 'socialist homeland', as he called the Soviet Union in his letter to Perriand.[267] A number of tasks were waiting for him in Kolli's studio, especially the design and construction of Moscow Metro stations. But Larsen could not wait for Sammer's return. She had been forced to change her plans suddenly, and left for her family in Honolulu for almost a year in order to look after her ill mother.[268] Despite the great distance separating them, the couple remained in touch by writing to each other regularly.[269] At the same time, Sammer stayed in touch with Perriand, having carried on correspondence with her since he left Paris. The intimacy with which they shared their beliefs about their professions and everyday life is evident not only in the written sources but also in the preserved photographs. Sammer's collection includes a number of photos taken by Perriand. Some of them are in her private archive, and are already known from other publications. Some of the published photos have enabled the identification of photos in Sammer's collection. The photographs found in Pondicherry differ from those in Perriand's personal Paris archive, particularly in that some have inscriptions addressed to Sammer. The fact that the exchange of photographs between Perriand and Sammer was mutual is attested to by a photo in Perriand's archive, which shows Sammer on board a ship.[270]

While Sammer was on his 'tour de cochon', Perriand was spending her summer in Dalmatia. He urged her to arrange a reunion with him during their travels,[271] but ultimately all he got was a photograph from the Dalmatian coast which she had taken of a fisherman's boat full of tuna.[272] 'I was helping out during an incredible catch of tuna, which had been pursuing a school of sardines. When I washed the salt off myself and made myself beautiful, I went onto the square in the village and danced to the accompaniment of a gypsy band or I bathed in the phosphorescent sea at midnight, lulled by choruses of men perched on the cliffs. Life truly was worth living'.[273] That is how Perriand recalled a summer holiday on the Dalmatian coast. From the seaside

267| Ibid.: 'Stephenson est parti pour Liverpool et moi j'étais bien content de pouvoir retourner, de nouveau voir Stamboul et puis la patrie Socialiste!'
268| Larsen, *Graffiti* (n. 122), pp. 288-314.
269| Ibid.
270| AChP. For their tracking down and providing me with the reproduction, I am indebted to Jacques Barsac and Pernette Perriand-Barsac.
271| AChP, letter Sammer to Perriand, 8 September 1934 (n. 250).
272| The same photograph is published in Barsac, *L'œil en éventail* (n. 164), p. 210.
273| Perriand, *Une vie de création* (n. 6), p. 58: 'Un été, j'allai sur la côte adriatique passer mes vacances dans une petite maison de vignes bordée par la mer, annexe d'une villa particulière où de proprietaires de Zagreb recevaient leurs amis. J'assistai à des pêches miraculeuses des thons qui suivaient des bancs des sardines. Après m'être dessalée et mise en beauté, j'allais danser sur la place du village au son d'un orchestre tzigane, où prendre un bain de minuit dans la mer phosphorescente, bercée par des chœurs d'hommes perchés sur des rochers. La vie valait vraiment la peine d'être vécue'.

∧ František Sammer in a photo from the Perriand's archive. AChP.

> Charlotte Perriand in a photo from Sammer's collection. Photograph, 5.3 × 5.4 cm. SAAA.

∨ Tuna in a fishing boat. On the back: 'In Dalmatia'. Photograph, 8.2 × 5.4 cm. SAAA.

< Pierre Jeanneret on the beach. On the back, written by Charlotte Perriand: 'My love'. Photograph, 7.8 × 6 cm. SAAA.

<< Swordfish. Contact print, 8.7 × 6 cm. SAAA.

v Fishing boat. Photograph, 8.4 × 5.5 cm. SAAA.

she sent Sammer a photograph of Pierre Jeanneret, with whom she was living at the time. The photo of a man, bare-chested and completely sprinkled with sand, has the words 'mon amour' written on the back.[274] She has thus shared an unusual portrait, and undoubtedly one of the most masculine looking, of this otherwise rather overshadowed architect.

Jeanneret also took photographs, and a number of shots of Perriand and of moments spent together are by him. In many cases, therefore, attribution is difficult, as it is with the pictures that Sammer took during shared moments with Larsen, Stephenson and other people. The importance of the Mediterranean region for Le Corbusier is generally well known.[275] The shore, the sea itself, swimming, fishermen, markets, fish and boats are among the subject matter that Sammer was intrigued with and often considered worth recording.

The photos by Perriand that have been preserved in Sammer's collection show the absolute interconnectedness of the modernists' private, as well as working lives, clearly. 'Housework. You remember cleaning up the kitchen. That is always a bore', Perriand comments on the back of a photo of the tiny kitchen of her studio in

[274] The same photo of Jeanneret on the beach, from Perriand's archive, is published in Barsac, *Charlotte Perriand* (n. 6), vol. 1, p. 286. A later xerocopy of it is deposited in the Pierre Jeanneret fonds, Canadian Centre for Architecture (CCA) Montréal, AP 156-085-19T.

[275] See *Le Corbusier et la Méditerranée* (exh. cat.), Marseille: Parenthèses – Musées de Marseille, 1987, and Benton, *Le Corbusier: mes années sauvages* (n. 39) and other sources (n. 110).

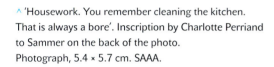

^ 'Housework. You remember cleaning the kitchen. That is always a bore'. Inscription by Charlotte Perriand to Sammer on the back of the photo.
Photograph, 5.4 × 5.7 cm. SAAA.

v Interior of Charlotte Perriand's studio in Montparnasse, including a smaller version of the Fauteuil Grand Confort (Easy Chair, 1928). Photograph, 5.2 × 5.8 cm. SAAA
>> The bedroom in the living area of Perriand's studio in Montparnasse. Inscription on the back: 'Pierre [Jeanneret] and Ch. [Charlotte Perriand]'.
Photograph, 5 × 5.2 cm. SAAA.
>>> Bedroom in a photo from Perriand's archive (see n. 277). AChP.

^ Mountains used as the background of a photomontage with a model of Perriand's design for a mountain resort. Photograph, 8.1 × 5.4 cm, in Sammer's collection. SAAA.

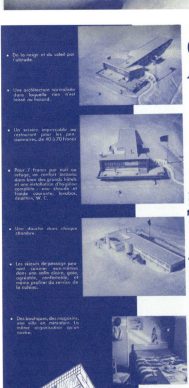

∧ Photomontage with a model of a ski resort designed by Charlotte Perriand in 1935. Photograph in Sammer's collection. Written on the back by Perriand: 'Project. Mountain Resort (the plan was very lovely)'. Both photographs, 5.4 × 5.4 cm. SAAA.

<< Photo of Charlotte Perriand as part of an advertisement for spring skiing, in the magazine *SKI, 1935, avec le guide-manuel des stations françaises de sports d'hiver* (see n. 278). AChP.

< Charlotte Perriand, a 1935 project for a mountain resort with small rooms modelled on her own studio (see the fourth photo from the top). *SKI, 1935* (see n. 279). AChP.

276| The same photograph from Perriand's archive is published in Barsac, *Charlotte Perriand* (n. 6), vol. 1, p. 176.

277| The same photograph from Perriand's archive, showing a smaller version of the *Fauteuil Grand Confort* (Easy Chair, 1928) inside, is published in ibid. (n. 6), p. 175. A second photograph, of the bedroom, shows a different arrangement of the furnishings, ibid., p. 174.

278| A portrait of Perriand together with her mountain resort project and a photograph of the arrangement of the interior of her studio in Montparnasse were published, for example, in *Ski, 1935, avec le guide-manuel des stations françaises de sports d'hiver*. Reproduced in Barsac, *Charlotte Perriand* (n. 6), vol. 1, pp. 312 and 313. See also Perriand Barsac (ed.), *Carnet de montagne* (n. 64), pp. 48–51.

279| Barsac, *Charlotte Perriand* (n. 6), vol. 1, pp. 312–15, and Perriand Barsac (ed.), *Carnet de montagne* (n. 64), pp. 48–51.

280| An identical shot of the model against the backdrop of a photograph of a massif is reproduced in Barsac, *Charlotte Perriand* (n. 6), vol. 1, p. 314, and Perriand-Barsac (ed.), *Carnet de montagne* (n. 64), p. 48. A second photo from Sammer's collection is of a photomontage with a different view, this time the side of the model with a rounded avant-corps containing the main hall and with a pedestrian ramp.

281| See pp. 52–55.

Montparnasse.[276] Sammer has preserved another two photos of the same format taken at her home, but these are shots of the bedroom and the living room.[277] The sharing of photos from one's private life may well be an expression of trust, but Perriand also uninhibitedly used them publicly as examples of the economical and first-rate organization of accommodations. The vitality and force with which she spread her 'joie de vivre' to her surroundings are radiated in some of her portraits, which she did not hesitate to use to accompany her projects.[278]

Perriand used her Montparnasse studio as the model for the guest units of the mountain resort that she designed in 1935.[279] The hotel, located 2,200 metres above sea level, was meant to be organized like a ship. Fourteen individual rooms offered privacy and modest comfort, which Perriand also intended to make accessible to poorer lovers of mountains and mountain sport.

She then took photographs of the project model and presented it in photomontages, two of which Sammer kept.[280] His collection even contains a photo of the snowy mountain peaks used in the photomontages as a backdrop for the model of the project.

Sammer started going to the mountains with Perriand as soon as they befriended each other at the Le Corbusier–Jeanneret atelier in the early 1930s.[281] Since that time, they shared a love of nature, sport, mountains, and the sea, and even after Sammer had left Paris, they shared their passions in their correspondence and photographs. Perriand was in the Soviet Union for the last time in 1934, so probably only informed Sammer of her 1935 project for a hotel in the mountains indirectly by mail. Considering the nature of the photographs that have been preserved in Sammer's collection, it is reasonable to assume that they could have discussed together the idea of a mountain resort earlier and may have also consulted on some aspects of the project by correspondence.

The project for the resort and other examples attest to the unbroken bonds that Sammer first formed in Paris. Despite changes in opinions and workplaces, his approach to life and to his profession did not change. Like a number of other architects of Le Corbusier's circle, at 35 rue de Sèvres Sammer acquired the principles that would be the basis of his professional thinking and of his future decision-making. Le Corbusier intentionally took on assistants of all nationalities and formed around himself an international community, a living atlas of the whole world, which he himself wanted to conquer. After gaining experience, the young architects left for other work, in all directions, sometimes returning back in their homelands. The network of people who remained linked to the atelier in Paris would eventually span nearly all the continents, yet continued to be a vibrant intellectual unit.

The land of 1,001 Sakakuras

The dynamics of the Le Corbusier galaxy, and the force with which it shaped the perspective of Sammer, is superbly demonstrated by his first trip to Japan in 1935. It was actually by chance that he went to this country with its deep traditions and exceptional sense of proportion so close to modern architecture in the West. It happened, he wrote, 'As if thrown into the bargain, [...] to see my girl after having been apart for eleven months'.[282] As the ideal place for a reunion after such a long time, the young couple chose Japan, a country on the way from Moscow to Honolulu. Larsen had already been to Japan before and Sammer had a certain idea of what it was like, especially from what he had learnt in the Paris atelier.

He had considered the journey well in advance and from the very beginning was discussing it with Perriand. He was enticing her to come to the Soviet Union in the summer of 1935: 'If you come [to Moscow] with Pierre, we'll go to Japan'.[283] He asked about Sakakura, who was still working at 35 rue de Sèvres: 'Write to me about Japan!!! Wouldn't it be lovely?!! [...] And how's little Saka?[284] Are you still sticking together?!'[285] Even shortly before his departure he tried to get Charlotte to join them: 'If you'd like to plan your vacation together with ours, write to me immediately [...] Greetings to Saka [...] And, listen, it's really a shame you can't come to Japan!'[286]

It remains a question whether Perriand even considered a trip to Japan in 1935. What is certain, however, is that she already had a certain notion of the country.[287] In sharing information and contacts, Japanese architects played a fundamental role at the Le Corbusier–Jeanneret atelier. Kunio Maekawa worked in Paris from 1928 to 1930 and Junzo Sakakura from 1931 to 1936. Both men later became not only pioneers of modern architecture in Japan, but also important intermediaries between East and West.[288]

Sammer gained first-hand experience of Japan before Perriand and got there well before Le Corbusier. He was in touch with both of them during his journey and shared his strong impressions with them. He travelled by the Trans-Siberian Railway from Moscow to Vladivostok, from where he continued on to Toyko by ship. Enchanted, he wrote his first impressions to his family in Pilsen: 'The Japanese are marvellous. [...] so clean that they seem like birds to me'[289] [see Excursus 3]. The locals, one and all, reminded him of his good friend from 35 rue de Sèvres and he immediately reported to Paris: 'My dear Charlotte, this country of 1,001 Sakakuras is amazing. You have made a big mistake by not coming, and you should realize that it is something you must experience!'[290] Thanks to Sakakura and Perriand, Sammer, immediately after his arrival, met with an art historian by the name of Tominaga, a painter called Sato[291] and Kunio Maekawa, and they kept him company during his sojourn.[292] Sammer spent a month in Japan with Larsen, 'still surrounded by a lot of friends. We knew three of them from Paris and we made a few new ones, Japanese, in Tokyo, and especially Mr Raymond, his wife and their little son'.[293]

Antonin Raymond (b. Reimann, 1888–1976), an architect of Czech origin, was known at Le Corbusier's in these years thanks particularly to his house in Karuizawa, which was built on plans heavily inspired by Le Corbusier's design of the unbuilt Errázuriz house in Chile. Le Corbusier publicly expressed his indignation about the Japanese project in the second volume of his *Œuvre complète*[294] and Raymond had a hard time defending why he had borrowed so much from Le Corbusier's design.[295] Sammer then wrote to Perriand from Japan that he had been 'invited to Mr Raymond's – the one who copied the Errázuriz house for himself'.[296] He also partly gave reasons justifying his new friendship: 'I can tell you that Raymond is a first-rate fellow – truly'.[297]

In Japan, Sammer was delighted not only with new friendships, but also with the unique culture, nature and appearance of traditional Japanese architecture. 'Japan

---

282| AMP, František Sammer Papers, letter home, 17 June 1935.

283| AChP, Sammer to Perriand, 2 December 1934: 'et si tu viendras avec Pierre, on irra au Japon'.

284| Amongst the friends from Le Corbusier's circle was Junzo Sakakura commonly known as Saka.

285| AChP, Sammer to Perriand, 28 February 1935: 'Et le petit Saka. Vous tenez encor [sic] ensemble?!'

286| Ibid., 5 June 1935: 'Si tu voudras arranger tes vacances en relation avec les nôtres, écris d'urgence. [....] Saluts à Saka. [....] Écoute – c'est tout de même malhereux que tu ne peux pas venir au Japon'.

287| See Jacques Barsac, *Charlotte Perriand et le Japon*, introduction by Germain Viatte, contribution by Sôri Yanagi; postface Yvonne Brunhammer; in collaboration with Pernette Perriand-Barsac, Paris: Norma, 2008. For an analysis of this relationship, see Yasushi Zenno, 'Fortuitous Encounters: Charlotte Perriand in Japan, 1940–41', in McLeod (ed.), *An Art of Living* (n. 6), pp. 90–153. For her dynamic relationship with Japan as exemplified in one particular piece of Perriand's furniture, see Charlotte Benton, 'From Tubular Steel to Bamboo: Charlotte Perriand, the Migrating "Chaise-longue" and Japan', 'Craft, Modernism and Modernity', special issue, *Journal of Design History* 11, no. 1, 1998, pp. 31–58.

288| Alfred Altherr, a Swiss colleague from the Paris atelier, describes Sakakura and Maekawa as the founders of modern Japanese architecture. Alfred Altherr, *Three Japanese Architects: Maekawa-Tange-Sakakura/Drei japanische Architekten: Maekawa-Tange-Sakakura*, New York: Architectural Book Publishing Co., 1968. Junzo Sakakura was presented at a Paris exhibition in 2013 as an example of cultural exchange between Japan and Paris: *Junzô Sakakura: Une architecture pour l'homme* (exh. cat.), Paris: Maison de la culture du Japon, 2017. For the importance of Japanese architects from Le Corbusier's circle to the Western scene, see Andreas Kofler, *Architectures japonaises à Paris 1867–2017*, Paris: Pavillon de l'Arsenal, 2017, esp. the chapter 'L'Apprentisage de la modernité 1867–1940', pp. 21–43. For more on Maekawa, see Jonathan M. Reynolds, *Maekawa Kunio and the emergence of Japanese Modernis Architecture*, Berkeley; Los Angeles; London: University of California Press 2001.

289| AMP, František Sammer Papers, Sammer to his aunt, 2 July 1935.

290| AChP, Sammer to Perriand, 22 July 1935: 'C'est formidable ce pays de 1001 Sakakuras. Tu as fait une grande faute de ne pas venir et met toi en tête que c'est une chose à vivre!' For a photograph and complete translation of the letter, see Excursus 3, pp. 172–174.

291| I discuss identifying Professor Tominaga and the painter by the name of Sato in my other research.

292| AMP, František Sammer Papers, letter to his parents, 27 July 1935, and also AChP, Sammer to Perriand, 22 July 1935.

293| AMP, František Sammer Papers, Sammer to his parents, 27 July 1935. Some scholars have assumed that Raymond had met Sammer even earlier, while visiting Paris in 1932. See Christine Vendredi-Auzanneau, 'Antonin Raymond and the Modern Movement: A Czech Perspec-

> 'We've travelled by train to Nara to see temples and pagodas, and to Kyoto, a cultural center. The landscape is diminutive – small mountains, small trees and houses. [...] Our old friend, Sakakura, from our Paris days, is working here as an architect'.

Agnes Larsen in a letter from Tokyo to Honolulu, 20 June 1935. Quoted in Larsen, *Graffiti*, p. 315 (see n. 122).

> Envelope from negatives developed in Ginza, Tokyo, 22–24 July 1935. SAAA.

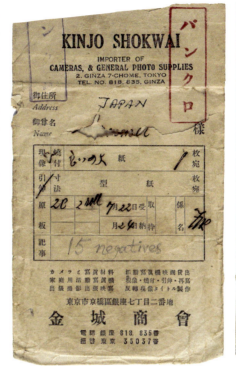 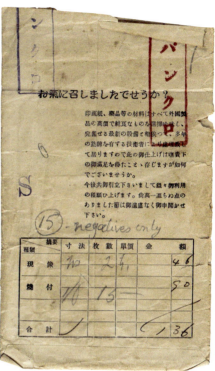

tive', in Kurt G. F. Helfrich and William Whitaker (eds), *Crafting a Modern World: The Architecture and Design of Antonin and Noémi Raymond*, New York: Princeton Architectural Press, 2006, p. 37. In his recollections of 1932, Raymond mentions Sammer, too: Antonín Raymond, 'Autobiography', *Kentiku*, October 1961, p. 21. The information in Sammer's correspondence, however, disproves this early date of meeting, as does Larsen's recollection from 1974, deposited in SAAA, as recorded by Mrityunjoy Mukherjee, a member of the ashram, who helped to build Golconde: 'in 1935 they [Sammer and Larsen] were already in Japan and met M. Raymond + his family and were their guests in their beach house for about a month in Tokyo'.

294 | Le Corbusier, 'Pas la peine de se gêner', in Boesiger (ed.), *Œuvre complète* (n. 41), vol. 2, p. 52.

295 | FLC, Raymond to Le Corbusier, 8 April 1935, and Le Corbusier's reply, 7 May 1935, deposited in the Architectural Archives of the University of Pennsylvania (AAUP), Antonin Raymond and Noémi Pernessin Raymond Collection. For details about Le Corbusier's project, see Christiane Crasemann Collins, 'Le Corbusier's Maison Errázuriz: A Conflict of Fictive Cultures', *The Harvard Architecture Review* 6, 1987, pp. 38–53. For more about Raymond's building and the debate with Le Corbusier, see Ken Tadashi Oshima, *International Architecture in the Interwar Japan: Constructing Kokusai Kenchiku*, Seattle; London: University of Washington Press, 2009, pp. 125–30. For Raymond's position on the dispute, see Antonin Raymond, *An Autobiography*, Rutland (VT), Tokyo: Charles E. Tuttle, 1973, pp. 130 and 131, which includes the above-quoted letters. For the debate in connection with Sammer, see Hrabová, 'Between Ideal and Ideology' (n. 18), pp. 148–51.

296 | AChP, Sammer to Perriand, 22 July 1935: 'Ecoute! Je suis invité chez Mr Raymond – celui qui a copié pour lui la maison Erazuris [*sic*])'. For a photograph of the original letter, see Excursus 3, pp. 173 and 174.

297 | Ibid.: 'Je peux te dire, que Raymond est un bon type – vraiment'.

298 | Ibid.: 'Japon et le pays de la pureté et le pays, où notre architecture comme nous le comprenons, est seulement un dévelopement très naturel d'une si bonne tradition'.

299 | Ibid.: 'J'ai aussi une idée d'un paralelisme [*sic*] entre le grec + Japonais'.

300 | Ibid.: 'On a presque peur de modifier la nature (parcs, recherche du site pour les temples + maisons, les types eux mêmes avec ses abris et les kimonos, les sabots, etc etc ––)'.

301 | Ibid.: 'C'est maintenant touchant de le regarder et songer combien du bon travail un Sakakura pourra faire mais au même temps combien des saloperies des autres ont fait'.

302 | Ibid.: 'On vie le paysage, (oui le paysage avant tout) puis les poissons qu'on bouffe, l'architecture, tous les types qu'on rencontre surtout à la campagne. Chaque chose a son dedans et c'est la nature où tout cela ce deroule [*sic*]'.

is the land of purity and a country where architecture – such as we [architects from Le Corbusier's circle] understand it – is only a very natural development of one remarkable tradition',[298] he wrote to Perriand. 'I have a certain idea about resemblances between Greek development and the Japanese [cultures]',[299] he wrote, attempting to find links with the European tradition. Sammer perceived how architecture was interwoven with the local landscape and he was reluctant to design in a way that would disrupt this: 'One is almost afraid to modify nature (parks, site surveys for temples and houses, the people themselves, with their dwellings and kimonos, wooden shoes and so on and so forth)'.[300] At the same time he dreamt about 'all the good work one Sakakura [Japanese modern architect] can do'.[301]

From the main Tokyo shopping district, Ginza, comes an envelope with 6 × 9 cm negatives. Sammer saved all 15 photos, developed towards the end of his first trip to Japan, between 22 and 24 July 1935, in his collection in Pondicherry. The wide-open spaces of the landscape correspond to the main perceptions Sammer describes in letters to friends and family in Europe. 'We are experiencing the landscape (yes, the landscape chiefly), then the fish, which we are stuffing ourselves with, the architecture, all the people we meet, mainly in the countryside. Everything here has its inner life and it is nature where it all takes place',[302] he wrote to Perriand. The photos of architecture Sammer took stealthily, and with accented attention to the surrounding natural environment. Evidence that he was discovering Japan in

Larsen's company is provided by photographs that they have taken of each other. We can see Sammer in a Japanese garden and Larsen on a path near a torii, a gate at the entrance to a shrine.

In the envelope with the negatives developed in Ginza there even remained a souvenir of the visit to Raymond's seaside home in Hayama. One negative shows a view from the house into an overgrown garden, with a hint of the horizon of the sea beyond a low wooden fence. In a second photo Larsen is posing on the verandah of the house, also enabling the identification of one of the printed photos in Sammer's collection. In the photo taken from the verandah we see Larsen in the shade of a pergola, gazing out towards the sea. At a garden table, on which there is a glass beer stein like the ones used in Bohemia, sits Raymond.

Meeting Antonin and Noémi Raymond was profoundly important to Sammer both professionally and personally, and it had an impact on a number of his future decisions. That does not mean that he forgot Le Corbusier, however. 'I think that it is very important that Corbu see Japan', he mentioned to Perriand and was convinced that their friend 'could do some good work' there.[303] According to Sammer's correspondence, it was Raymond who was behind the idea and together they were trying to figure out how to get Le Corbusier to Japan. Raymond was willing to take care of matters on the Japanese side and Sammer saw to organizing the trip. He was planning to link Le Corbusier's visit with his trip to the Moscow congress of architects.[304] Sakakura, who was supposed to leave 35 rue de Sèvres and return to Japan for good, could, Sammer believed, look after Le Corbusier.[305]

'Sir, [...] I wish to bring to your attention an opportunity [...] to spend some time in Japan. I talked once with Mr Raymond, who is the initiator of this idea. [...] And amongst my friends [...] there is great enthusiasm for the project. I [...] wish only to arouse your interest',[306] Sammer wrote to Le Corbusier shortly before leaving Japan. He confided to him that he had originally wanted to write the letter in a 'calmer environment, in Karuizawa, at the house inspired by your Erazuris [sic] project, [...] [where I] could spend a few days'.[307] Raymond had invited Sammer there to help work on the project for the dormitory of the Sri Aurobindo Ashram in Pondicherry.

^ František Sammer and Agnes Larsen in Japan, 1935. Negatives, 5.7 × 8.5 cm. SAAA.

> View into the garden of the Raymonds' summer home in Hayama. Negative, 5.7 × 8.5 cm. SAAA.

> Agnes Larsen on the verandah of the Raymonds' summer home in Hayama. Negative, 5.7 × 8.5 cm. SAAA.

>> Agnes Larsen with Antonin Raymond in Hayama, summer 1935. Photograph, 8 × 11.2 cm. SAAA.

303| Ibid.: 'Je crois que c'est très important que Corbu voie Japon [...] Corbu pourra faire un bon travail au Japon'.

304| According to the correspondence, where, however, it is not specified which congress was being held in Moscow. Most likely it was the international conference of architects, already being planned for several years and finally held in 1937. See below, p. 127.

305| AChP, Sammer to Perriand, 22 July 1935 (n. 296). FLC, Sammer to Le Corbusier, sent from Japan, 25 July 1935: 'Imaginez-vous, que probablement vous pourriez aller avec Saka'.

306| FLC, Ibid.: 'Monsieur je veux vous écrire surtout d'un chose. C'est seulement que je veux réveiller votre attention à une occasion que je trouve, pour passer quelque temps au Japon. J'ai parlé une fois avec Monsieur Raymond qui est iniciateur de cette idée. Moi, je l'ai attrapé et me voilà qui la vous présente. Monsieur Raymond en tout cas pourra vous expliquer mieux que moi tous les details. Moi, je pourrais vous dire, que entre mes amis anciens et nouveaux que j'ai fait ici au Japon, il y a un grand enthousiasme pour ce projet. Moi, seulement comme j'ai dis plus haut, je veux seulement réveiller votre attention'.

307| Ibid.: 'J'ai voulu l'écrire dans un état plus tranquil, à Karuizawa, dans la maison inspiré par votre projet Erazuris [sic]. C'est Monsieur Raymond qui a été pendant tout mon séjour formidablement gentil et grâce à qui j'ai pu avoir de la chance de passer quelques jours juste dans sa maison à Karuizawa'.

'François knows a Czech architect, Antonin Raymond, and his French wife [Noémi Pernessin Raymond], who is a sculptor. They came here after the earthquake to work with Frank Lloyd Wright, stayed on, and have done well. We spent a few days at their vacation house at a sea resort. In town they have a modern villa'.

Agnes Larsen in a letter from Tokyo to Honolulu, 20 June 1935. Quoted in Larsen, *Graffiti*, p. 315 (see n. 122).

'We are laying the foundations of a new architecture based on principles, not on habits of mind. As you do in your philosophies: first of all, free thinking, open, and as unburdened of preconceived ideas as possible'.

Antonin Raymond in a letter to Philippe Barbier Saint-Hilaire, called Pavitra, which accompanied the first variant of the Golconde design, 9 October 1935. SAAA.

^ 'Pas la peine de se gêner', Le Corbusier's reaction to Raymond's house built in Karuizawa. From Boesiger (ed.), *Le Corbusier et Pierre Jeanneret: Œuvre complète 1929–1934*, vol. 2, p. 52 (see n. 41).

< The initial design of the Golconde, a dormitory for the Sri Aurobindo Ashram in Pondicherry, on which Raymond's office worked in Karuizawa from July to October 1935. SAAA.

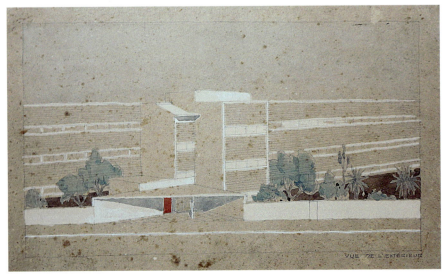

His office was just beginning to work on the assignment and Sammer was supposed to join in the first phase of the design together with Antonin Raymond and Kunio Maekawa,[308] a former assistant at the Le Corbusier–Jeanneret atelier in Paris. Because of visa difficulties, however, Sammer and Larsen, instead of travelling to Karuizawa in the mountains, had to board the SS *Siberia Maru* to Vladivostok and return to the Soviet Union. Raymond, together with Maekawa, started working on the Golconde without Sammer, who, with heavy heart, was leaving, having decided to return to Japan as soon as possible.[309] 'We merged with the Japanese landscape, made discoveries in architecture – in short, we lived extremely intensely and <u>we will never forget it</u>',[310] he wrote to his parents on the return journey.

Sammer's trip to Japan in 1935 was largely that of a tourist's. But at the same time, it reveals a network of people who were linked by the same profession and a similar outlook on life. Through Sammer, there was an attempt to reconcile two rivals in the world of modern architecture, Le Corbusier and Raymond. Sammer also deserves the credit for a very early formulation of the idea of Le Corbusier visiting Japan. As with Perriand, however, the question remains whether Le Corbusier at the time even considered such a journey. As Sammer had foreseen, Le Corbusier eventually did do 'good work'[311] in Japan, but that was not until the 1950s, and thanks to his first and only assignment there – the National Museum of Western Art in Tokyo, built from 1956 to 1959.[312]

One finds many parallels between traditional Japanese architecture and modern architecture in the West and several figures of Le Corbusier's calibre have substantially affected the formation of modern architecture in Japan. Information among the distant countries circulated in various ways; not every creative person from the West was able to visit Japan, of course. Perriand did not set out for Japan until the confluence of various crises during the Second World War, and did so thanks to an invitation from her old friend, Sakakura.[313] It was his invitation that enabled her to leave France just before the German invasion and to get to the country in which she would find an inexhaustible source of inspiration for the rest of her life.[314] The former assistants at 35 rue de Sèvres also arranged Le Corbusier's visit to Japan in the 1950s. The big assignment that brought him there was carried out largely thanks to Maekawa and Sakakura.[315]

In July 1935, Le Corbusier replied promptly to Sammer's letter,[316] but without considering the invitation at all, just as he did not consider Sammer's later questions regarding the trip to Japan.[317] He had other worries – namely, things related to the big Soviet commission, which Sammer was supposed to supervise on site. 'My dear Sammer, on the train between Warsaw and Vienna I learnt from two passengers from Moscow that Centrosoyuz is already in operation. [...] I would have been happy if it had been you who told me and, more specifically, you had given me your opinion and some photographs, too'.[318]

---

308 | AChP, Sammer to Perriand, 22 July 1935 (n. 296): 'Je travaillerai 5 jours à peu près avec Maiekawa + son équipe sur un logement à Pondicherry'. This refers to the beginning of work on the Golconde project in July 1935, which is also confirmed by entries in the ledger of Raymond's office, deposited in the AAUP, Antonin Raymond and Noémi Pernessin Raymond Collection. The same document provides evidence that Kunio Maekawa was involved at the beginning of the project. In October of that year, Raymond's office had already prepared the first variant of the design, which Raymond sent to Pondicherry in a letter to Philippe Barbier Saint-Hilaire (1894–1969), called Pavitra, 9 October 1935. SAAA, Pondicherry.

309 | AChP, Sammer to Perriand, 22 July 1935 (n. 296).

310 | AMP, František Sammer Papers, Sammer to his parents, 27 July 1935. Emphasis in original.

311 | See n. 303

312 | For Le Corbusier's relationship with Japan, see Gérard Monnier (ed.), *Le Corbusier et le Japon*, Paris: A. & J. Picard, 2007.

313 | For literature on Perriand and Japan, see n. 287.

314 | Perriand was in Japan first for two years, from 1940 to 1942, after which she repeatedly went back to the country. She played a key role in providing mutual inspiration between East and West. See above, p. 114 and n. 287.

315 | See above, p. 114 and n. 288.

316 | FLC, Sammer to Le Corbusier, from Japan, 25 July 1935, and FLC, Le Corbusier to Sammer, from Paris to Moscow, 31 July 1935.

317 | FLC, Sammer to Le Corbusier, from Japan, 17 September 1935.

318 | FLC, Le Corbusier to Sammer, from Paris to Moscow, 31 July 1935: 'Mon cher Sammer, J'ai appris dans le train entre Varsovie et Vienne, par deux voyageurs venant de Moscou, que le Centrosoyuz était occupé. [...] J'aurais eu du plaisir à ce que se soit vous qui me l'annonciez et, plus particulièrement, à ce que vous me faissiez parvenir votre opinion et également quelques photographies'.

The Soviet Union, 1935–37

Sammer supervised the construction of Le Corbusier's large Soviet assignment at the same time as working on a number of projects at Kolli's office. The construction work was made more complicated by political pressure for the implementation of socialist realism, which put modern architects in the Soviet Union in a difficult spot. Le Corbusier watched the work only indirectly. That is why he asked each of his friends who had made it to Moscow, and could keep an eye on the construction work as it proceeded, to send him photographs. Charlotte Perriand and Josep Lluís Sert brought him photographic documentation from their visits to the Soviet Union. 'More visitors from the West. This time it was Luis [sic] Sert, the Spanish architect who was so nice to us in Barcelona last year. He was here with some friends for a few days, staying at the Metropole. François saw them every day',[319] Larsen wrote in a letter to Honolulu.

Sammer made an active part of the information exchange[320] and repeatedly promised photographs to Le Corbusier. 'I am going to photograph the Centro[soyuz]. I will also write to Corbu and send him photos',[321] Sammer wrote to Perriand. Sammer's collection does not include such material, but it is possible that he could have taken some of the photos that are now in the Le Corbusier archive.[322]

Owing to his links to Le Corbusier, Sammer found himself in a difficult position in Moscow, even though from the start they had never shared the same political views. Le Corbusier's political views are distinguished by considerable fluctuation[323] and in the clash with Sammer's confirmed left-wing idealism they remained a point of contention.[324] That, however, did not prevent Sammer from continuing to respect Le Corbusier as an authority on modern architecture.[325] Similarly, for Le Corbusier the political views of his former colleague were not so decisive as to prevent him from respecting Sammer as an architect.[326]

Seen from the Soviet Union, Le Corbusier's activity seemed to Sammer like banal theorizing and he could not resist making a comparison. 'It is difficult to write to you in Paris about things that can be judged only by the Moscow yardstick',[327] Sammer wrote, explaining the lateness of his correspondence regarding the Centrosoyuz. At the same time, he did not forget what he had learned in Paris, and in the Soviet Union he had a hard time reconciling himself to compromises in the quality of the built architecture. 'What we are most busy with now is socialist realism in art. Perhaps justifiable as a concept, but really a vexing matter of development',[328] he wrote to Le Corbusier.[329]

At the beginning of 1934 Sammer often accompanied Perriand during her second visit to the Soviet Union.[330] 'We've had a visitor from Paree [sic]: Charlotte Perriand. You may recall, she's Le Corbusier's interior designer and was a colleague of François. After a week in a hotel, she spent several days with us',[331] Larsen wrote in a letter home to Honolulu. In Moscow, Perriand acquainted herself with the current state of the construction of the Centrosoyuz and attended talks by André Lurçat, in which he openly attacked Le Corbusier, calling him a fascist.[332] In Kolli's office, she joined in the work on the last phase of the project for the Trade Unions Theatre. Sammer wrote about the failure of this project to Pierre Jeanneret in Paris: 'Tovarisch Kaganovich[333] is now pushing verticalism in architecture and our façade was lengthwise!!!'[334] Regarding Lurçat, he added: 'You would in any case agree with me that he was less dangerous in Paris than here'.[335]

The political pressure to apply the state-dictated architectural style in the Soviet Union increased month after month, and the number of architects courageous enough to continue the struggle for the ideals of avant-garde architecture declined.

[319] Larsen from Moscow to her family in Honolulu, 3 May 1934, in Larsen, *Graffiti* (n. 122), p. 282.

[320] FLC, Perriand to Le Corbusier, 18 January 1934.

[321] AChP, Sammer to Perriand, 2 December 1934: 'J'irrai fotografier Centro l'un de ces jours. J'écrirai aussi à Corbu et j'enverrai les photos'.

[322] FLC, photos of the Centrosoyuz under construction, particularly FLC L3(19)34; L3(19)35. I continue to work on the identification of the photographs in my other research.

[323] A conference on the problematic topic of Le Corbusier and politics, *Le Corbusier: Mesures de l'homme*, was held at the Centre Georges Pompidou, Paris, in 2016. The papers are published in Baudouï (ed.), *Le Corbusier 1930-2020* (See n. 32).

[324] See above, pp. 59–61.

[325] For more on this, see Hrabová, 'Between Ideal and Ideology' (n. 18).

[326] See below, p. 138, especially the correspondence between Sammer and Le Corbusier after the Second World War.

[327] FLC, Sammer to Le Corbusier, from Moscow, 17 September 1935: 'C'est si difficile d'écrire à vous qui est à Paris, les choses qui doivent être mesuré par l'échelle de Moscou'.

[328] FLC, Sammer to Le Corbusier, from Moscow, 7 January 1934: 'Le chose qui nous occupe actuellement beaucoup, c'est le réalisme socialiste en art. Peut être juste comme conception, mais clairement une chose vraiment embêtante de developpement, répondante à la periode de la dictature du proletariat'.

[329] Socialist realism was officially defined at the First Congress of Soviet Writers, in August 1934, thus rubberstamping Stalin's decree of two years before. Concerning the implementation of socialist realism and the split inside the community of Russian architects during the course of the 1930s, see the pioneering essay, based on research in Russian archives, by Danilo Udovički-Selb, 'Between Modernism and Socialist Realism: Soviet Architectural Culture under Stalin's Revolution from Above, 1928-1938', *Journal of the Society of Architectural Historians* 68, no. 4, December 2009, pp. 467–95, and, more recently, id., *Soviet Architectural Avant-Gardes: Architecture and Stalin's Revolution from Above, 1928-1938*, London: Bloomsbury Visual Arts, 2020. For an explanation of socialist realism, see Catherine Cooke, 'Beauty as a Route to "the Radiant Future": Responses of Soviet Architecture', *Journal of Design History* 10, no. 2, 1997, pp. 137–60.

[330] Concerning Perriand's trips to Moscow, see above, pp. 85 and n. 203.

[331] Larsen to her family from Moscow to Honolulu, 19 February 1934, in Larsen, *Graffiti* (n. 122), p. 278.

[332] See above, p. 56 and n. 96.

[333] Lazar Moiseyevich Kaganovich (1893–1991) was a Soviet politician and close colleague of Stalin. For Kaganovich's role in pushing through socialist realism and for context, see Vendula Hnídková,

^ Centrosoyuz under construction, 1934. Photographs in the Le Corbusier archive. FLC L3(19)34 and L3(19)35.

Moskva 1937: Architektura a propaganda v západní perspektivě, Prague: Institute of Art History, Czech Academy of Sciences, 2018, esp. pp. 15–19.

334 | FLC, František Sammer to Pierre Jeanneret, from Moscow, 27 March 1934: 'Tovarich Caganovitch force maintenant du verticalisme en architecture et notre façade était en longueur!!!'

335 | Ibid.: 'Vous seriez en tout cas de mon avis qu'à Paris il était moins dangereux qu'ici'.

336 | AChP, Sammer to Perriand, 27 March 1936: 'Les seuls architectes qui ont quelque chose à dire sont les frères Vesnin avec Ginsbourgh et toute la jeunesse autour'.

337 | Ibid.: 'C'était très beau à entendre [the Vesnins and Ginzburg] et en comparaison avec des différents trucs diplomatiques de Colley, pleine de character et de sûreté'.

338 | Ibid.: 'Nous sommes fiers de notre passé' (constructiviste) - Oh oui la maison de le Corbusier (sur la Miasnitskaia) est la meilleure chose qu'on a bâti et qu'on va bâtir dans 50 années'.

339 | Ibid. See also FLC, Sammer to Le Corbusier, 23 April 1936.

340 | FLC, Ibid. '"Nous" – c'est à dire tous qui étions autour de vous les quatres dernières années'.

341 | Ibid.: 'Mais aujourd'hui on est bien prêt pour faire une révision. [...] Les Vesnins + Ginsbourgh [*sic*] + Leonidov et plusieurs d'autres avec un programme très net et puis le reste en désorientation. [...]. Et si je parlerai à propos de nous-jeuns soyez assuré, que nous sommes prêts de s'engager dans les luttes avec vous'.

342 | Viktor Valeryanovich Kalinin (1906-2003) was a close colleague of Sammer's in Russia, and, according to the available information in the AMP, František Sammer Papers, they remained in touch even during the Second World War.

343 | AChP, Sammer to Perriand, 27 March 1936: 'Mon ami Kalinin qui est le seul qui semble noir – d'ailleurs l'un des architectes des plus appréciés à l'atelier Colly'.

344 | AMP, František Sammer Papers, Sammer to his parents, 6 October 1936.

345 | This was a study for a tuberculosis sanatorium and a sanatorium for senior bureaucrats in Gagra by the Black Sea, in what is today Abkhazia/Georgia. These projects were never built.

Kolli eventually became the head of the Union of Socialist Architects, and in his studio the opportunities to try and preserve modernist forms were also declining. 'The only architects who have anything to say are the Vesnin brothers and Ginzburg and all the young people around them',[336] Sammer wrote to Perriand in spring 1936, when he had already decided to leave Kolli and his 'various diplomatic affairs'.[337] He was moved by the openness of the Vesnin brothers and the courage with which they came out in support of Constructivism, which was becoming more and more restricted. 'We are proud of our (Constructivist) past – and, yes, Le Corbusier's [Centrosoyuz] building (in Myasnitskaya) is the best we have built and will build in the next 50 years',[338] wrote Sammer in a letter to Perriand, praising a talk by the Vesnins at the Club of Architects in Moscow, where they had met for discussions about the state of Soviet architecture.[339]

In the Soviet environment, the authority of Le Corbusier and Jeanneret acquired symbolic importance in the struggle to preserve the ideals of modern architecture. The more the state bureaucracy interfered in architecture, the more strongly Sammer realized the value of his base in the Paris atelier. Not only did he maintain contact with people from Le Corbusier's circle, but in Moscow he openly joined the side of Le Corbusier's defenders. '"We"', Sammer wrote to Le Corbusier from Moscow, 'means everyone who has been around you during the last four years'.[340] At the same time he sought an ally in Le Corbusier in the struggle for the rescue of modern architecture in the Soviet Union: 'We are ready for a review [...] the Vesnins + Ginzburg + Leonidov and a few others [...] we are ready to join you in the struggle'.[341]

Together with his friend Viktor Valeryanovich Kalinin,[342] he planned to go to another office. Sammer described Kalinin to Perriand as 'one of the most appreciated architects in Kolli's studio, [...] the only one who seems to be black [probably meaning opposed to socialist realism]'.[343] In 1936, Sammer joined the planning office of Narkomzdrav (Narodnyi Komissariat Zdravo-okhraneniia – People's Commissariat of Public Health), which was run by Moisei Yakovlevich Ginzburg (1892-1946) in collaboration with the brothers Alexander (1883-1959) and Viktor Vesnin (1882-1950). He worked on projects for health facilities there, and with Kalinin designed a sanatorium in Yalta[344] and two sanatoriums in Gagra.[345] Together with Ivan Leonidov

(1902–59)³⁴⁶ he worked on the 'planirovki', a territorial plan for the south coast of the Crimea, and spent some time in Kislovodsk in the foothills of the Caucasus. There, the office was finishing work on a large sanatorium, which, despite the prescribed classicizing style, includes concealed avant-garde forms.³⁴⁷ Two other architects from Czechoslovakia, Jaromír Krejcar (1895–1950) and Josef Špalek (1902–42), were involved in planning and construction, too.³⁴⁸ Like Sammer, Špalek came from Pilsen and their paths crossed not only in the Soviet Union but also through their relatives and friends in their home town, who kept in touch with them.³⁴⁹

After his departure from Kolli's office, Sammer spent a lot of time in the south of the Soviet Union, in the mountains and on the 'Soviet Riviera' – places that had enchanted him while on his travels with Stephenson in 1934. In the summer of 1936 he planned to visit 'the Caucasus, by plane and on foot – with mountains and glacier heads – and then sea and sun, nakedness and fruit'.³⁵⁰ He shared his dreams about future travels with Perriand, writing to her: 'Maybe Stephenson will come too. Part of the Caucasus we are going to conquer with a professor of material culture [Sammer probably means his colleague and friend, the architect Timofeyi Ignatevich Makarychev (1904–1980)], who was born there, and then, we will do some of the mountaineering madness alone. Doesn't that remind you of something? On foot, with all the other things on our backs. [...] I think about it constantly'.³⁵¹ He was reminding Perriand of times together while they were working in the Paris atelier, and was trying to entice her to join the journey.

Photographs from Sammer's collection show that the only woman hiking with them and other friends in the Caucasus was Larsen. The intensity of the experiences that Sammer brought back with him from his travels comes across in his draft letter to Makarychev.³⁵² More than 30 years later, Sammer poetically reflected on that trip hiking with friends, recalling the donkey that they satirically called Adolf. Photographs from the trip remained deposited in Pondicherry, so the illustrations to the preserved written sources had previously long remained hidden. All the more, then, did Sammer draw on his imagination to describe the shared experiences in a letter to his old friend Makarychev written in 1968, wishing to return with him to the same places [see Excursus 4, p. 176].

When planning the summer trip in 1936, Sammer had not seen his family in Pilsen since 1933, when he left for work in the Soviet Union. He was feeling the distance between himself and his friends elsewhere in the world as well. Photographs were one of the rare means to share the current appearance of the people close to him and the atmosphere in which they were living. 'I really cannot imagine Honza [his brother Jan, also called Jenda] going to dance classes, or how tall he is', Sammer wrote in a letter home. 'I cannot imagine how he talks, what he thinks about, and so on [...] I received a letter from Milča, too. I was better able to imagine that. Perhaps because I have photographs'.³⁵³ He confided similarly to Perriand, 'You know, one loses perspective and soon I won't know what interests you [Perriand and Jeanneret]',³⁵⁴ and he describes his impressions of the photos that he was shown, probably in Moscow by Kolli, after he returned from his trip to Paris: 'I saw a photo of you and Pierre in front of the Salvation Army building – and it moved me greatly. [...] We hear from you so seldom. And then the great event – the congress of architects, which will not take place. Oh, how I had looked forward to seeing you all again'.³⁵⁵ Planned for a number of years and constantly postponed, the international congress of architects in Moscow seemed to haunt Sammer from the moment he decided to leave to work in the Soviet Union. Not only was he unable to take part in the fourth

346| Ivan Ilyich Leonidov was a leading talent of Constructivism in Russia, but most of his designs remained solely on paper. One of the few projects he lived to see built was the set of steps on the grounds of the Kislovodsk sanatorium.
347| The Ordzhonikidze Sanatorium in Kislovodsk was completed in 1938. For details, see Udivički-Selb (n. 329). See also Richard Pare, 'Ginzburg at Kislovodsk: The Ordzhonikidze Sanatorium and the End of Modernism in Russia', a paper delivered at Princeton University on 10 May 2013, https://mediacentral.princeton.edu/media/Ginzburg+at+KislovodskA+The+Ordzhonikidze+Sanatorium+and+the+End+of+Modernism+in+Russia/0_jz0cvvbz/13468701 Accessed 13 January 2024.
348| Concerning Czechoslovak architects who went to the Soviet Union to work, see Hrabová 'Between Ideal and Ideology' (n. 18), pp. 162–66. For more, based on research in Russian archives, see Dofková, 'Avantgarda 20.–30. let: Praha–Moskva' (n. 222).
349| I examine the link between František Sammer and Josef Špalek in my other research.
350| AChP, Sammer to Perriand, 27 March 1936: 'Le Caucase par avion et au pieds – avec les montagnes et attagnes [sic] des glaciers – et puis la mer avec soleil - nudité et fruits'.
351| Ibid.: 'Peut-être Stephenson va venir. On va faire une partie de Caucase avec un professeur de la culture materielle qui est né là bas et puis des folies alpinistes on fasse seuls. Ça ne te dis rien? Au pieds, avec un tant [sic] et toutes les autres choses sur le dos. [...] Je pense tout le temps à cela'.
352| AMP, František Sammer Papers, draft letter, Sammer to Makarychev, spring 1968. For a photo and translation of the letter, see Excursus 4.
353| Ibid., Sammer to his parents, 13 January 1937.
354| AChP, Sammer to Perriand, 27 March 1936: 'Tu sais on perd de l'échelle et bientôt je ne saurais pas que ce qu'il vous intéresse!'
355| Ibid.: 'J'ai vu un photo de toi et Pierre devant L'Armée du salut – qui m'a touché beaucoup. [...] On entend si peu de vous. Et puis grand événement – le congrès des architectes qui n'aura pas lieu. Oh comme j'ai attendu de vous revoir'.

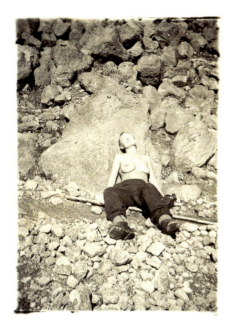  

^ Agnes Larsen and František Sammer during the trip to the Caucasus, on the way to Mount Elbrus, 1936. Photographs, 4.1 × 2.9 cm. SAAA.

< Krugozor base camp, before climbing Mount Elbrus, 1936. First from the left: Agnes Larsen, the only woman on the trip, together with: Misha, Yurka, Timofei, Aptekar and František Sammer, according to Larsen, *Graffiti*, p. 346 (see n. 122).
Photographs, 4.1 × 2.9 cm. SAAA.

'The excitement in our lives these days is the trip we're planning for this summer – to the Caucasus Mountains in the Soviet Republic of Georgia (Gruzia in Russian). There'll be six of us – five about our age and our leader, about forty, who knows the territory well. I'm the only woman'.

Agnes Larsen in a letter to Honolulu, 10 January 1936. Larsen, *Graffiti*, p. 343 (see n. 122).

congress of the CIAM because of the empty promises from the Soviet side, but in the coming years he lived in the hope that he would get his Paris allies to come to Russia on the occasion of the next planned congress. After returning from Japan in the summer of 1935 and in the course of 1936, however, he understood that if he wanted to maintain contact with them, he was the one who would have to set off on a trip, and go to Europe.

v Gurzuf, the Crimea. Postcard, 13.7 × 8.5 cm. SAAA.
> Simeiz, the Crimea. Postcard, 14 × 8.3 cm. SAAA.

< František Sammer (first from the right) with Charlotte Perriand and two unidentified friends in Paris, 1937. Contact print, 3 × 3.8 cm. SAAA.

^ Postcard from František Sammer home to Pilsen, 13 February 1937, with his address c/o Charlotte Perriand, Paris: F. Sammer chez Ch. Perriand, 135bis Bd Montparnasse. AMP.

Paris,
January–February 1937

'I am leaving for Paris, where we are expected – by the whole Internationale, including Le Corbusier',[356] Sammer wrote to his parents in Pilsen in early 1937. He had gone to Paris so that after his long absence he could 'see everything that an architect has to know',[357] looking around at all the recently-built projects, attending exhibitions, buying books and spending lots of time with friends from Le Corbusier's circle, who played host to him in Paris.[358] 'Le Corbusier has a lot of work. We have already been to some building sites, continuously telling one another about things that interest us. There is a great, great deal that's new'.[359] For the first time in years, he was reunited with the core of the Paris atelier, and also with Sakakura, Sert and Adam. These three men were no longer working for Le Corbusier and had come to Paris as professional architects on the occasion of preparations for the 1937 Exposition internationale.[360]

Shortly afterwards, Sert achieved fame at the Exposition with his Spanish pavilion, in which Picasso's *Guernica* was shown, and Sakakura gained acclaim on the international architecture scene with his Japanese pavilion.[361] Czechoslovakia was represented at the Exposition by the Constructivist pavilion designed by Jaromír Krejcar, and the Soviet Union demonstrated its power with a monumental classicizing building. Sammer did not affiliate himself with either the Czechoslovaks or the Russians.

356| AMP, František Sammer Papers, Sammer to his parents, 13 January 1937.
357| Ibid., Sammer on a postcard to his parents, 13 February 1937.
358| Ibid., Sammer in letters to his parents, January and February 1937. See also n. 1 and the quotation on p. 41.
359| Ibid., Sammer to his parents, 30 January 1937.
360| The Exposition internationale des arts et des techniques dans la vie moderne took place in Paris from 25 May to 25 November 1937.
361| For the Japanese pavilion Sakakura was awarded the Grand Prix de jury de l'Exposition, thus becoming the first Japanese architect to win on the international scene of modern architecture. See p. 114 and n. 288.
362| AMP, František Sammer Papers, Sammer to his parents, postcard, 17 February 1937: 'For the 1937 exhibition, I am working on a plan for Moscow, which will be exhibited in the Pavillon des Temps Nouveaux

> Photos from a visit to the construction site of the Cité de la Muette by Eugène Beaudouin and Marcel Lods, in Drancy, near Paris, designed and built from 1929 to 1940. In the first photo, second from the right, Muncha Sert; in the second, first from the right, Agnes Larsen. Photographs, from 1937, 3 × 3.8 cm and 8 × 5.1 cm. SAAA.

organized by the Society of Modern Architects [*sic*]'. In the form of a tent, the Pavillon des Temps Nouveaux housed an exhibition of photomontages, models and dioramas, particularly about society during the Great Depression and about urban-planning solutions that had come out of the CIAM congresses. The plan for Moscow which Sammer mentions could have been part of the exhibition of urban plans for a 'functional city', but that remains a topic for future research. For an analysis of the pavilion in the context of the politics of the times and Le Corbusier's work, see Danilo Udovički-Selb, 'Le Corbusier and the Paris Exhibition of 1937: The Temps Nouveaux Pavilion', *Journal of the Society of Architectural Historians* 56, no. 1 (March 1997), pp. 42–63. The pavilion was not opened until 17 July, after the fifth congress of the CIAM, which was held in Paris. See Mumford, *The CIAM Discourse on Urbanism* (n. 190), pp. 115 and 116.

363 | AMP, František Sammer Papers, Sammer to his parents, 18 April 1937.

He demonstrated his role in the international field of modern architecture by working on the plans for Moscow at the exhibition to be held in the Pavillon des Temps Nouveaux,[362] which was built by the team from the Le Corbusier–Jeanneret atelier outside the main exhibition grounds. Sammer spent the whole month in Paris with Larsen, who came down from Norway, where she had spent Christmas with her Norwegian relatives. The couple then travelled back to Moscow, with a stop in Pilsen, where they visited the Sammer family. During his first years in the Soviet Union, Sammer used to send Soviet publications everywhere, seeking to enlighten his friends in the West. Now, at the start of 1937, he was bringing back to Russia a great deal of European printed matter. 'We had a visitor – our friend Gordon Stephenson [...] We are just beginning to sort out all kinds of packages from Paris and Pilsen for relatives of our acquaintances. Tomorrow we will begin to deliver them',[363] he wrote home in the spring.

'PAVILLON des Temps Nouveaux. Le Corbusier and P. Jeanneret, architects.
An attempt at a museum of the public education (urbanism).
VISITOR: This is the rigorous science of urbanism.
Urbanism brings woe to towns and the countryside. But it can – in future – bring essential happiness.
Urbanism as the total manifestation of the lyricism of an era'.

Introduction to the presentation of the Pavillon des Temps Nouveaux, in Le Corbusier, *Des canons, des munitions? Merci! Des logis, s. v. p.*, Boulogne-sur-Seine: Éditions de l'architecture d'Aujourd'hui, 1938, p. 26.

< Agnes Larsen and František Sammer in the Jardin des Tuileries, Paris, 1937. Contact prints, 3 × 3.8 cm. SAAA.

v Le Corbusier and Pierre Jeanneret, Pavillon des Temps Nouveaux at the Exposition internationale des arts et des techniques dans la vie moderne, Paris, 1937. FLC L2(13)74. Photo: Albin Salaün.

^ The Louvre, the Seine and a figure on the horizon, Paris, 1937. Contact prints, 3 × 3.8 cm. SAAA.

'We both changed – Paris and I. People talk of unemployment, the war in Spain, and the Nazis. [...] We're invited to Le Corbusier's for dinner – an informal evening at their new villa'.

Agnes Larsen in a letter to Honolulu, 17 January 1937. Larsen, *Graffiti*, p. 392 (see n. 122).

From 15 to 26 June 1937, the long-awaited international congress was finally held in Moscow. Leading architects from all over the world came to the First All-Union Congress of Soviet Architects in order to discuss the current state of architecture in the country. The Soviet side also seized the opportunity to confirm formally the establishment of socialist realism in the country and to condemn the modern manifestations of Soviet Constructivism. The Western world learnt about the congress proceedings from leading figures of modern architecture like Frank Lloyd Wright.[364] Le Corbusier had received a formal invitation, too, but quickly declined it, explaining that while the Soviet congress was being held he had to prepare the fifth CIAM congress in Paris, which would take place in late June and early July of that year.[365]

From his correspondence we know that Sammer had also been involved in the preparations of the Moscow congress. At the same time he continued to work on projects that had already begun. He wrote to his parents: 'Now, before the congress of architects there are so many worries and tasks of all kinds that it has not been possible to get distracted. The sanatorium is in full swing and many other things are too. Everything is going very well'.[366] In letters sent to places outside the Soviet Union, however, he could hardly write what was really happening during this period. The week before the opening of the congress Sammer received a telegram from Raymond with an invitation to Tokyo.[367] By then, Larsen had left the Soviet Union and was in Vienna, and Sammer had his hands full trying to arrange his departure from the country as quickly as possible. The circumstances around their sudden departure remain unclear. Much later, Larsen and Sammer said that they had left for administrative reasons. Foreigners living in the Soviet Union were no longer able to extend their visas[368] and were given the choice of either applying for Soviet citizenship or leaving the country.[369] Sammer took the second option, which brought to a close his struggle, begun with the Vesnin brothers, for the principles of Constructivist architecture in Russia. Most of the foreign architects who chose to remain in the country soon faced serious difficulties. By leaving, Sammer most probably saved his life and could thus set out on another journey to achieve the ideals of modern architecture.

364 | Frank Lloyd Wright, 'Architecture and Life in the U.S.S.R.', *Architectural Record* 82, no. 4 (October 1937), pp. 58–63. For more details about the congress, see Simon Breines, 'First Congress of Soviet Architects', ibid., pp. 63–65, 94 and 96. For details about invitations and the participation of foreign delegates, with Frank Lloyd Wright as the example, see Donald Leslie Johnson, 'Frank Lloyd Wright in Moscow: June 1937', *Journal of the Society of Architectural Historians* 46, no. 1, March 1987, pp. 65–79. For an overview of the available sources and information about the congress from the Western perspective, see Hnídková, *Moskva 1937* (n. 334).

365 | FLC, letter of invitation from the Union of Soviet Architects, 10 May 1937, and Le Corbusier's reply, 22 May 1937. For details about the CIAM 5 congress, see Mumford, *The CIAM Discourse on Urbanism, 1928–1960* (n. 190), pp. 105–16.

366 | AMP, František Sammer Papers, Sammer to his parents, 18 April 1937. By 'sanatorium' Sammer was probably thinking of the project in Gagra, led by Moisei Ginzburg, on which he had worked with Viktor Valeryanovich Kalinin, a former colleague from Nikolai Kolli's office.

367 | Ibid., 7 June 1937: 'This morning I received a telegram from Raymond, [inviting me] to come at the end of the summer'

368 | SAAA, Pondicherry, a recollection of Larsen, recorded by Mrityunjoy Mukherjee in 1974: 'All foreigners were to leave Russia, as Russians knew the war was coming, so the foreigners' visas were not renewed'.

369 | For information about Czech architects in the USSR in the 1930s as written up by František Sammer at the request of the architect and theorist Vítězslav Procházka, see Hrabová, 'Between Ideal and Ideology' (n. 228), pp. 162–66.

Japan revisited

Sammer travelled to Raymond's office in Tokyo with a busy itinerary. As before, he was driven by curiosity and a thirst for knowledge, regardless of the distance he had to go. From Moscow he travelled to Vienna, where he spent a few days with Larsen, and, after a stop in Pilsen, he continued on travelling from Switzerland to Paris: 'It must be beautiful there now. The exhibitions. Chats, walks – and what about Charlotte, is she doing better? And maman and papa Perriand?' Agnes wrote to Sammer, inquiring about their friends from Le Corbusier's circle in a letter from Hungary, where she had gone to work for a few months. 'Greetings to them all from me, all right? The Serts, Pierre, Saka, Polak [sic], Ione, Bob and Jenny, the Kertesz [sic] and so on'.[370] As always, Sammer was a guest of Perriand in her Montparnasse studio. He arrived in Paris shortly after the fifth CIAM congress and after the recent opening of Le Corbusier's Pavillon des Temps Nouveaux at the 1937 world exhibition.[371] What he didn't know then, was that it would be his last opportunity to meet with all his friends from the Le Corbusier–Jeanneret atelier before many of them parted ways under the pressures of the Second World War.[372]

From Paris, Sammer continued on to Marseille, where, now with his costs covered by Raymond, he boarded the SS *Hakozaki Maru* for Japan.[373] The voyage would take almost a month and he used every opportunity to tour the places the ship took

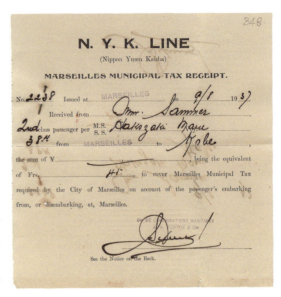

'Tomorrow morning I travel to Marseille and on the 13th I leave from there. – It was really hard to get a ticket – but I have one now – all the ships are full. – The ship is called the Hakozaki, a 10,000-ton (quite small) steamship of the N.Y.K. [Line], – a Japanese company – on 17 September I will be in Yokohama'.

František Sammer to his parents, from Paris, 7 August 1937, shortly before his journey to Japan. AMP.

^ Confirmation of Sammer's having paid embarkation tax in Marseille, 9 August 1937, before boarding the SS *Hakozaki Maru* of the N.Y.K. Line. SAAA.

< A letter from Larsen to Sammer, of 2 August 1937, addressed to the apartment of Charlotte Perriand in Paris, where he regularly stayed when visiting Paris. SAAA.

370| SAAA, Pondicherry, Larsen to Sammer, from Keszthely, 2 August 1937: 'Cela doit être beau maintenant. Ces expos. Les bavardages, les promenades – Alors Charlotte va mieux? Et mamman et papa Perriand? Saluts tous le monde pour moi, oui? Les Serts, Pierre, Saka, Polak [sic], Ione, Bob et Jenny, les Kertesz [sic] etc, etc'. Agnes was asking about Charlotte Perriand and her parents, Josep Lluís Sert and his wife Muncha Sert, Pierre Jeanneret, Junzo Sakakura, an architect by the name of Georges Pollak, the Kertészes (relatives of Alex Adam) and other friends.
371| See AMP, František Sammer Papers, Sammer to his parents, 18 April 1937 (n. 363).
372| At the invitation of Sakakura, Perriand left for Japan in 1940. Jeanneret spent the war years in Grenoble and, beginning in 1951, worked in India. Sert emigrated to the United States in 1939. Adam left France for England (though we do not know when exactly).
373| AAUP, Antonin Raymond and Noémi Pernessin Raymond Collection: accounts for the Golconde project, as of 31 December 1937. For August 1937, Raymond paid Sammer 300 yen.

˅ Before the steamship passed through the Suez Canal, Sammer was able to explore Cairo and the pyramids of Giza. He most likely travelled with some Dutch fellow-passengers. Photographs from August 1937, 8.5 × 5.3 cm. SAAA.

'I said goodbye to the Dutch with whom I'd spent a few pleasant days aboard the ship. – They are travelling to Java – to trade. – They are special people, these ones from the colonies. – What is interesting about them is how they cling to the superficialities characteristic of European bourgeois life. And then the difference between the white man and the native. It is sometimes astonishing – The white man is a god!! I caught a whiff of that'.

From Sammer's letter to his parents, sent from Singapore, 5 September 1937. AMP.

'Suez, 19 August.
Dear Milána,
It is already midnight – we are waiting for our ship to arrive at two o'clock[.] We left her in Port Said and went to have a look at Cairo and the pyramids. –
It was really lovely but tiring. – We have been up since four in the morning. –
Soon we will have been awake for 24 hours and we are very active. We went swimming in a gorgeous pool at the pyramids and right now we got [an offer] to go and bathe in the sea in the moonlight. – We accepted. – Goodnight!
Frantík. –'

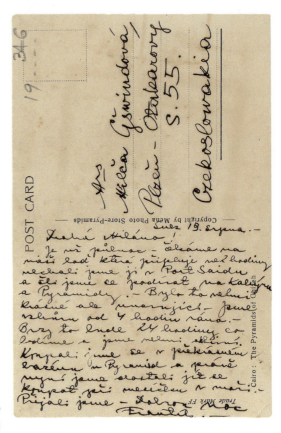

port at. Before sailing through the Suez Canal, Sammer managed to explore Cairo and the pyramids of Giza. 'The voyage already seems very long, but there are still many interesting things. Yesterday I spent the whole afternoon in the town – tremendously exotic with a gorgeous tropical park full of monkeys', he wrote in a letter to Pilsen, describing his experience of the 24-hour stop in Singapore, adding: 'I am now looking forward to Tokyo and work. If I go bust, I will at least have an opportunity to beg in all languages'.[374]

Already in September 1937 the Ministry of the Imperial Household of Japan granted Sammer permission to visit Nijō Castle and the Shugakuin Imperial Villa in Kyoto.[375] At the same time, Sammer joined the ranks of the main architects of Raymond's office in Tokyo, working on the final stage of the plans for a dormitory for the Sri Aurobindo ashram in Pondicherry.[376] Sammer was already acquainted with the project from his first visit to Japan in 1935.[377] At that time, however, circumstances did not allow him to take part in the first phase of the design, for which Raymond had invited him to his house in the mountain resort town of Karuizawa.

Raymond may have borrowed something or other from Le Corbusier for his own house, but in the design of the Indian dormitory he surpassed the Parisian architect in several aspects. Golconde, as the dormitory is called, represents a pioneering work in the use of concrete in India, and recent research shows that it is fair to call it the first major work of modern architecture in the country [see Research Diary, pp. 30–31].[378] Golconde anticipates the important modern buildings erected after the Second World War by Le Corbusier in Chandigarh and Ahmedabad. Sammer joined in the planning and building work of Raymond's design, and went to a faraway country, once again long before his former Paris boss did. 'We are working, finishing a certain stage. I arrived towards the end of Raymond's eighteenth year in Tokyo. My shirtsleeves are rolled up from dawn to dusk. [...] Probably in the first half of January we are going to Pondicherry. We will stop in Manila, Saigon, Penang and Colombo.[379] [...] A nice reward for a job well done. I am otherwise very well, seeing a lot, and they tell me I contribute a lot',[380] Sammer wrote home to Pilsen from Tokyo in December 1937.

374| AMP, František Sammer Papers, Sammer, from Singapore, to his parents, 5 September 1937.
375| SAAA, Pondicherry, permission expressly for Sammer to enter Nijō Castle and the Shugakuin Imperial Villa in Kyoto, 29 September 1937.
376| AAUP, Antonin Raymond and Noémi Pernessin Raymond Collection: accounts for the Golconde project, as of 31 December 1937. AMP, František Sammer Papers, Raymond's confirmation of 18 October 1939 that Sammer was employed in his Tokyo office from 10 October 1937 to 10 February 1938.
377| See above, pp. 116–119, n. 308.
378| Pankaj Vir Gupta, Christine Mueller, and Cyrus Samii, *Golconde: The Introduction of Modernism in India*, New Delhi: Urban Crayon Press, 2010.
379| Raymond later described in detail the itinerary of the journey via Manila (the Philippines), Saigon (today's Ho Chi Minh City, Vietnam), the Malaysian island of Penang and the city of Colombo (in today's Sri Lanka), describing in detail visits to Singapore, Angkor Wat (Cambodia) and Bangkok (Thailand). Raymond, *An Autobiography* (n. 295), pp. 160-62.
380| AMP, František Sammer Papers, Sammer, in Tokyo, to his parents, 14 December 1937.

<> František Sammer, a postcard, not sent, for his sister, Milča, with a description of his experiences from his stop in Egypt at the Suez Canal, from a visit to Cairo and the pyramids of Giza, 19 August 1937. SAAA.

ˇ The envelope and permission to enter Nijō Castle and the Shugakuin Imperial Villa in Kyoto, issued expressly to František Sammer by the Ministry of the Imperial Household, on 29 September 1937. SAAA.

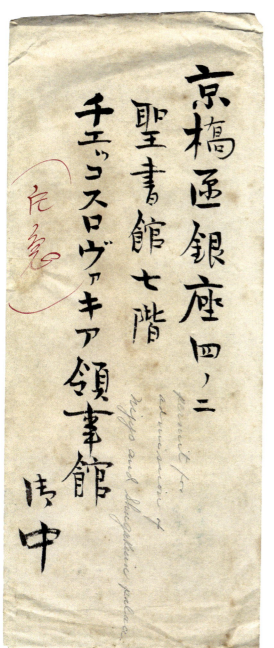

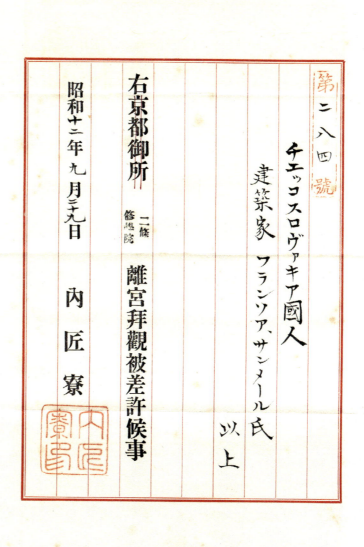

India

František Sammer joined Antonin and Noémi Raymond in the turbulent years leading up to the Second World War. His meeting with them during his first visit to Japan, in 1935, was the start of both a lifelong friendship and their strong support of him during the difficulties he faced in the following years. It was also this couple who acquainted him with a spiritual dimension of lived experience. Raymond invited Sammer on a journey to India, during which they saw, as he wrote, 'so many unusual things that merely enumerating them would be a lot of work. [...] I hope that once we meet, or even sooner, once I have a few photographs, it will be easier for me'.[381] The journey remained too in Raymond's memory and many years later he would write about it in his autobiography, in which he used this opportunity to introduce Sammer to his readers.[382]

Sammer's photographic collection appears to contain only one souvenir of his journey to India – namely postcards of the Angkor Wat temple complex in Cambodia. Sammer and the Raymonds arrived in Pondicherry in early February 1938 and shortly afterwards Larsen came from Europe, where she had been working. In these new places they encountered a dramatic change of environment and with it a complete change of rhythm in their daily lives. Sammer's experience of Pondicherry, where he would spend four years, is best described in his own letters home: 'We are in an unusually interesting environment. In a circle of thinkers influencing all of India and also renowned in Europe. Thanks to these new acquaintances we have managed to study everything about India – from its history right up to our times and the future. [...] Pondicherry is a nice town – a port, founded by the Dutch in the sixteenth century. Since those days it has been Dutch, then French, and at times English. Now it is the remainder of French India. The European part of the town is

> *'We spent about a week in Angkor Wat tirelessly surveying this wonderful Khmer civilisation [...] We sympathised with the optimistic French explorers who had tried so valiantly to wrest the ruins from the always encroaching jungle'.*

Antonin Raymond recalling his journey with František Sammer from Japan to India in late 1937 and early 1938. Quoted from Raymond, *An Autobiography*, p. 161 (see n. 295).

^ Agnes Larsen, *Flowers*, watercolour on paper, 1938 or 1939. Sri Aurobindo Ashram Art Gallery.

\> František Sammer, view from the terrace of the house in the Bay of Bengal, Pondicherry, watercolour on paper, between 1938 and 1942. Sri Aurobindo Ashram Art Gallery.

< Angkor Wat. Postcards from Sammer's collection, 13 × 8.2 cm, 13 × 8 cm, and 13.4 × 7.8 cm. SAAA.

381| Ibid., 25 February 1938.
382| Raymond, *An Autobiography* (n. 295), p. 160. See also AMP, František Sammer Papers, Sammer, in Tokyo, to his parents, 14 December 1937 (n. 380).
383| AMP, František Sammer Papers, Sammer to his parents, 25 February 1938.
384| Ibid., 25 February 1938.
385| Ibid., 3 May 1938.
386| AAUP, Antonin Raymond and Noémi Pernessin Raymond Collection, Sammer in Pondicherry to Endoh San in Raymond's Tokyo office, 27 May 1938, in which he asks for some watercolour paper and paints, eventually bought with the help of Professor Tominaga.
387| SAAA, František Sammer Papers, 'Description des travaux à exécuter à Golconde', in which Sammer notes even the smallest technical details of the building. For more on this, see Hrabová, 'Between Ideal and Ideology' (n. 18). While studying the project documents of Golconde, deposited in Pondicherry, I succeeded in identifying a number of Sammer's drawings. In my other research I am looking at his share in the project and his specific work on the building.

imposing, full of historically and architecturally interesting buildings, planned around the square where a fortress once stood. The port is nothing special – shallow. The ships remain in the roadstead. [...] The land is of course tropical. We have a low plateau nearby, from which we can survey the whole wide plain – there are no mountains. [...] It is warm and now in winter there are pleasant breezes from the sea and in the evening from the mainland. We have a lovely small apartment with a beautiful terrace with a view of the garden and the sea'.[383]

The bright colours of India, the tropical climate and the slow tempo and calm in the heart of the spiritual community could not suitably be depicted with black-and-white film or the shutter speed of a camera. In his first letter from Pondicherry Sammer wrote to his family in Pilsen: 'We are painting a lot in order to remember all the beauty of the light and colours. Agnes is of course sculpting and making beautiful things'.[384] In another letter, he wrote: 'I cannot send you any sketches or photos yet. There are all kinds of difficulties with developing etc'.[385] Sammer was ordering paper and watercolour paints from Japan, with the help of friends and through regular correspondence with Raymond's office in Tokyo.[386] A large part of the building material for Golconde was also being imported from Japan.

Sammer supervised the construction of Golconde for more than four years. Of all the architects in Raymond's office, he worked in Pondicherry the longest and was behind many of the solutions that had been arrived at on the spot.[387] Raymond and his family left Pondicherry for the United States in July 1938. The following year an American architect, furniture designer and woodworker with Japanese roots, George Nakashima (1905–90), who had been employed in Raymond's office and worked on the Golconde construction site since 1937, left for the States as well. During his first two years in Pondicherry, Sammer was, together with Nakashima, in charge of construction. Again, he was standing in for a great master of modern architecture, who entrusted him with full responsibility for carrying out his own project. Though Sammer's own architectural work is difficult to identify, it is fair to consider the master's trust in him to be evidence of his professional qualities.

Shortly after arriving in Pondicherry, Sammer became a fully-fledged member of the spiritual community. Later, he also designed furniture for the rooms of the heads of the ashram and a concrete pergola supporting the sacred tree in the heart of the ashram complex.

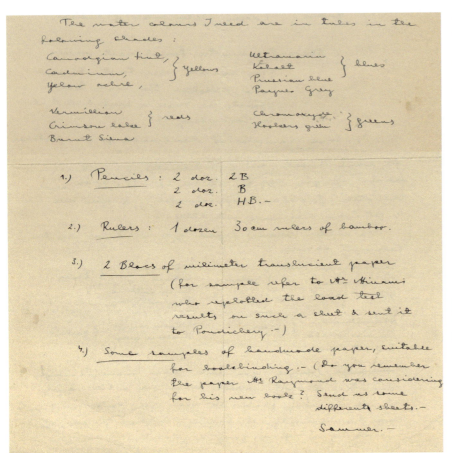

< Sammer's list of art supplies to order from Japan, sent from Pondicherry to Endoh San in Tokyo, 27 May 1938 (detail). Architectural Archives of the University of Pennsylvania (AAUP), Masanori Sugiyama Collection.

< František Sammer at the construction site of the Golconde, in Pondicherry, c.1938. AAUP, Antonin Raymond and Noémi Pernessin Raymond Collection.

> František Sammer with friends shortly before joining the British Army, Pondicherry, 1942. From the left: William Lovegrove (the brother of Mona Pinto), Nishta (Margaret Woodrow Wilson), Ambu Patel, Mona with Gauri and František Sammer. Private archive of Gauri Pinto, Pondicherry.

'Ashram? A retreat for adherents of a distinct philosophical belief. Scores of new words soon enhanced my vocabulary: yoga, karma, guru, jiva, prana, purusha, prakriti. They, and more, remain a part of my glossary. [...] Sri Aurobindo, the guru, or spiritual teacher, of the Pondicherry ashram, had his own course: Purnayoga. [...] Many became his disciples and joined the ashram, among them two elderly women from the West. One was [Olga Herzen], the widow of French historian Gabriel Monod and daughter of Alexander Hertzen [sic], Russian revolutionary thinker who lived in Paris, and the other, President Woodrow Wilson's daughter, Margaret.'
Agnes Larsen, recollection of the ashram in Pondicherry. Larsen, *Graffiti*, p. 408 (see n. 122).

^ Photograph from a Christmas Party in Pondicherry, 1939; from the left: František Sammer, Nishta (Margaret Woodrow Wilson, the eldest daughter of US President Woodrow Wilson), Mona Pinto with her daughter Gauri and Ambu Patel, a teacher of hatha yoga. Photograph, 5.6 × 5.8 cm. SAAA.

^ The ceremony of Agnes Larsen's being received into the spiritual community of the Sri Aurobindo Ashram, Pondicherry, when she was given the name 'Agni', 1938 or 1939. From the left: Shanti Doshi, George Nakashima, Dilip Kumar Roy, Agnes Larsen. Second and third from the right: Kalyan and Nolini Kanta Sarkar. Photograph, 5.9 × 8.3 cm. SAAA.

He tried to explain his new address to his family in Pilsen in the following words: 'SAMMER chez Ashram de Sri Aurobindo. PONDICHERRY – INDE FRANÇAISE. Ashram = university; Sri = Holy; Aurobindo = the name of our host. That is, he is holy'.[388]

Although Sri Aurobindo (1872–1950) was born in India, he was educated in Great Britain, at grammar schools and at King's College, Cambridge. He became known in his native land firstly by his involvement in politics and the struggle for Indian liberation from British colonial rule. After he was imprisoned on suspicion of terrorist attacks, however, he chose, in 1910, a life in seclusion and left British India for the French enclave of Pondicherry. Shortly after that, he was joined by Mirra Alfassa (1878–1973). Born in France of Sephardic Jewish parents, she became known as the the Mother or la Mère, and soon took over responsibility for the operation and organization of the whole community. In Pondicherry, beginning in 1926, an international community developed under the Mother, based on Sri Aurobindo's teaching.

Sri Aurobindo believed in the equality of all people and all nations and promoted the creation of the unity of the whole world in freedom. As a means to liberation not only of the individual but also of society as a whole, he believed it was necessary to suppress material ambitions and the ego. He saw the search for balance between personal freedom and collective life as the ideal of the organization of human society. At the same time, however, he was certain that such a society could not be achieved by the State exerting its power from above, and that transformation begins with the inner growth of individual members of the community. In a scholarly study of the life and teaching of this holy man, the historian Peter Heehs points out that Sri Aurobindo had formulated these ideas even before the October Revolution in Russia and before the Nazis took power in Germany.[389]

Nevertheless, Sammer, an architect forged by the international avant-garde and still embracing socialist ideals, saw a link between the ideology being applied in the Soviet Union and Aurobindo's teaching. He perceived it as a sign of a natural progression towards a better society: 'For him [Sri Aurobindo] the reforms carried out in the USSR after the revolution, which are taking too long to develop, and also all the reforms that Europe must now carry out, are the basis for the spiritual evolution of man',[390] Sammer wrote to his parents in one of his first letters from India. Aurobindo's teaching strongly resonated with Sammer and he saw it as offering a way to carry out the ideals he had been striving for in previous years. 'It is the beautiful development of acquiring knowledge – first Russia and now India, which, considering the Russian (Soviet) experiment to be the basis, is going very, very far',[391] he wrote to his parents in Pilsen. A bit later he reflected on the path he had travelled so far: 'I am thinking about the chronology of all my actions. For example, that I came from the USSR, the nature of the bond between the firm ideological commitment there and here [in India], and yet how everything is different and closer to the result'.[392]

In Pondicherry, Sammer found another international community, which became his new home. But he also felt so far away from his native land, and so completely isolated, that for the first time since leaving Czechoslovakia he was homesick: 'I love my country and I realized all the patriotic ties during the difficult moments that you have endured and I with you – believe me',[393] he confided in a letter to his sister, now a Red Cross volunteer. He was reacting to the recent news of political events during the past few months of 1938, when two Czechoslovak allies – Great Britain and France – signed the Munich Agreement allowing Germany to annex areas along the Czechoslovak border. Nevertheless, Sammer's newly-awakened patriotism soon became the Achille's heel of his decision-making.

388 | AMP, František Sammer Papers, Sammer to his parents, 25 February 1938.
389 | Peter Heehs, *The Lives of Sri Aurobindo*, New York: Columbia University Press, 2008, p. 289.
390 | AMP, František Sammer Papers, Sammer to his parents, 3 May 1938.
391 | Ibid.
392 | Ibid., Sammer to his sister Milča, 17 January 1939.
393 | Ibid.

Real w

In 1939,
that yea
nounce
prompt
Tokyo:
unexpe
when N
betwee
lunch
voyage
'You k
has be
his soj
securi
the w
tinued
portu

^ Agnes Larsen, *Flowers*, watercolour on paper, 1938 or 1939. Sri Aurobindo Ashram Art Gallery.

> František Sammer, view from the terrace of the house in the Bay of Bengal, Pondicherry, watercolour on paper, between 1938 and 1942. Sri Aurobindo Ashram Art Gallery.

< Angkor Wat. Postcards from Sammer's collection, 13 × 8.2 cm, 13 × 8 cm, and 13.4 × 7.8 cm. SAAA.

---

381 | Ibid., 25 February 1938.
382 | Raymond, *An Autobiography* (n. 295), p. 160. See also AMP, František Sammer Papers, Sammer, in Tokyo, to his parents, 14 December 1937 (n. 380).
383 | AMP, František Sammer Papers, Sammer to his parents, 25 February 1938.
384 | Ibid., 25 February 1938.
385 | Ibid., 3 May 1938.
386 | AAUP, Antonin Raymond and Noémi Pernessin Raymond Collection, Sammer in Pondicherry to Endoh San in Raymond's Tokyo office, 27 May 1938, in which he asks for some watercolour paper and paints, eventually bought with the help of Professor Tominaga.
387 | SAAA, František Sammer Papers, 'Description des travaux à exécuter à Golconde', in which Sammer notes even the smallest technical details of the building. For more on this, see Hrabová, 'Between Ideal and Ideology' (n. 18). While studying the project documents of Golconde, deposited in Pondicherry, I succeeded in identifying a number of Sammer's drawings. In my other research I am looking at his share in the project and his specific work on the building.

---

imposing, full of historically and architecturally interesting buildings, planned around the square where a fortress once stood. The port is nothing special – shallow. The ships remain in the roadstead. [...] The land is of course tropical. We have a low plateau nearby, from which we can survey the whole wide plain – there are no mountains. [...] It is warm and now in winter there are pleasant breezes from the sea and in the evening from the mainland. We have a lovely small apartment with a beautiful terrace with a view of the garden and the sea'.[383]

The bright colours of India, the tropical climate and the slow tempo and calm in the heart of the spiritual community could not suitably be depicted with black-and-white film or the shutter speed of a camera. In his first letter from Pondicherry Sammer wrote to his family in Pilsen: 'We are painting a lot in order to remember all the beauty of the light and colours. Agnes is of course sculpting and making beautiful things'.[384] In another letter, he wrote: 'I cannot send you any sketches or photos yet. There are all kinds of difficulties with developing etc'.[385] Sammer was ordering paper and watercolour paints from Japan, with the help of friends and through regular correspondence with Raymond's office in Tokyo.[386] A large part of the building material for Golconde was also being imported from Japan.

Sammer supervised the construction of Golconde for more than four years. Of all the architects in Raymond's office, he worked in Pondicherry the longest and was behind many of the solutions that had been arrived at on the spot.[387] Raymond and his family left Pondicherry for the United States in July 1938. The following year an American architect, furniture designer and woodworker with Japanese roots, George Nakashima (1905–90), who had been employed in Raymond's office and worked on the Golconde construction site since 1937, left for the States as well. During his first two years in Pondicherry, Sammer was, together with Nakashima, in charge of construction. Again, he was standing in for a great master of modern architecture, who entrusted him with full responsibility for carrying out his own project. Though Sammer's own architectural work is difficult to identify, it is fair to consider the master's trust in him to be evidence of his professional qualities.

Shortly after arriving in Pondicherry, Sammer became a fully-fledged member of the spiritual community. Later, he also designed furniture for the rooms of the heads of the ashram and a concrete pergola supporting the sacred tree in the heart of the ashram complex.

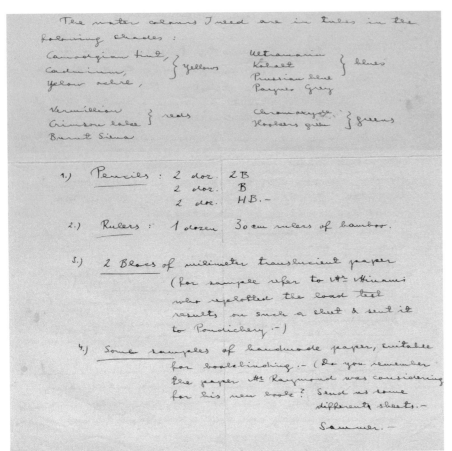

< Sammer's list of art supplies to order from Japan, sent from Pondicherry to Endoh San in Tokyo, 27 May 1938 (detail). Architectural Archives of the University of Pennsylvania (AAUP), Masanori Sugiyama Collection.

< František Sammer at the construction site of the Golconde, in Pondicherry, c.1938. AAUP, Antonin Raymond and Noémi Pernessin Raymond Collection.

> František Sammer with friends shortly before joining the British Army, Pondicherry, 1942. From the left: William Lovegrove (the brother of Mona Pinto), Nishta (Margaret Woodrow Wilson), Ambu Patel, Mona with Gauri and František Sammer. Private archive of Gauri Pinto, Pondicherry.

'Ashram? A retreat for adherents of a distinct philosophical belief. Scores of new words soon enhanced my vocabulary: yoga, karma, guru, jiva, prana, purusha, prakriti. They, and more, remain a part of my glossary. [...] Sri Aurobindo, the guru, or spiritual teacher, of the Pondicherry ashram, had his own course: Purnayoga. [...] Many became his disciples and joined the ashram, among them two elderly women from the West. One was [Olga Herzen], the widow of French historian Gabriel Monod and daughter of Alexander Hertzen [sic], Russian revolutionary thinker who lived in Paris, and the other, President Woodrow Wilson's daughter, Margaret.'
Agnes Larsen, recollection of the ashram in Pondicherry. Larsen, *Graffiti*, p. 408 (see n. 122).

^ Photograph from a Christmas Party in Pondicherry, 1939; from the left: František Sammer, Nishta (Margaret Woodrow Wilson, the eldest daughter of US President Woodrow Wilson), Mona Pinto with her daughter Gauri and Ambu Patel, a teacher of hatha yoga. Photograph, 5.6 × 5.8 cm. SAAA.

^ The ceremony of Agnes Larsen's being received into the spiritual community of the Sri Aurobindo Ashram, Pondicherry, when she was given the name 'Agni', 1938 or 1939. From the left: Shanti Doshi, George Nakashima, Dilip Kumar Roy, Agnes Larsen. Second and third from the right: Kalyan and Nolini Kanta Sarkar. Photograph, 5.9 × 8.3 cm. SAAA.

388| AMP, František Sammer Papers, Sammer to his parents, 25 February 1938.
389| Peter Heehs, *The Lives of Sri Aurobindo*, New York: Columbia University Press, 2008, p. 289.
390| AMP, František Sammer Papers, Sammer to his parents, 3 May 1938.
391| Ibid.
392| Ibid., Sammer to his sister Milča, 17 January 1939.
393| Ibid.

He tried to explain his new address to his family in Pilsen in the following words: 'SAMMER chez Ashram de Sri Aurobindo. PONDICHERRY – INDE FRANÇAISE. Ashram = university; Sri = Holy; Aurobindo = the name of our host. That is, he is holy'.[388]

Although Sri Aurobindo (1872–1950) was born in India, he was educated in Great Britain, at grammar schools and at King's College, Cambridge. He became known in his native land firstly by his involvement in politics and the struggle for Indian liberation from British colonial rule. After he was imprisoned on suspicion of terrorist attacks, however, he chose, in 1910, a life in seclusion and left British India for the French enclave of Pondicherry. Shortly after that, he was joined by Mirra Alfassa (1878–1973). Born in France of Sephardic Jewish parents, she became known as the the Mother or la Mère, and soon took over responsibility for the operation and organization of the whole community. In Pondicherry, beginning in 1926, an international community developed under the Mother, based on Sri Aurobindo's teaching.

Sri Aurobindo believed in the equality of all people and all nations and promoted the creation of the unity of the whole world in freedom. As a means to liberation not only of the individual but also of society as a whole, he believed it was necessary to suppress material ambitions and the ego. He saw the search for balance between personal freedom and collective life as the ideal of the organization of human society. At the same time, however, he was certain that such a society could not be achieved by the State exerting its power from above, and that transformation begins with the inner growth of individual members of the community. In a scholarly study of the life and teaching of this holy man, the historian Peter Heehs points out that Sri Aurobindo had formulated these ideas even before the October Revolution in Russia and before the Nazis took power in Germany.[389]

Nevertheless, Sammer, an architect forged by the international avant-garde and still embracing socialist ideals, saw a link between the ideology being applied in the Soviet Union and Aurobindo's teaching. He perceived it as a sign of a natural progression towards a better society: 'For him [Sri Aurobindo] the reforms carried out in the USSR after the revolution, which are taking too long to develop, and also all the reforms that Europe must now carry out, are the basis for the spiritual evolution of man',[390] Sammer wrote to his parents in one of his first letters from India. Aurobindo's teaching strongly resonated with Sammer and he saw it as offering a way to carry out the ideals he had been striving for in previous years. 'It is the beautiful development of acquiring knowledge – first Russia and now India, which, considering the Russian (Soviet) experiment to be the basis, is going very, very far',[391] he wrote to his parents in Pilsen. A bit later he reflected on the path he had travelled so far: 'I am thinking about the chronology of all my actions. For example, that I came from the USSR, the nature of the bond between the firm ideological commitment there and here [in India], and yet how everything is different and closer to the result'.[392]

In Pondicherry, Sammer found another international community, which became his new home. But he also felt so far away from his native land, and so completely isolated, that for the first time since leaving Czechoslovakia he was homesick: 'I love my country and I realized all the patriotic ties during the difficult moments that you have endured and I with you – believe me',[393] he confided in a letter to his sister, now a Red Cross volunteer. He was reacting to the recent news of political events during the past few months of 1938, when two Czechoslovak allies – Great Britain and France – signed the Munich Agreement allowing Germany to annex areas along the Czechoslovak border. Nevertheless, Sammer's newly-awakened patriotism soon became the Achille's heel of his decision-making.

Real war

In 1939, an important chapter in Sammer's personal life came to a close. In April of that year, after having left Sammer and Pondicherry, Larsen showed up unannounced in Japan. Endoh San, an assistant manager at Raymond's office in Tokyo, promptly informed his boss, already in the United States, about Agnes's visit to Tokyo: 'Well, we never expected to see Mrs. Sammer here in Tokyo so soon. Her unexpected visit was as much surprising to us as snow that we had on the very day when Mrs. Sammer arrived in Tokyo from Kobe'.[394] During the 24-hour stopover between the ports of Kobe and Yokohama, Larsen visited Raymond's office, had lunch with Professor Tominaga and Junzo Sakakura, and then continued on her voyage home to Hawaii.[395]

'You know, we have been living in peace here, which during those European events has been a bit awkward',[396] Sammer wrote in a letter home during the first year of his sojourn in Pondicherry. Being isolated in India, far from Europe, may have offered security, but, particularly after Larsen's departure, looking on idly at the events of the war became unbearable for Sammer. He remained in Pondicherry and continued working on Golconde, but at the same time he persistently sought any opportunity to serve his native land.[397]

^ Miloslava (Milča) Gschwindová, František Sammer's sister. Photograph, undated. Private archive.

< Confirmation of František Sammer's volunteering to serve his country, issued by the Consulate of the Czechoslovak Republic in Marseille, 18 October 1939. AMP.

394| AAUP, Antonin Raymond and Noémi Pernessin Raymond Collection, letter from Endoh San of Raymond's office in Tokyo to Sammer in Pondicherry, 12 April 1939.

395| Ibid., Endoh San to Raymond, 6 April 1939.

396| AMP, František Sammer Papers, Sammer to his parents, 3 November 1938.

397| Ibid., confirmation of Sammer's volunteering for military service, issued at the Consulate of the Czechoslovak Republic in Marseille, 18 October 1939.

398| SAAA Pondicherry, František Sammer Papers, correspondence with the Consulates of the Czechoslovak Republic in Marseille and in Bombay. As is clear from a draft letter of early August 1940, in which Sammer requests assistance in his efforts to serve his country, he even turned to President Edvard Beneš, who at that time was with the Czechoslovak Government-in-Exile in London.

399| AMP, František Sammer Papers, Sammer in Singapore to his mother in Pilsen, 9 December 1945.

400| Military History Institute Prague – Vojenský historický ústav (VHÚ), file 24-20/4/106, a document issued by the Consulate of the Czechoslovak Republic in Bombay, 8 June 1944.

401| VHÚ, file 24-20/4/106, Czechoslovak Consul in Bombay to Sammer, sent to a training camp in Lahore, the Punjab, 21 April 1944.

402| VHÚ, file 4-20/4/106, Sammer's request to join the Union of Anti-Fascist Fighters (Svaz protifašistických bojovníků) with a summary of wartime events, 21 April 1965.

∧ The last letter Sammer received from Milča, written on the day she was guillotined in Berlin, 4 September 1942. AMP.

'Milča Gschwindová, Königsdamm 7, Plötensee, Berlin, 4 September 1942.
*Dear Franti,
I have been praying for you for almost four years, that I would be fortunate enough to see you again and I will in a moment know where you are and when we will meet. Please accept my thanks for everything nice and beautiful you gave me in life. I was truly a happy sister! Be happy, my dear little brother, if you're alive – otherwise, see you in a moment.
Yours,
Milča*'

---

403 | VHÚ, file 24–20/4/106, Sammer's file from the Czechoslovak Ministry of National Defence, No. 6217/VHÚ-1965, and a request for acknowledgement of his involvement in the fight against fascism.
404 | AMP, František Sammer Papers, letters from Noémi Raymond, 1945.
405 | Ibid., Noémi Raymond to Sammer's relatives in Pilsen, 24 August 1945.
406 | Ibid., notes for a reply to a letter of 3 July 1946 from Agnes. For more details about Milča's life see n. 176.

It was not easy to join an Allied army from the tiny French enclave in India. The mere fact that he managed to do so is evidence that Sammer did his utmost to enlist.[398] 'Soon after war broke out [in September 1939] I signed up for any future Czechoslovak Army organized abroad. When the Germans attacked the Soviet Union [22 June 1941], I made various efforts to get into the Red Army, but that was impossible',[399] he wrote to his mother a few months after the war had ended. As a Czech wishing to sign up in India, he had only one possibility, and that was to join the British Army.[400] In October 1942, he enlisted in the East Yorkshire Regiment as an engineer-architect. His sojourn in Asia did not end with that though. After almost five years spent in the tropical climate of the south-east coast of India, he would spend three more years in other parts of India and experience arduous times in an Asian jungle.

Sammer first went through training in Kirkee (today, Khadki), now part of the city of Pune, at the Royal School of Military Engineering. After training in Lahore, he was promoted to lieutenant, but did not go into battle until nearly the end of the war. 'I understand that you would rather be somewhere on the Russian front today, or in England, but military responsibilities demand discipline and serving where one has been sent. Believe me, you are carrying out very praiseworthy work also at the other end of the earth',[401] was the answer Sammer received from the Bombay consulate of the Czechoslovak Government-in-Exile in reply to his request to be transferred. Beginning on 1 November 1944 he served as the commander of a company of engineers in the most difficult of conditions in Burma and then, as a captain, in British Malaya, driving out the last of the Japanese Army.[402] The circumstances were desperate, and the wounds Sammer received in battle could not be properly treated until almost a year later.[403]

The years of military service mark the end of the part of his story that we can follow in Sammer's correspondence with his father, his sister Milča and other family members in Pilsen. It was a period in which he could not communicate with almost anyone. The only person Sammer was turning to in confidence while in the army was the Mother, the head of the ashram in Pondicherry. From her, Antonin and Noémi Raymond received news about Sammer, which they would then send on to others, including Sammer's relatives in Pilsen.[404] Sammer's reports from the battlefield thus had to surmount great distances, travelling across India to the United States and from there to Czechoslovakia. Noémi Raymond tries to explain the circumstances in a letter to the relatives of Sammer in Pilsen: '[He] has a home in India, at the Ashram, where he can always find refuge. The person who is called the Mother is one of the heads of the Ashram and she is devoted to François. As you know he is a fine architect and we are very devoted to him also'.[405]

By leaving Pondicherry, Sammer left behind not only his home, but also all his personal belongings, including the collection of photographs that form the core of this publication. Thanks to the great care provided by the Mother and other members of the ashram, his things have remained there in safekeeping to the present day. Sammer did not write to his family in Pilsen until he was in hospital in Singapore, where, at the end of 1945, he was waiting to be transferred to doctors in Great Britain. It was there that he learnt the sad news that he would never again see his father and his beloved sister Milča. He later wrote to Larsen, in his self-taught English, about his sister's fate: 'About Milča I have learned first in Singapore. Her case is that of spirit and defiance and love as of many others. She had with Pepa [probably Josef Sammer, František's elder brother] organized printing of underground news, which as you perhaps know have been at home [in Czechoslovakia] communist. They have been caught. Pepa escaped with bare life. Milča had been imprisoned for almost three years and finally executed. Many of my friends had similar fate'.[406]

Great Britain, 1946–47

Beginning in January 1946, Sammer was recuperating in the best British hospitals and sanatoriums, but he had to undergo a serious operation on his lungs. Yet even before his treatment began, he drew on all his strength to track down his close friends and colleagues from before the war. He turned to the Royal Institute of British Architects (RIBA) in London, requesting contact information for Le Corbusier, Nikolai Kolli, Gordon Stephenson, Pierre Jeanneret and Charlotte Perriand.[407] 'The French and the Russians are particularly hard to find, because it takes so long before one gets on the right track. Nobody knows their addresses. But I am quite patient. The English are easy to track down',[408] he wrote to his mother in Pilsen. In his first letters to Stephenson he asked not only about the friends he hoped the RIBA would help him find, but also about Jane West Clauss, Alex Adam and William Holford.[409]

Fortunately, Le Corbusier's address had not changed, so Sammer sent one of his first letters to 35 rue de Sèvres. To his great relief, he resumed the dialogue of earlier years with ease: 'My dear sir, the most recent bit of news I have of you is that you were swimming in the sea and a motorboat ran over you [...] That appeared in some Indian newspaper in, I think, 1940. Of your work, I have not heard anything since the last time we saw each other, in 1937. [...] Have you been working on anything? Anything big?'[410] Fortunately, Le Corbusier survived the injury from the motorboat propeller, and immediately assured Sammer that he had 'not stopped fighting for modern architecture'. During the war, he added, he had been forced to 'limit himself to writing books, because all his work was rejected'.[411] He also seized the first opportunity to renew his ancient political dispute with Sammer, and defended himself: 'I am not at all accusing you of being a Communist (that, by the way, is very much the 'in' thing), and I was just joking a bit, so as not always to be talking so seriously'.[412] For Le Corbusier, political opinions were not decisive in obtaining commissions or even looking for new colleagues. That is confirmed by, among other things, the fact that despite these jabs, he was trying to entice Sammer back to the atelier at 35 rue de Sèvres after the war: 'our organization lacks those who had been formed earlier and then all scattered. There are only young people here, who have the best intentions but we lack those who are more experienced'.[413] In the war years Le Corbusier's atelier only operated in a makeshift way, but after the war he renewed its activity with marked changes in staff and the way work was organized. These changes were fundamentally affected by the departure of Pierre Jeanneret, Charlotte Perriand and most of his other closest colleagues.

As in most architectural firms, the main task at 35 rue de Sèvres was now the reconstruction of the war-torn country and repairing the vast damage. After the war, at the same time as the big commission for the housing project of the Unité d'habitation in Marseille, the Atelier des Bâtisseurs (ATBAT) was established, in which work was efficiently divided up between administrators, engineers and architects. 'We have very important tasks in La Rochelle-Pallice, in a valley of the Pyrenees and perhaps in St-Dié and elsewhere. Other things are appearing too',[414] Le Corbusier reported to Sammer, who was lying in hospital after part of his lungs had been removed. Sammer asked Le Corbusier mainly for architectural news and to send him new books. The last work he had read was Le Corbusier's *Quand les cathédrales étaient blanches* (1937),[415] about a trip to the United States in 1935, and after the war Sammer was hungry for knowledge: 'I am eager to reimmerse myself in this living water of ideas and works, which for me are now the essence of the present and the rediscovered future as well'.[416]

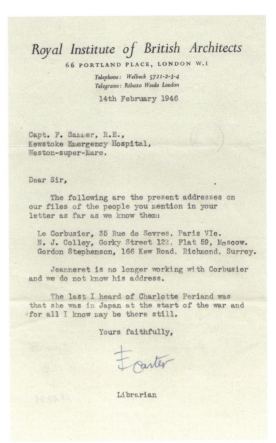

407| Ibid., RIBA reply to Sammer, 14 February 1946.
408| Ibid., Sammer to his mother in Pilsen, 24 February 1946.
409| Ibid., Stephenson to Sammer, 30 April 1945 and 25 February 1946.
410| FLC, Sammer to Le Corbusier, 24 February 1946: 'Mon cher Monsieur, la dernière nouvelle que j'ai de vous c'est que vous avez plongé dans la mer et un bateau à moteur vous a traversé en vous blessant. [...] Cette nouvelle est paru dans un journal quelconque [sic] de Indes quelque temps en 1940 je crois. De votre travail je ne sais rien depuis que je vous ai vu en 1937. [...] Est-ce que vous travaillez sur quelque chose? Grand?' Sammer is referring to the injury Le Corbusier suffered in 1938.
411| Ibid., Le Corbusier to Sammer, 7 March 1946: 'Je n'ai pas cessé de combattre pour l'architecture moderne. J'ai dû me limiter à écrire des livres puisque tout travail m'a été refusé'. For a photograph of the letter, see p. 139.
412| Ibid., 6 April 1946: 'Je ne vous accuse pas du tout d'être communiste, (c'est très bien porté d'ailleurs), et je plaisantais un peu, afin de ne pas toujours parler sérieusement'.
413| Ibid., 7 March 1946: 'Reviendrez-vous un jour en France pour travailler? Il y aurait de la place pour vous dans notre organisation à laquelle manque ceux qui ont été formés autrefois, et qui sont tous dispersés. Nous n'avons que des jeunes qui sont de très bonne volonté, il manque des échelons'.
414| Ibid., 7 March 1946: 'Nous avons des tâches très importantes à La Rochelle-Pallice, dans la vallée des Pyrénées, à Marseille, et peut-être à St Dié et ailleurs. D'autres choses s'annoncent'.
415| Le Corbusier, *Quand les cathédrales étaient blanches: voyage au*

< After returning from battle in Burma, and during his convalescence for wartime wounds in hospitals in Great Britain, František Sammer searched for his close friends and colleagues from before the war.
A reply to František Sammer from Edward Carter, Librarian, the Royal Institute of British Architects (RIBA), London, 14 February 1946. AMP.

> Le Corbusier's letter to František Sammer, 7 March 1946. Private archive.

---

pays de timides, Paris: Plon, 1937. Published in English as *When the Cathedrals Were White: A Journey to the Country of Timid People*, translated by Francis E. Hyslop. New York: Reynal & Hitchcock, [1947]. During the war Le Corbusier published a number of books, including *Sur les quatre routes*, Paris: Gallimard, 1941; *La Charte d'Athènes*, Boulogne-sur-Seine: l'Architecture d'Aujourd'hui, 1943; and *Les Trois établissements humaines*, Paris: Denoël, 1945.

416| FLC, Sammer to Le Corbusier, 26 March 1946: 'Considérant la lacune, pouvez vous me confier quelques de vos livres récents? Depuis le 'Quand les cathédrales ....' je n'ai rien lu. [...] Je suis sérieux, vous demandant les livres – croyez-moi que l'avidité de ces années militaire a été grande et que je suis avide de me retremper dans cette eau vive des idées et travaux qui sont pour moi maintenant toute éssence du présent et aussi future retrouvé'.

417| For Pierre Jeannerct, scc n. 4.

418| FLC, Le Corbusier to Sammer, 7 March 1946: 'Pierre Jeanneret est à Grenoble. Charlotte Perriand était à Indochine pendant la guerre. On m'a écrit qu'elle revenait de là-bas avec un enfant sur les bras, mais je ne l'ai pas vue encore'.

419| Ibid.: 'Et vous-même n'êtes-vous pas marié? Donnez-moi de vos nouvelles...'. See above, pp. 60–66.

420| Ibid., Sammer to Le Corbusier, 26 March 1946: 'Quant-à-moi, nous avions des différences avec Agnes et elle est partie pour Honolulu en 39. Depuis je n'avais pas encore de la chance de me marier, étant soldat'.

421| AMP, František Sammer Papers, Sammer to his aunt, 7 January 1931 (n. 27). See above, p. 45.

František Sammer intensively tried to find Pierre Jeanneret and Charlotte Perriand, both of whom had loosened their tight bonds with Le Corbusier and his atelier before the war. Perriand worked in Japan from 1940 to 1942, where she laid the foundations for her lifelong relationship with Japanese culture. Jeanneret spent the war years in resistance in Grenoble and he pursued his own practice. After the war, his professional path crossed with Le Corbusier again, this time, however, not in Paris but in India. There, from 1951 to 1965, Jeanneret supervised the building of Le Corbusier's large project for the city of Chandigarh in northwest India. Afterwards, he remained there almost until the end of his life. Apart from work for Le Corbusier, he established himself as an architect in India and saw many of his own designs built. He was also appointed the head of the Chandigarh College of Architecture.[417]

In 1946, Le Corbusier wrote to Sammer that 'Pierre Jeanncret is in Grenoble. Charlotte Perriand was in Indochina during the war. They wrote to me that she had returned from there with a child in her arms, but I haven't seen her yet'.[418] He did not refrain from then asking a personal question: 'And what about you? Have you not married? Write to me with your news [...]'.[419] At that moment Sammer could only reply that he and Agnes 'had disagreements and she left for Honolulu in 1939. As a soldier in active service, I had no opportunity to marry'.[420]

At that moment Sammer particularly needed to figure out where he really wanted to live. At the beginning of his travels, he wrote to his family in Pilsen that he would choose a place to live once he had seen the whole world.[421] It could hardly have occurred to him then how strongly he would later desire to settle down in the country from which he was so keen to escape.

Returning

Regarding his future employment, Sammer had a wide range of possibilities. He was offered work not only by Le Corbusier, as well as by Antonin and Noémi Raymond, who invited him to the United States.[422] He might also work with Gordon Stephenson in Great Britain[423] and he still had to put the finishing touches on Golconde in Pondicherry.[424] But, while recovering in sanatoriums, Sammer, eager to recall his mother tongue, devoured classic works of Czech literature, particularly historic novels by Alois Jirásek and proletarian verses of Jiří Wolker. He turned down all offers of employment abroad. He was convinced that his place now was in his native Czechoslovakia.

Nevertheless, his ideas about home and the world had not changed. 'I believe', he wrote to his mother in Pilsen, 'that it would be lovely if it were possible to make a synthesis of all cultures. For that, it would be necessary for people to travel abroad and visit each other, and of course, to return home afterwards. Well, I am returning. Home is quite a broad term, because after having been starved of culture, after wandering amongst Indians and Mamelukes, a Russian song sounds as much like home as a French or German symphony, as pretty as a Czech song. [...] There are of course other things as well – a pious pilgrimage to Prague and to live from spring to summer and from autumn to winter as it is supposed to be, as when I was growing up and as is proper and fitting for me to say what I think. These things are not abroad; also one must be careful what one says when abroad. And, God willing, we will travel to Paris, because they paint well there, and to our dear mother Moscow, because we have friends there'.[425]

At the start of 1947, he returned to his native country still believing in an interconnected world and open borders, that is, with the same ideals he had when he first set out on his career before the war. Shortly afterwards, he married Ludmila Müllerová, a doctor, and later in 1954, they had one child, Petr. After the Communist takeover in February 1948, however, the Czechoslovak borders were closed to free travel and there was little appreciation of Sammer's earlier experiences and achievements. His days working in the Le Corbusier-Jeanneret atelier in Paris now carried as much negative weight on his CV as his rank of captain in the British Army. He was spared the worst of these negative associations thanks to his contributions to building socialism in the Soviet Union and to the intercession of his Soviet colleagues and friends. These circumstances also seriously affected Sammer's place in the history of architecture in his native land, where, until recently, he was remembered primarily as the founder of the Pilsen branch of Stavoprojekt (the state-run organization of most architecture and engineering offices in the country)[426] and as one of the 'most active proponents of socialist realist architecture in Pilsen'.[427]

Sammer, back in his native Pilsen, fought for his place in the profession, and joined in the first phase of designing the Slovany housing estate. He demonstrated that he could easily master the socialist realist style. Soon, however, he found a way to circumvent the state-dictated aesthetic directives. He found the least restrictions in urban planning, to which he then devoted himself for the rest of his life. With his close friend, the architect and urban planner Jindřich Krise (1908–89), he spent years working on Master Plan for the Development of Pilsen (Směrný územní plán města Plzně), which reflects his knowledge of the radical solutions of Le Corbusier's urban planning.

Soon after the Czechoslovak Communists seized power, the secret police began to keep Sammer under surveillance.[428] In order to protect himself, his wife and his little son, he had to break off all contact with friends abroad. He often did so without any explanation and many people assumed that he was long dead. All the greater then

422| AMP, František Sammer Papers, Noémi Raymond to Sammer, 1 October 1945. Even before the war, Sammer had planned to move to the United States. The Raymonds looked after all the visas and documents he needed to enter the country, but he ultimately did not use them.

423| Ibid., Stephenson to Sammer, 3 March 1946: 'If you don't go back to Czecho.Slovakia [sic], there is work here for you!'

424| Ibid., the Mother in Pondicherry to Sammer in Great Britain, 24 January 1947: 'Inutile de dire que nous serrions enchantés de vous avoir de nouveau ici. Il y a beaucoup, beaucoup de travail à faire, même seulement pour finir Golconde. Tant de détails restent à décider!'

425| Ibid., Sammer to his mother in Pilsen, 16 March 1946.

426| Most of what has been written about Sammer's post-war work has been in the context of socialist realism in Czechoslovakia. See Josef Pechar, *Československá architektura 1945-1977*, Prague: Odeon, 1979, pp. 21, 26, 81; Radomíra Sedláková, *Sorela: Česká architektura padesátých let*, Prague: National Gallery, 1994, pp. 12, 38, 39; Pavel Halík, 'Architektura padesátých let', in Rostislav Švácha and Marie Platovská (eds), *Dějiny českého výtvarného umění*, vol. 5: 1939-1958, Prague: Academia, 2005, pp. 324–25; and Petr Domanický, 'Navzdory malomyslné okresní zatvrdlosti: SZVU a architektura', in Petr Jindra (ed.), *Umění českého západu: Sdružení západočeských výtvarných umělců v Plzni 1925-1951*, Řevnice, Pilsen: Arbor Vitae and Západočeská galerie, 2010, pp. 13 and 14. The artistic quality of Sammer's work is highlighted in Jindřich Vybíral, 'Majáky převratných idejí', in Sedláková,

^ František Sammer in a photograph from 25 January 1947. Private archive.
^> František Sammer, a housing complex from the first phase of the construction of the Slovany housing estate in Pilsen, Czechoslovakia, called the Superblok. Designed and built in c. 1951–55. AMP.
v> František Sammer and Jindřich Krise, perspective drawing of the urban plan for the eastern part of Pilsen, Czechoslovakia, 1948–49. AMP.

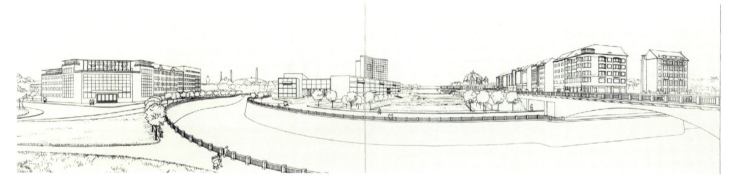

Sorela, p. 64, and, in greater detail, in Jindřich Vybíral, 'The Beacons of Revolutionary Ideas: *Sorela* as Historicism and Rhetoric', *Centropa* I, no. 2, May 2001, pp. 99-100; Martina Koukalová, 'Plzeň – Slovany', in Lucie Skřivánková, Rostislav Švácha, Eva Novotná and Karolina Jirkalová (eds), *Paneláci 1: Padesát sídlišť v českých zemích: kritický katalog k cyklu výstav Příběh paneláku*, Prague: Uměleckoprůmyslové museum, 2016, pp. 108-15.

427| Domanický, 'Navzdory malomyslné okresní zatvrdlosti' (n. 427), p. 14.
428| Security Services Archive (Archiv bezpečnostních složek – ABS), archive report of the Pilsen Regional Department of the Interior Ministry, archive no. 790. This information was provided to me by the archive after a search done on 1 April 2015. Sammer was under the closest surveillance by the Czechoslovak secret police from 1957 to 1965. For more see n. 49.

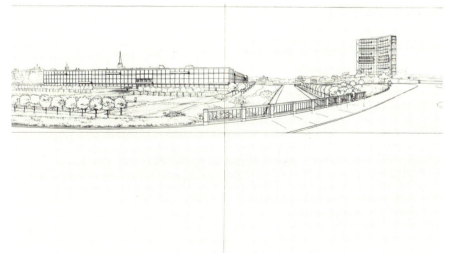

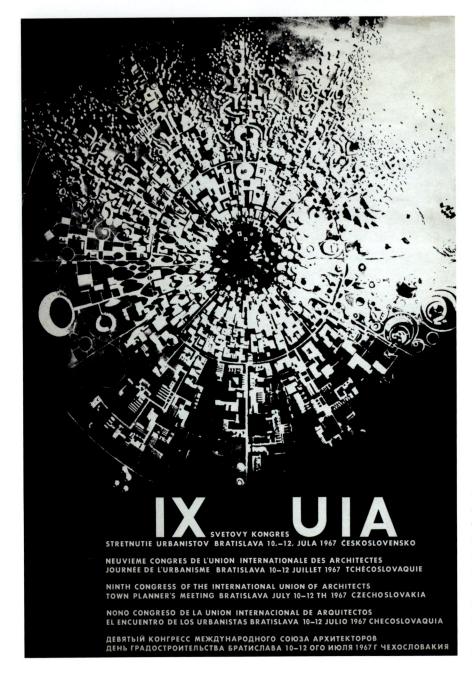

< Roger Anger, the Nebula plan, 1967. A preliminary draft of an urban plan for the soon-to-be founded Auroville, India, on a poster for the Ninth Congress of the International Union of Architects (UIA). The congress was held in Prague and Bratislava in 1967. Poster collection of Terryho ponožky, Prague.

> Roger Anger, model of the resulting urban plan for Auroville, based on the shape of a galaxy, 1968. Reproduced from Fassbender, *Auroville Architecture*, p. 56 (see n. 433).

was their surprise when Sammer contacted them almost 20 years later, during the political thaw in the late 1960s. He could then begin to try to return to an international community of people who were dear to him.

Sammer's British colleagues immediately invited him and his whole family for a visit. 'How well you have retained your English! I only wish I could write a letter like yours in French, or Russian, or modern Greek, or any of the other languages I have tried to speak in the past',[429] Holford wrote to him in reply to his letter of August 1966. Offering to cover the costs, he invited Sammer and his family to Great Britain: 'We should like you to stay with us at Brighton [...], and, of course to visit London and other places of architectural interest; so that you can re-visit some of the places which we saw together when we were working on the Antwerp competition in 1930 [*sic*, 1933] with Gordon Stephenson'.[430] Holford, now Lord Holford, was working in the Republic of South Africa and Gordon Stephenson was living in Australia, but both of them planned to be in Great Britain in the summer of 1967, the time for which Sammer was invited.

[429] AMP, František Sammer Papers, William Holford to František Sammer, summer 1966. Sammer to Holford, 4 August 1966.
[430] Ibid., Holford to Sammer, 20 March 1967.
[431] Ibid., Raymond to Sammer, 30 August 1966. Private archive, Antonín Raymond to Eda Kriseová, 30 July 1966: 'The letter from František [Sammer] made us happy, and moved us – we were almost absolutely certain that he was no longer in this world. The last we heard of him he was in England during the war – that is about twenty years ago – we wrote to Pilsen and in other ways tried to find out something

'It is increasingly bigger in Pondichery. Now they have the idea of building a whole new city. They call it "Auroville" and apparently some young French architect is working on it. They wanted me but I don't want to go there – it's hot there – in many senses – but I designed, only as a sketch so far, the Japanese Pavilion – modern of course, air-conditioned etc. – and over it a "kasa", something like a parasol of concrete'.

Antonin Raymond in a letter letter written in Czech to František Sammer, 9 December 1966. AMP.

Antonín and Noémi Raymond described rediscovering Sammer as a 'resurrection'.[431] At his request, they willingly looked after Eda Kriseová, the daughter of the architect Krise, when she visited Japan in the summer of 1966. In their resumed correspondence they acquainted each other with the main events of the past years and Raymond updated Sammer on what was now happening in Pondicherry. Sammer had left the construction of the ashram dormitory unfinished in 1942. Following his instructions, other members of the ashram completed the job, having been taught by Sammer while working together. The construction was now supervised by Udar Pinto. His wife, Mona, then managed the building: 'Golconde is as wonderful as ever', Pinto wrote to Sammer, after they resumed their correspondence in 1968. 'Mona has kept it like a jewel and it is as fresh today as when it was built 25 years back. It is indeed a marvel to everyone who sees it and to me it is a constant reminder of you, François. I learned so much from it and you, and this is reflected in what I do now'.[432] The letter included a postcard from Mona with a photograph of the garden of Golconde and an invitation to return to Pondicherry [see photo on p. 31].

In the 1960s, the ashram continued to prosper under the direction of the Mother. In 1967, she even founded a new town in the name of the ideals of Sri Aurobindo's philosophy. The winning design for Auroville, an ideal town for inhabitants of every nationality in the world, was on a galaxy-shaped plan by the French architect Roger Anger (1923–2008).[433] One of the design variants, the 'Nebula' model, from 1966, was featured in the main theme of the promotional material for the 9th Congress of the International Union of Architects (UIA), which was held in Prague in 1967. At the congress, Sammer presented the results of his urban planning for Pilsen and, after catching sight of Anger's spectacular plan, he immediately got in touch with his friends in Pondicherry.[434]

---

about him – nothing – and now, a miracle – a resurrection. That is wondeful – a resurrection'.
432 | Ibid., Udar Pinto to Sammer, 1 October 1968.
433 | Franz Fassbender, *Auroville Architecture: Towards New Forms for a New Consciousness*, 5th edn, (2004) Auroville: Prisma, 2014, pp. 24–31.
434 | AMP, František Sammer Papers, Sammer to Raymond, draft letter, 26 March 1968. AAUP, Antonin Raymond and Noémi Pernessin Raymond Collection, Sammer to Raymond, 26 March 1968.

'Auroville was opened on 28 February. You are right to say that the event has a cosmic significance',[435] Pavitra, one of the heads of the ashram, replied without delay to Sammer's interest in news about the ashram.[436] The plan of Auroville is centred around a galactic core – Matrimandir, the spiritual heart of the community with rooms for meditation. The branches of the galaxy contain the individual zones of the town. They are divided by function, which was meant to ensure the utterly self-sufficient operation of the community. Individual nations were given space for their own pavilions, some of which have already been erected while others are still awaiting construction. So it is with the Japanese Pavilion, which was designed by Raymond, who described it to Sammer as 'modern, air conditioned, etc. – and above it is a "kasa," a kind of concrete parasol'.[437]

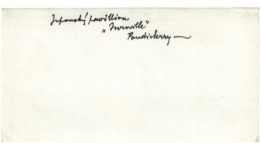

^ Antonin Raymond, a model of the Japanese pavilion for Auroville, after 1966. The intention to build the pavilion, on Raymond's design, remains. Private archive.

In 1969, two years after the conference, Sammer tried to explain to the Communist authorities, why he wanted to return to India: 'I knew that it [the ashram] is my second home even back then and they assure me of it now when they invite me to their place'.[438] He wanted to go to Pondicherry with his wife and son, and to participate in its planning. He discussed that in his correspondence with the Mother, who was then 95, and with other heads of the ashram. 'You should think of an "International House" grouping together countries that cannot have a big house for themselves, and you would come to build it!',[439] Gabriel Monod-Herzen, the head of the French-based Association for Auroville, wrote to Sammer in late 1970. By that time it was already clear that Sammer would never be granted permission to travel to take part in a 'synthesis of all cultures'[440] and enjoy the freedom of movement and speech that he had dreamt of since the end of the war.

A closer look at the plans for Auroville suggests a comparison with ideas advocated by the avant-garde movements in the West. The organization of the town into zones according to purpose evokes the idea of the functional city as formulated at the CIAM architectural congresses between the two world wars. The notion of the co-existence of all nations in one place and their representation by national pavilions recalls the tradition of world fairs. The idea of a supranational pavilion, about which Monod-Herzen wrote to Sammer, has much in common with Le Corbusier's project

435| AMP, František Sammer Papers, Philippe Barbier Saint-Hilaire, called Pavitra, to Sammer, 9 April 1968: 'L'inauguration d'Auroville a eu lieu le 28 février dernier. Vous avez raison de dire que l'événement a une signification cosmique'.
436| Philippe Barbier Saint-Hilaire (1894–1969), called Pavitra, was from 1925 until the end of his life the general secretary of the Sri Aurobindo Ashram.
437| AMP, František Sammer Papers, Raymond to Sammer, 9 December 1966.
438| Ibid., František Sammer to Jan Pelnář, 13 January 1969.
439| Ibid., Gabriel Monod-Herzen in Pondicherry to Sammer in Pilsen, 27 December 1970: 'Vous devriez penser à une "Maison internationale" groupant les pays ne pouvant pas avoir une grande maison pour eux seuls, et vous viendriez la construire!'
440| Ibid., Sammer to his mother in Pilsen, 16 March 1946. See above, p. 140, and n. 425.
441| For a description and comparison of the two pavilions, see McLeod, 'Urbanism and Utopia' (n. 32). For more on Mundaneum see p. 45 and n. 35. For pointing out the parallel of the project of Mundaneum with the idea of the supranational pavilion for Auroville I am grateful to Mary McLeod.

of Mundaneum. It also resembles the way Le Corbusier presented his visions at world fairs. His pavilions from 1925 and 1937 were international in their program and design.[441] Moreover, the gathering of representatives of the countries of the whole world, who were drawn to one another by a similar way of seeing the world and how to co-exist in it, brings to mind the milieu of the Le Corbusier–Jeanneret atelier. All of that, but with the difference that the core of that galaxy was not the indisputably charismatic and turbulent personality of Le Corbusier, but a quiet temple for meditation.

The galaxy reflected in the 'Livre noir'

In the 1960s it would have been hard to encounter the whole 'Internationale' assembled in one place,[442] as Sammer described the gathering of the Le Corbusier's circle in Paris in 1937. During the brief period when Sammer could renew contacts abroad, Le Corbusier was already dead.[443] The addresses or telephone numbers of some of his friends were just as difficult for him to find as they had been after the Second World War and many of them did not expect to see Sammer ever again. 'I have been trying to get news of you from time to time since 1940. But no one has any. I believed you to be in the USA. All those who disappear from Europe are picked up by the "Big Grinder"',[444] wrote the architect Jean Bossu to Sammer in early 1969. This former assistant at 35 rue de Sèvres, who at that time was working in Algeria, thus replied to Sammer's letter, expressing his desire to meet with him 'in order to recall the others they had worked with and whom they liked'.[445]

In 1967 and 1969, thanks to an invitation from William Holford, František Sammer was finally able to travel to Great Britain. He met with his closest friends and colleagues, Gordon Stephenson and Alex Adam. He visited France and in the summer of 1967 tried, without success, to see Charlotte Perriand at her new address at 26 rue Las Cases.[446] He was not sure whether he had the correct contact information, and kept looking for it in his correspondence; he also kept looking for news about Pierre Jeanneret.

It was generally known in Czechoslovakia that Le Corbusier had died in August 1965. However, the news that 'quiet Pierre' Jeanneret[447] had died in December 1967 had not reached Sammer behind the Iron Curtain. 'Is Pierre still in Chandigarh?', Sammer asked Perriand in March 1968, naturally recalling the years spent in India: 'It is strange how we just missed meeting each other in Asia. Because of one old epistle from my dear Corbu [Chandigarh], I keep thinking that it would not have taken much for us to have met there'.[448]

Even after the 30-year silence, he wrote to Perriand just as before 'My dear Charlotte, we must see each other', and tried to explain why he was incommunicado for so long: 'They were also hard years […] with all kinds of persecution, but eventually everything worked out and since 1965 I have been working as an architect – town planner. The results of recent events in the country, which are advocating a more democratic, more efficient economic system, can have only a good influence on our work – and on our travel opportunities'.[449]

Nevertheless, the promises of a 'more democratic system' in Czechoslovakia were left unfulfilled because of the Soviet-led military intervention in August 1968. Sammer succeeded in travelling out of the country in 1969, but the prospects of other trips soon vanished during the period called 'normalization', that is, the reinstatement of a hard-line Communist regime in the course of 1969–70.

Nevertheless, Sammer would enjoy one more personal meeting of great importance. In the summer of 1972, Agnes Larsen, after not having seen Sammer for 33 years, came to Czechoslovakia to visit him for a week. At that time, she was living in

---

442| Ibid., Sammer to his parents, 13 January 1937. See p. 124 and n. 356.

443| Le Corbusier was born Charles-Édouard Jeanneret in La Chaux-de-Fonds, on 6 October 1887, and died in Cap Martin, in the South of France, on 27 August 1965.

444| AMP, František Sammer Papers, Jean Bossu to Sammer, 2 February 1969: 'J'essayais d'avoir de tes nouvelles de temps en temps depuis 1940. Mais personne n'en avait … Je te croyais aux U.S.A. Tous ceux qui disparaissent d'Europe sont recupérés par la "grande Broyeuse"'.

445| Ibid., Sammer, draft letter, to Jean Bossu, December 1968: 'J'aimerai beaucoup te rencontrer même si cela ne sera que pour nous souvenir des autres avec qui on a travaillé et qu'on a aimé'.

446| Perriand's former Paris studio now houses her archive. See the Research Diary, p. 37.

447| See above, p. 41 and n. 4.

448| AMP, František Sammer Papers, Sammer to Perriand, draft letter, 26 March 1968: 'Est-ce que Pierre est toujours à Chandigarh? C'est curieux comme nos chemins se sont croisés en Asie. À cause d'une ancienne épître de mon vieux Corbu j'entretiens toujours une idée qu'il aurait suffi très peu pour nous rencontrer là'. It is possible that Sammer refers to an earlier correspondence concerning the Chandigarh project, yet the 'ancienne épître' he mentions remains unknown to me.

449| Ibid., Sammer to Perriand, draft letter, 26 March 1968: 'Ma chère Charlotte nous devons nous voir. […] Il y avait aussi des années dures, […] diverses persécutions, mais à la fin tout a été mis en ordre et depuis 1965 je travaille en architecte – urbaniste de la ville. Les résultats des événements récentes dans notre pays, qui préconisent un ordre plus démocratique et plus efficace en économie générale du pays ne peuvent que d'avoir un bonne influence sur notre travail – et sur nos possibilités de voyager'.

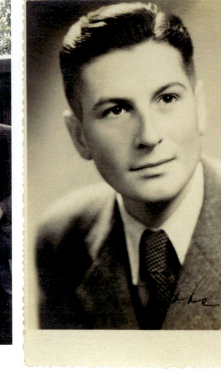

^ Boba, Sammer's childhood friend, 1930s.
Photograph, 8.3 × 12.1 cm. SAAA.

Photo from Agnes Larsen's visit to Prague, summer 1972. All the photos are deposited in the UWA, Gordon Stephenson Papers.

^ << From the right: Agnes Larsen, František Sammer and his childhood friend Boba on the terrace of the Hanavský pavilon (Hanau pavilion) in Letná Park, Prague.

^ < From the right: František Sammer, Agnes Larsen, Boba with his sister and brother-in-law.

< From the left: Agnes Larsen and František Sammer with Boba at his cottage at Špičák in the Bohemian Forest.

Florence and travelled to Czechoslovakia by way of Vienna, where she tried in vain to find Georges Pollak, one of their architect friends from 35 rue de Sèvres.[450] Larsen and Sammer had renewed their correspondence after more than a 20-year break, by way of the ashram in Pondicherry,[451] with which both had stayed in touch. They now met again, and spent several days in Prague and its environs, as well as a couple of days in South Bohemia in the company of Sammer's childhood friend 'Boba' and his family.[452] Why Agnes Larsen and František Sammer split up after the outbreak of the Second World War remains an open question, and even their closest friends wondered about it in correspondence they maintained until the end of their lives. A partial explanation appears in a letter from Larsen, sent in 1994 to Stephenson in Perth, Australia, where he was living and working at that time:

> Re François – it's not easy to write about what happened. I was liable for part of it, and have never discussed it with anyone. It still hurts, even though

[450] Ibid., Larsen in Vienna to Sammer, 18 June 1972. According to the 'Répertoire des collaborateurs', the architect Georges Pollak worked at 35 rue de Sèvres from 1935 to 1936. See also above, p. 128, and n. 370. Despite considerable effort, I have unfortunately not been able to find more information about Pollak.

[451] Gordon Stephenson Papers, 1942–97, MS 144, Special Collections, University of Western Australia (UWA), Larsen to Stephenson, 31 May 1994: 'In 1971 I took a trip to Pondicherry. The ashram wanted news of him [Sammer] and gave me his address'. For a photograph of the letter, see p. 147.

[452] Ibid.: 'François was there (déjà vu?) with Boba, his oldest friend,

> A letter from Agnes Larsen to Gordon Stephenson, 31 May 1994, explaining her breaking up with Sammer and then meeting up again much later. The letter was accompanied by the three photos, shown on the opposite page. UWA, Gordon Stephenson Papers.

whom I knew. But no Ludmila. The four of us went out to Boba's dacha'. Despite serious efforts to find it out, Boba's full name remains unknown.
453| Ibid.
454| For having found and providing me with documents, I am greatly indebted to Professor David Massey of the University of Liverpool, Professor Jenny Gregory of the University of Western Australia and Deanne Barrett of the University of Western Australia in Perth.
455| Pierre-André Emery (1903–82), Swiss architect, worked at 35 rue de Sèvres from 1924 to 1926. According to 'Répertoire des collaborateurs', at the FLC (n. 8).

François and I later figured out "it was written" and, for some karmic reason beyond our human understanding, had to be. In Pondicherry, 1939, we disagreed about something – nothing irreparable – and I returned to Honolulu to visit my family. I had to earn my fare back to India but before I could leave, the Pacific war blocked me. The war dragged on. Endless years passed. [...] The tragedy of more than half of his life, and not of his making, is painful to contemplate – much more than one person can bear. I'm glad to share it at last, with someone as close as you. [...] We were going to change the world! Remember? Out of danger, into [a] stranger space without escape.[453]

To the letter Larsen attached a few colour photos of that meeting in 1972, which are now part of Stephenson's papers held in the archive of the University of Western Australia in Perth.[454]

In 1973, Sammer was approached by Pierre-André Emery, an architect who had been an assistant at 35 rue de Sèvres in the early years, and later worked for years in Algeria.[455] Emery was turning to him with a request for help in finding information

ASSOCIATION INTERNATIONALE LE CORBUSIER

L'ASSOCIATION INTERNATIONALE LE CORBUSIER répond à un désir maintes fois et très explicitement défini, de son vivant, par Le Corbusier lui-même.

En effet, au cours des dernières années de sa vie, il a été préoccupé par le destin des idées et des théories qu'il a constamment développées et qu'il a matérialisées à travers son architecture, son urbanisme, sa peinture, son éloquence persuasive et son génie poétique. Cinquante années d'attaques et de polémiques n'ont pu opposer de réfutation valable à ces idées. Une impulsion créatrice aussi généreuse a toutes les chances de survivre à son auteur. Encore faut-il qu'elle ne soit pas détournée de son objet et ne soit pas utilisée à des fins partisanes ou tendancieuses.

La Fondation Le Corbusier, chargée — entre autres tâches — de gérer le patrimoine qui lui a été légué, répond déjà à ce souci de persistance et de pérennité. Cependant, il est clair que ni la Fondation, ni les Associations nationales ou locales, ne peuvent assumer une vocation qui soit à proprement parler internationale.

Les buts de l'Association Internationale sont clairement exprimés dans ses statuts, et le règlement intérieur proposé définit les moyens dont elle pourra disposer.

Pour atteindre ces buts, il est évident que l'Association ne saurait se contenter d'être un groupement statique de défense, de conservation ou de sauvegarde, ou plus simplement une réunion d'anciens combattants de l'architecture moderne évoquant leurs souvenirs sous une glorieuse bannière.

L'Association Internationale entend s'inspirer de l'exemple de Le Corbusier, de son dynamisme et de sa totale ouverture d'esprit à tous les problèmes contemporains.

Elle souhaite donc pouvoir faire face à des tâches toujours renouvelées et poursuivre une action que la référence à la pensée de Le Corbusier ne peut que vivifier. Cette action pourra prendre des formes multiples, parfois originales et inédites.

Pour cela, l'Association doit acquérir l'audience nécessaire, devenir un instrument ferme et souple tout à la fois, avoir la possibilité de réagir rapidement et efficacement à l'événement, où qu'il se produise.

L'Association ne s'adresse pas, dans le cas présent, à des bonnes volontés, mais à des volontés déterminées et éprouvées.

L'Association Internationale souhaite tout d'abord coordonner les nombreuses initiatives spontanées — parfois touchantes — qui se sont manifestées au cours de ces dernières années. Elle désire leur apporter son appui, les faire profiter des moyens dont elle dispose, et créer un climat favorable à l'éclosion d'initiatives nouvelles et de manifestations conséquentes.

Elle conserve, dans son action, des rapports constants avec la Fondation, dans une complète identité de vues. Les résultats obtenus depuis trois ans sont appréciables et ils encouragent l'A.I.L.C. à poursuivre et développer son action.

Une telle entreprise est certainement ambitieuse. Mais sa réussite est nécessaire, en tant qu'elle sera le témoignage le plus marquant de l'attraction et de la vitalité de la pensée de Le Corbusier.

Mai 1971

Adresser la correspondance au secrétariat :

16, rue Sismondi - 1201 Genève - Tél. (022) 31 93 40

Extrait des statuts de l'Association :

51 b) Les cotisations des membres actifs sont fixées à Fr. S. 100.— (pour les membres résidants en France Fr. FR. 125.—). Paiement par virement bancaire.

Compte bancaire : Union de Banques Suisses - Genève (No 202.89900 Z).

Les membres français ont la faculté de verser le montant de leur cotisation annuelle : (Fr. FR. 125.—) au compte No H 23-056-13.

Association Française des AMIS DE LE CORBUSIER

Crédit Industriel & Commercial, 48, bd Malsherbes - PARIS 8ème.

De ce fait ils deviennent membres de l'Association Française.

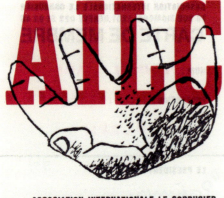

^ Statutes of the Association Internationale Le Corbusier (AILC), founded for the protection and development of Le Corbusier's legacy, dated May 1971. Private archive.

< Sammer's AILC membership card, sent in a letter from Pierre-André Emery, 13 January 1973. For political and financial reasons, however, the Czech architect was unable to participate at all in the activities of the international organization. Private archive.

> Letter from Pierre-André Emery to František Sammer, in which he requests help in drawing up a 'Répertoire des collaborateurs' (List of assistants) from 35 rue de Sèvres' (see n. 8 and 464), and explains how the list is being made. Letter of 13 January 1973. Private archive.

Adresser correspondance
et communications au
SECRETARIAT
16, rue Sismondi - 1201 Genève
Tél. (022) 31 93 40

ASSOCIATION INTERNATIONALE LE CORBUSIER
11, RUE TŒPFFER 1206 GENÈVE SUISSE TÉL. (022) 46 46 32

le 13 janvier 1973

Monsieur François S A M M E R.
architecte

Alesowa 3

P L Z E N.

Tchécoslovaquie.

Cher Monsieur.

L'Association Internationale Le Corbusier cherche, en ce moment, à établir la liste la plus complète et la plus détaillée possible des collaborateurs de Le Corbusier qui ont travaillé à ses côtés à l'atelier du 35 rue de Sèvres. Ils sont très nombreux, environ 270, et sur certains d'entre eux, nous ne possédons que très peu de renseignements, ou même pas du tout.

C'est la raison pour laquelle nous faisons appel à vos souvenirs car, pour la période au cours de laquelle vous étiez vous-même à l'atelier, nous relevons sur le "cahier noir" où étaient inscrits les plans, à côté de votre signature, certaines sur lesquelles nous souhaiterions qu'il vous soit possible de nous donner quelques éclaircissements. Ce sont:

Mlle BURCKHARDT. suissesse
POURSAIN. Français ayant travaillé au Ministère de l'Equipement
          et à la Caisse des Dépôts et Consignations.
ADAM. ayant travaillé chez Lubetkin, à Londres.
OSWALD. Tchéque
DAVID. hongrois.
BADER.

Je joins à cette lettre une photocopie d'un extrait du "cahier noir", ainsi que votre carte de membre de l'A.I.L.C. à laquelle vous avez droit comme ayant fréquenté l'atelier, ainsi qu'une documentation sur notre Association.

Nous vous remercions par avance de ce que vous pourrez nous communiquer au sujet de ces quelques personnes, et nous vous prions d'agréér, chère Monsieur, l'expression de nos sentiments les meilleurs.

le vice-président
Pierre-A EMERY.

PaEmery

1 carte de membre
1 photocopie
1 documentation.

A.I.L.C. Compte No 202.89900 Z - U.B.S. Genève

'The copies of the pages of the 'Livre noir' with the signatures of my friends and my own have awakened vivid feelings, and, on the screen of my memory, portraits of the people you are looking for'.

František Sammer in reply to Pierre-André Emery for having sent copies of pages from the 'Livre noir'. Letter of 24 January 1973. AMP.

about other former assistants at the atelier. He was doing so as the vice president of an organization established after Le Corbusier's death, which aimed to preserve his intellectual legacy. The Association Internationale Le Corbusier (AILC), based in Geneva, Switzerland, was founded in 1968, at the same time as, and in collaboration with, the Paris-based Fondation Le Corbusier (FLC) and the Association des amis de Le Corbusier (AALC). Unlike the organizations in France, the AILC in its statutes and by-laws was international in its mission.[456]

'The Association cannot be satisfied with being a static group for defence, conservation or safeguarding or, simply, a reunion of old warriors for modern architecture, recalling their memories under a glorious banner. The International Association intends to draw inspiration from the example of Le Corbusier, his dynamism and his complete openness to all contemporary problems'.[457] As such the AILC sought to bring together everyone well acquainted with the methods and thinking of the famous architect and inspired by them. All the former assistants at 35 rue de Sèvres were entitled to a membership card,[458] and the attempt to reunite the architects from that community was a logical step in the programme of the association. Emery's letter included Sammer's membership card. Due to of a lack of funds and the nature of membership, incompatible with the restrictions imposed by the Communist regime in Czechoslovakia, Sammer could not participate in AILC activities.[459]

'At this moment the Association Internationale de Le Corbusier seeks to establish the most complete and detailed list possible of Le Corbusier's collaborators who worked beside him at the atelier at the 35 rue de Sèvres. There are many of them, about 270, and about some of them we have very little information, or even none at all',[460] Emery wrote to Sammer, asking him for help in locating assistants 40 years after his practice at the Le Corbusier-Jeanneret atelier. Information about the operation of the Le Corbusier–Jeanneret atelier in the years before the Second World War was harder to find than information about the post-war period. 'That is why we are appealing to you for your recollections, because in the 'Livre noir', for the period when you were at the atelier, we have noticed your signature next to some of the plans registered there, and we hope that it might be possible for you to provide us with clarification about some of them [the assistants]',[461] Emery wrote to Sammer, explaining why he had sent him copies of selected pages of the 'Livre noir', and highlighted their names in colour.

The international community of friends and colleagues from the 1930s could hardly meet in person in the early 1970s. All the greater, then, was the testimony about their interconnectedness, which remained preserved on the pages of the 'Livre noir'. On the copies of the pages from 1932, František Sammer, more than 40 years later, saw his name together with those of Gordon Stephenson, Jane West, Alfred Altherr, Junzo Sakakura, Charlotte Perriand, Alex Adam and many others. He was thus given a chance to glimpse again into the Le Corbusier Galaxy, which he had first entered in the early 1930s.

In his reply, Sammer expressed his gratitude: 'Dear Mr Emery, dear friends, I was profoundly moved by your having kindly made me a member of the Association

> Copy of page 39 of the 'Livre noir', with the circled names of architects who had been signed next to František Sammer, and about whom Pierre-André Emery was seeking further information. Enclosed in a letter from Emery to Sammer, 13 January 1973. Private archive

---

456| Private archive, Statutes and By-laws of the Association Internationale Le Corbusier, May 1971, attachment to a letter from P.-A. Emery to Sammer, of 13 January 1973: 'Cependant, il est clair que ni la Fondation, ni les Associations nationales où locales, ne peuvent assumer une vocation qui soit à proprement parler internationale'. For a photo of the document, see p. 148.

457| Ibid.: 'il est évident que l'Association ne saurait se contenter d'être un groupement statique de défense, de conservation où de sauvegarde, ou plus simplement une réunion d'anciens combattants de l'architecture moderne évoquant leurs souvenirs sous une glorieuse bannière. L'Association Internationale entend s'inspirer de l'exemple de Le Corbusier, de son dynamisme et de sa totale ouverture d'esprit à tous les problèmes contemporains'.

458| Private archive, P.-A. Emery to Sammer, 13 January 1973: 'Je joins à cette lettre [...] votre carte de membre de l'A.I.L.C. à laquelle vous avez droit comme ayant fréquenté l'atelier, [...]'. For a photo of the letter, see p. 149.

459| AMP, František Sammer Papers, František Sammer to Václav Rajniš, draft letter, 13 January 1973.

460| Private archive, P.-A. Emery to Sammer, 13 January 1973: 'L'Association Internationale de Le Corbusier cherche, en ce moment, à établir la liste la plus complète et la plus détaillée possible des collaborateurs de Le Corbusier qui ont travaillé à ses cotés à l'atelier du 35 rue de Sèvres. Ils sont très nombreux, environ 270, et sur certains d'entre eux, nous ne possèdons que très peu de renseignements, où même pas du tout'.

461| Ibid.: 'C'est la raison pour laquelle nous faisons appel à vos souvenirs car, pour la période au cours de laquelle vous étiez vous-même à l'atelier, nous relevons sur le "cahier noir" où étaient inscrits les plans, à côté de votre signature, certaines sur lesquelles nous souhaiterions qu'il soit possible de nous donner quelques éclaircissements'.

Sammer

Avoir

2930	B	Cloisons à R. d. ch.	9.5.32	Sam.
2931	?	Façade, ~~Rue~~ ? Tourelle	9.5.32	Bade
2932	B	Lanterneaux dans cour	11.5.32	Osw.
2933	C.U.	Chambre type - panneaux 1:20	12.5.32	West
2934	C.U.	Corridor - panneaux - 1:20		
2935	B	Cloisons niveau garage		
2936	B	" caves.		Sam
2937	B	Escalier garage - R.d.ch		12.5.32
2938	B	" caves - garage		
2939	B	Coupe Lanterneaux 1:1	14.5.32	Osw.
2940	B	Escalier caves 1:10	18.5.32	Osw.
2941	B	3ème étage N. et Ferd 2ème ét. Tourelle	30.5.33	Ferrand
2942	C.U.	Plan et coupe des douches - 1:5	23.5.32	West
2943	C.U.	Coupe de douche et mi-cloison - lavabo 1:5		
2944	C.U.	Coupe des placard - 1:5		
2945	B	Cloisons des étages (2 app)	23.V.32	Sam
2946	B	Entrée Boulogne 1:20	27.5.32	Oswald
2947	C.U.	Plaques de lynol. Plafond. Rez de Chaussée 1:50	28.5.32	West
2948	C.U.	Plaques de lynol. Plafond 4ème Etage		
2949	B	Développement façade cour 1:20	29.V.32	Sam
2950	C.U.	Plaques - Plafond - Etage Courant 1:50	31.5.32	West
2951	CR	Balustrade ateliers	1:20 8.6.32	Sam
2952	CR	" Rotonde		
2953	CR	Loge Portique 1:20	9.6.32	Oswald
2954	B	Passerelle (Grandeur) 1:1	10.6.32	Sam.
2955	C.U.	4e Etage. Apt. Directeur. Plan 1:20	16.6.32	West
2956	C.U.	" " Coupes		
2957	C.U.	Rez de Chaussée. Cuisine. Concierge 1:20	16.6.32	West
2958	CR	Perspective Portique	17.6.32	Oswald
2904-T	C.U.	Plan du Rez de Chaussée et Jardin		
2959	B	Façade latérale petite cour	22.6.32	Sam

Internationale Le Corbusier [...] The copies of pages from the "Livre noir" with the signatures of my friends and my own awakened vivid feelings, and, on the screen of my memory, portraits of the people you are looking for'.[462]

The evidence of the drawings and the archaeological layers of interlinked projects did more than just summon up vivid recollections in Sammer, however. Despite the time that had passed, the geographical distance and the political restrictions, he was able to send an exhaustive up-to-date reply to Geneva. When he was not in direct contact with a former colleague, he had news from others or knew where to ask further. 'The list of assistants in the atelier at 35 rue de Sèvres, which you are drawing up, will definitely be a praiseworthy work. I would very much like to own [a copy], and will be grateful to you for one',[463] he wrote to Emery in March 1973.

Shortly afterwards, on 18 October 1973, Sammer died. Nevertheless, towards the end of his life, he was able, even from his isolation in a totalitarian country, to contribute to the creation of a source vitally important for understanding the operation of the Le Corbusier–Jeanneret atelier at 35 rue de Sèvres.[464] He provides us with evidence that, even after Le Corbusier's death, the system of creative people interconnected and bound together as if by the force of gravity did not cease to move around the personality of this Swiss-French architect. Together, they constituted, and continue to constitute, a living organism operating according to laws similar to those of a galaxy.

> Copy of page 40 from the 'Livre noir' with the circled names of former colleagues and friends from 35 rue de Sèvres. Enclosed in a letter from Emery to Sammer of 13 January 1973. Private archive.

'The list of assistants in the atelier at 35 rue de Sèvres, which you are drawing up, will definitely be a praiseworthy work. I would very much like to own [a copy] and will be grateful to you for one'.

František Sammer in reply to Pierre-André Emery for sending copies of pages of the 'Livre noir', 23 March 1973. AMP.

462| AMP, František Sammer Papers, draft letter from Sammer for P.-A. Emery, 24 January 1973: 'Cher monsieur Emery, chers amis, je suis très touché de votre attention de m'avoir fait membre de l'Association Internationale Le Corbusier, [...] Les facsimilés des pages du cahier noir avec signatures de mes amis et de moi même ont reveillé vives émotions, et sur l'écran de mon mémoire des portraits de ceux, que vous cherchez'.

463| Ibid., 23 March 1973: 'La liste de collaborateurs à l'atelier du 35 Rue de Sèvres que vous préparez, sera certainement une oeuvre méritaire at j'aimerai bien de l'avoir et vous en serai bien reconnaissant'.

464| FLC, 'Répertoire des collaborateurs de Le Corbusier ayant travaillé à l'atelier 35 rue de Sèvres ainsi qu'aux travaux executés à l'étranger'. The so called 'Emery List of Assistants' which was compiled in the 1970s is the main and, for now, the most comprehensive document for research on the people who worked with Le Corbusier the whole time he had his atelier in Paris. Though made with considerable effort, it contains a number of inaccuracies. Some names are still missing and a number of those included are often listed with partly misleading information. Consequently, the list must be used judiciously and requires a critical analysis.

SAMMER **Avoir**

~~2931~~	~~B.F.~~			
~~2932~~			1:50	
2991	CR	Entrée Chevaleret	13 septembre	Sam
2992	CR	Petit bâtiment de centrée		
2993	B	Balcon 6e étage 1:10	15 septembre	Sam
2994	CR	Bacs à fleurs Chevaleret	15.9.32	Sam
2995	B }	Volets avec chassis	18 9.32	Sam
2996	B }	détails grandeurs } plan		
2997	CR	Balustrades Rue Chevaleret	26..9.32	Sam
2998	CR	Corrigée du N° 2855 (cuisine)	29.9.32	Sam
2999	CR	Plan des chambrettes 6e	3.X.32	Sam
3.000	DAL	Plan d'ensemble, 1:200	11.X.32	Sam
3.001	DAL	Perspective vers la mer, nord		Salsa
~~3002~~				Sam
3.003	CU	Situation (proposition de vue de ciel)	14.X.32	Sam
3004	DAL	Plan d'appartements - Série 4m 1e et 2e et	19.10.32	Poussin
3005	DAL	do Série 4m 3e et 4e et	19.10.32	Poussin
3006	DAL	Axonométrie générale	19.10.32	Adam
3007	CU	Plan du jardin de circulation	26.10.32	Adam
3008	CH	Pilotis		
3009	CH	R. d. ch		
3010	CH	étage		
3011	CH	Coupe		
3012	CH	Perspective		
3013	DAL	Coupes	28/X.32	Sam
3014	KAP	Kaplan transformation	1. nov. 1932	Adam
3015	DAL }			
3016	DAL } perspectives	8 nov. 32	
3017	DAL }	exclusion	
3018	DAL } plans 4ème Étage	7 décembre 1932	
3019	DAL } " (1er et second)		

Excursuses

Excursus 1 | Great Britain, 1931

František Sammer first travelled to Great Britain – England to be precise – in the summer of 1931, after which he returned several times for work and to see the friends he had made thanks to the network formed at the Le Corbusier–Jeanneret atelier. He corresponded regularly with friends and colleagues in England, and exchanged photographs with them. The question of who took some of these photos and when they were taken is therefore sometimes difficult to answer, and remains a task for future research. In letters home to his native Pilsen, Sammer expresses the enthusiasm he felt for his first encounter with the sea while crossing the English Channel and describes his impressions of England.

A letter to Sammer's sister, Milča. AMP.
Paris, 25 August 1931

Dear Milča & Co.,
[...]
In August, I had a second pair of shoes resoled, bought only one book, and with the end of the course [in French at the Sorbonne], and the beginning of Le Corbusier's vacation, I also set off for England with two Swiss men (who work at Corbus's and we are good friends).[1] The whole thing cost slightly more than 800 francs and took ten days. – To this, I would only add that we were equipped with recommendations from Le Corbusier.

∧ Regent Street, London. Contact print, 4 × 3 cm. SAAA.

We set out by express train on a beautiful evening and tore along to Dieppe at a speed of sometimes more than 120 km per hour. At two in the morning we were on board the ship. You can imagine, Milča, that in the smell of the sea and the harbour I suddenly again experienced those moments and evenings when, as a little boy, I read about Captain Kidd[2] and the others. Aboard the ship there was a sign stating that it was forbidden to walk on the upper deck because it is stormy. You can imagine that I utterly ignored that lovely sign and as we were leaving the harbour I climbed up on the upper deck, took cover by the bow rail, and watched. It was a starry night without a moon. One could see the lighthouse on the breakwater in front of us and the lights of the waterfront at Dieppe slowly fading in the distance. And then came the first wave, full of the sea, just as we were leaving the last lighthouse. You can guess that my eyes were bulging with wonder as I watched, taking cover from the salty spray of the waves that crashed all the way to the upper deck. I tasted the saltiness of the water on my tongue and tried to stand up without holding on to anything. That was possible of course as long as the ship was rocking in rhythm. But when a big wave came, tossing the ship, I went flying from one side to the other. We were passing lightships with the sound of sirens and in that dance I felt like someone who was first experiencing the beauty and grandeur of the sea. An hour later I was wet and tired enough to go down and have some tea, which was extremely brown, fragrant and sweet, and that accompanied me for the full ten days.
Both my friends below were downcast when I came and one of them began to get sea sick – it was Bosshardt,[3] who had crossed the Atlantic four times before.
Then I fell asleep while being rocked, and trying to savour that rocking as much as possible. I didn't wake up till we reached Newhaven, when we were landing. Crossing the Channel (Dieppe–Newhaven) takes four hours but we sailed for four and half. After disembarking, tea with milk again, already in England, good cakes with raisins and we boarded miniature carriages (quite long but low), which are all fitted up the same (first, second and third class) and we sped through the beautiful English countryside to London. I slept a bit again, but in London I was already refreshed enough to devour everything with my eyes. Terribly old taxis, double-decker buses, trams, old houses, Whitehall, Piccadilly, Trafalgar Square and other places. We drove to the YMCA, rested for about half an hour, and set out at about nine o'clock for our first hunt for impressions. Milča, it's terribly difficult to write about everything we saw in a definite order. We didn't have any plans and perhaps thanks to that we saw a great deal of London.

1| See p. 51-52 and n. 53 in 'The Le Corbusier Galaxy' part of this publication.

2| The story of the legendary pirate William Kidd (c.1645-1701) inspired, for instance, a novel by Robert Louis Stevenson, the Scottish writer, which was first serialized from 1881-82, and became a cult novel about searching for buried treasure. Translated several times into Czech, under various titles, *Treasure Island* is best known today in that language as *Ostrov pokladů*. The first translations were published by Vilímek, in Prague, as *Zlatý ostrov* [Island of Gold], and from Sammer's other correspondence it is clear that he knew the novel under that title. For the awareness of the book in the Le Corbusier's circle see p. 68 and n. 154 in 'The Le Corbusier Galaxy' part of this publication.

3| According to the 'Répertoire des collaborateurs', FLC (n. 8 in the main text), Edwin Bosshardt (1904-1986), a Swiss architect, worked at the atelier in 1931. See p. 51-52 and n. 53 in 'The Le Corbusier Galaxy' part of this publication.

4| Here, Sammer is referring to the trilogy by John Galsworthy, *The*

> On an excursion to the environs of London. Contact prints, 4 × 3 cm. SAAA.

Bits and pieces of the English language began to come back to me and I had no trouble at all asking for whatever I wanted. The English are terribly polite, different from the French, much more polite. They are annoying with their politeness, but they are helpful and will help to organize everything you wish. Absolutely everything is done very naturally and casually. One is surprised by the cleanness and making one feel at home, far more developed than in Paris. I was looking for places from [The Forsyte] Saga and imagined the inhabitants of those beautiful old homes on Bedford Square like Soames and so on.[4] We went to the National Gallery, the Docklands, Hyde Park and everywhere we could go. The evening in Hampstead was lovely, clear, cool and windy, with the yellow sunset, the little sailing boats and eventually with the grey calm of full evening in the quiet streets, with the lights in the windows and the inkling of lovely comfortable interiors, the scrumptiousness of apple pie and kind company.

That was the first day, followed by the second, just as eventful and lovely, ending with a no less atmospheric evening in Richmond Park and Robin Hill, returning on the upper deck of the bus, with the calm streets of the garden city and the hustle and bustle of Regent Street. Milča, even now, when I recall all of that, I get sentimental.

And then a visit to the architect Easton, a very kind old gentleman with whiskers and good cigarettes, who gave us a recommendation to many architects (he's President of the Architectural Association),[5] but mainly to a friend of his in Oxford, and the architects Louis Soissons[6] and Mr Warren.[7]

The visit to Mr Warren was also something special. Mrs. Warren, who had been a painter before she married, works together with her husband. Petite, French and couldn't have been any kinder. She told us, in a merry French (with an English accent, which is so endearing that you can't keep from laughing all the time) how it was when she and Mr Warren married, how they found a stable in St James's Street from the reign of Queen Victoria, which they converted into a home, how they ate on the balcony on the first day and everyone was looking at them. – Vous savez, nous avons pensé, que nous sommes tous seules dans le monde. (You know, we thought we were all alone in the whole wide world.) Eventually, we were invited to lunch; terribly good and entertaining, with laughing and chatting all the while. You'd like to know what we ate, wouldn't you? Pea soup, then some kind of pie made from pastry like crumbly strudel and inside was kidney and liver, and it was hot with brown sauce, and awfully good. Then the requisite apple pie, which is a dream, and, at the end, good tea. That apple pie is another story. I don't think a pie like that can be made in Europe. It's like strudel, but the apples are quite different and it's eaten hot, covered in a special syrup and vanilla cream. Then we continued talking till about two o'clock, looked at architecture and eventually I was assured: I hope that my husband succeeds at finding you a position here. Milána [Milča], the lady was so

---

Forsyte Saga (first serialized, 1906-21), which has been published in Czech translations since the 1920s, as Sága rodu Forsytů.
5| From 1919-31, the architect John Murray Easton (1889-1975) worked with Howard Robertson at the office of Easton & Robertson, in London. In 1925, he and his firm designed the British Pavilion for the Exposition internationale des arts décoratifs et industriels modernes, in Paris. In the 1930s, Easton was President of the Architectural Association in London, and in 1955, he was awarded the Royal Gold Medal of the Royal Institute of British Architects (RIBA).
6| Louis de Soissons (1890-1962) was an architect and the town planner of Welwyn Garden City (1920-60).
7| Edward Prioleau Warren (1856-1937) was a British architect and archaeologist. He designed mainly in a late-seventeenth-century Revivalist style. His main works were lodgings for Oxford colleges and residential houses in London and the countryside. He was married to Margaret Morrell and among his friends was the writer Henry James.

∧ Hyde Park, London, first photo from the left: Rotten Row; photo on the right, the Peter Pan statue. Contact prints, 2.8 × 3.7 cm. SAAA.

nice; she acted like a countess, yet was as cordial and cheerful as she was beautiful. Then we were in the editorial offices of *Studio*,[8] where we were received by a young woman on behalf of the editor, and she took us on an excursion to a private home. (It was a very lovely house and again recalled the Saga.) The next day we were in Oxford, had a tour of the colleges and several private homes, and thanks to a recommendation from Mr Easton, we had a good lunch free of charge. The weather was beautiful all day, and we had a walk through the now-silent colleges and lovely parks. Then Welwyn Garden City with its charming little houses; driven around all day by Mr Batticombe (a recommendation from Mr Warren). The viaduct, across which Queen Victoria didn't want to cross and preferred to take to her coach, old 'cottages' (little village houses with unparalleled comfort). One little house like that had the sign of a little grocery shop. I went there to buy a two-penny sweet just so I could look inside. Milána, I was astonished. It was quite cool, a log was burning in the fireplace, a small child was sleeping in a pram with little wheels [a sketch of the pram], a comfortable armchair with chintz upholstery, everything was absolutely clean, and the shopkeeper herself was a plump, pretty, young mummy. So I got the impression that that is probably what happiness looks like. Then the return by express train. We spent the other days touring London: the Tower, the British Museum and other places of interest.

We again left on a cold day, with intermittent rain. We travelled to Newhaven by bus. I will not forget that journey either. (It was recommended to us by Mrs Warren and it is cheaper than the train.) So much beautiful countryside. Halfway through the journey at about eight o'clock we stopped at an old (but modernized) inn, on which a sign said:
Apple pie.
Toasts
Cakes, home-made.

We drank tea with milk and ate apple pie, toast and home-made cakes, now really with reverence, because we were aware that it was getting late. Then, at dusk we drove to Brighton, with the beautiful grey roaring sea all around us, being questioned by a beautiful little girl, about ten years old, until we reached Newhaven.

The boarding and crossing were even more turbulent, with a sea-sick Bosshardt and one Swiss woman we had made friends with. We arrived in Dieppe, where we spent two days looking at the surroundings. And then the journey home, not merry, but not sad, aware that it had to be. Gare St Lazare, the Métro, to bed and sleep from six in the morning to two in the afternoon, and doing the bills, and then back to work in the office like before London.

8| *The Studio: An Illustrated Magazine of Fine and Applied Art* was published in London from 1893 to 1964. It played a key role in spreading the ideas of the Art Nouveau and Arts and Crafts movements and, in the 1920s, Modernism. In 1935, on a commission from the editors, *The Studio* published Le Corbusier's *Aircraft: The New Vision*. For pointing out this connection, I am indebted to Irena Žantovská Murray.

9| See p. 157 and n. 7 in the Excursus.

Excursus 1 | Great Britain, 1931

∧ George Frederic Watts, *Physical Energy* (1882–1904), bronze equestrian statue in Kensington Gardens, London. Contact print, 3 × 4 cm. SAAA
> The Tower of London and a photo from a car trip to the environs of London. Contact prints, 3 × 4 cm. SAAA

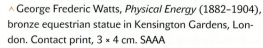

[...] Loads of greetings to Otakar Sr and Jr, Alan and Kamil
Yours, Frantík. –
P.S. Write!

A letter to Sammer's parents. AMP.
28 August 1931

Dear Dad and Mum,
[...] As you can see, I also returned from England to Paris almost as if it were my home port.
[...] Now I shall write something about London. I'll begin with my visit to the architects Louis Soissons and Warren. I explained to Mrs. Warren how extraordinarily interested I am in English architecture, and the dear lady eventually assured me that she would manage to find something. –
She said: I hope that my husband and I manage to find a job for you. Of course I am being a pest and I have already written the dear couple a letter from Paris. They are, however, also now on holiday in Vienna for a few days. You can see that I won't stop till I get a job. Apart from that, London, indeed all of England, has almost bewitched me.
Imagine that I go to a foreign country and everything I see is just as I imagined it. In England I see a strong country where remembered tradition forms the backbone of everything. Everything has a tradition and everything is good. These people do not have a reason to change good things. If Paris astonished me, in London I felt at home from the first moment. The politeness of people is different, not annoying. We went to visit a few architects and everyone received us very kindly, the Warrens[9] most of all, who organized an excursion to Welwyn Garden City for us. I would gladly write to you about everything, but I know that I'd be repeating the letter I wrote to Milča,[10] which she surely will give you to read.
The British Museum, the National Gallery, the Docklands, and many other things each deserve to be described separately. You also have to try and imagine that I saw for the first time the sea and seafaring ships, things I had dreamt of doing long ago. I'm not a poet, so cannot describe to you everything that I saw and all the emotions I felt when I got sprayed by my first salty wave.
At the British Museum, all of Egypt, the Parthenon, objects collected by Lord Carnarvon[11] and lots of lovely china; at the National Gallery, wonderful Gainsboroughs[12] – you can understand that I was in ecstasy every one of these days.
And the English countryside, Oxford, Brighton, Richmond, Hampstead, Windsor – unfortunately, we had very little time, but it was, as I wrote to you before, enough to make me excited about it. The Tower, with all its important things, with the most beautiful treasure in the world, the English crown jewels – it's impossible to write about it all and you've no doubt noticed that the disjointedness [of this letter] is the result of my good will to write a lot about this.
[...] With best wishes, Yours,
Frantík. –

10| See the previous letter from Sammer to Milča of 25 August 1931.
11| George Herbert, the 5th Earl of Carnarvon (1866–1923), was, among other things, a collector of Egyptian antiquities and the financial backer of the Egyptologist Howard Carter in the search for Tutankhamun's tomb and its excavation in the Valley of the Kings in 1922.
12| Thomas Gainsborough (1727–88) was a leading eighteenth-century British painter of portraits and landscapes.

Excursus 2 | Spain and the Maghreb, 1933

After leaving the Le Corbusier–Jeanneret atelier and Paris, František Sammer set off for Spain and the Maghreb. The journey, which he took with his partner, Agnes Larsen, was a landmark between Sammer's work at 35 rue de Sèvres and the beginning of his independent career as a professional architect. From the Maghreb, the young couple headed straight to West Kirby, an English coastal town near Liverpool, where Sammer was going to work on a competition entry for an urban plan for Antwerp.

A letter from Sammer to his parents. AMP.
Toledo, 15 March 1933

Dear Dad, Mum and Honza. –
This evening I leave Toledo, where I've spent the past two days. –
I began my visit to Spain with Barcelona. I began to get interested on the journey between the Pyrenees and the sea. – It was night and the moon was shining very brightly. – But in the morning, when I awoke in the train, the picturesqueness of nature and architecture was supplemented by colours. I first saw oranges. – [...] And then Barcelona: functioning disorder and filthy splendour. – A warm reception by my friend Sert, trips to the surrounding area and, fish and crabs and wine and oranges for lunch – the best things I have ever eaten in my whole life. – Then came Valencia, a city that gives you an inkling of Andalusia. From Valencia to Madrid, a very clean city, just as magnificent as the preceding one, but more orderly. – Again, welcomed by friends, and a visit to the Prado with its famous Velázquezes and an El Greco I'd never seen before. –
In the afternoon: from Madrid to the Escorial, a very nice little town for daytrips in the Sierra de Guadarrama. Again, travelled by train, which was very amusing, with merry people. Before they begin to eat, they ask if their neighbour would like to have a taste. – And then the Escorial, a former monastery, now a secondary school and private flats. Beautifully maintained, first-class architecture. There is still snow in the Sierras. – In the evening we ran through the Escorial. In the morning, up at six o'clock and a run straight into the mountains. – I ran up in three hours, waded through the snow, and ran down before the clock struck ten. – A visit to the library and the church and in the afternoon, we left for Toledo. –
Toledo, the city-museum. – The people keeping shop, making marzipan and weapons. – The same work as in the Middle Ages. The city is not well maintained, which makes it even more picturesque. From the surrounding hills, full of vineyards and olive groves, a splendid view of that beautiful medieval town rising up on a promontory surrounded by the River Tagus on three sides. – A magnificent cathedral, the El Greco Museum and his house, and the Alcázar, where there is a military museum.
In the morning three street urchins attached themselves to us, and showed us absolutely everything. – We wandered everywhere, every little place. – In the evening, a walk to the other bank of the river Tagus with beautiful views of the town. – But ultimately the second evening arrived too and we are leaving – for new stories and things to admire. – Our next destination is Córdoba, then Granada and Seville, where we will see bullfights. – Then Málaga, Algeciras, crossing through the Strait of Gibraltar and on to Tétouan, which must, according to Pierre Jeanneret, be seen. – And then to London for two or three days, and to Liverpool for work, where I'll stay till the end of May. But I'll return home in May, so that on the first of June I can go to Moscow for the congress. – I hope that we'll all see one another for a few days and that we'll have enough time to talk. –
I will definitely write to you from England. – But not from Spain, I don't think, because there really is not enough time.

Many greetings,
Frantík

^ Photograph from Spain.
Contact print, 6 × 8.7 cm. SAAA.

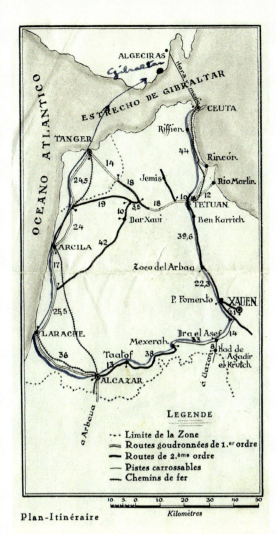

^ Itinerary of František Sammer and Agnes Larsen's travels in north Morocco. AMP.

1| Xauen, also known in Spanish as Chefchauen, Chefchaouen or Chauen or Chaouen.

2| A short version of the Spanish name of the city of Alcazarquivir, meaning the big castle, today's El-Ksar el Kebir.

A letter from Sammer to his sister, Milča. AMP.

26 March 1933, Rio Martin [today's Martil Valley]

Dear Milána,
This morning we arrived here in Rio Martin from Tétouan, in search of sun and sea. Rio Martin is a little seaside village with a lovely beach. We'll stay here for a few days. Why am I writing you this letter? Some Spanish women infuriated me. This is what happened: Agnes and I bought three beautiful eels for 0.50 peseta, about 1.50 Czech crowns. I took the eels home and told the women to cook them. But I had to kill the eels because the women found them repulsive. – So, I thought about you, and how you would cook them. Their kitchen stove only uses charcoal and they only eat salad, fried things and steaks done rare. – One day, Agnes and I had had enough of that, so we bought half a litre of denatured alcohol. I made a tripod from wire and on an aluminium plate we fried twelve eggs with onion and stuffed ourselves very nicely. –

That was in Tétouan. I have to write to you about how things really are with our travels. – I last wrote to you from Toledo. – From Toledo [we travelled] to Córdoba and from Córdoba to Granada. Those are beautiful cities, except that they're not at all adapted to a modern way of life. The streets are unsuited to modern motor traffic. That is also why the city remains as it was hundreds of years ago and beside it, a modern city is beginning to be built. – But that is a phenomenon only of the main cities like Seville, Barcelona, Valencia. – Córdoba and Granada are museum cities. Granada with the Alhambra, a Moorish palace of fairy-tale splendour. The city is located below the Sierra Nevada (Snowy Mountains), which shine all day because of their glaciers. – Life in such a town is like it is in rural Bohemia, in, say, the town of Rokycany. – From Granada we travelled to Algeciras, a small town in the Strait of Gibraltar. There, we boarded a steamboat and sailed to Ceuta, about one hour and thirty minutes away. – We spent two days in Ceuta, the main port of Spanish Morocco. From Ceuta [we went] to Tétouan, an original African town, 50 per cent Arab. Very interesting walks through the town, with all of its oriental life and never-ending sun, despite the fact that astronomical spring began a few days ago. –

This morning, as I mentioned, we arrived here in Rio Martin to bask in the sun and get our fill of swimming. – Now, I am going to stop writing and go out and get some fresh air. – Now I have taken some fresh air. There is a strong wind and it wasn't possible to take off my clothes, but I hope that it will be great tomorrow. –

This morning we see that it won't be better and we're leaving for Tétouan with the intention of leaving at noon for Xauen.[1] – We are buying tickets for the bus and now we are drinking coffee. –

I have drawn a small map for you, showing the trip that we will go on in an hour.
Tétouan–Xauen by bus,
Xauen–Alcazar[2] on horseback,
because it is uninhabited, and without roads, one rises through the steppe at the beginning of a desert. –

From Xauen to Mexerah, it is about 50 km; and from Mexerah to Alcazar another 50 km. – It will, I hope, be interesting because it will show us what life is like in Africa.
From Alcazar to Larache, 36 km by bus.
From Larache to Arcila [today's Asilah], 45 km by bus.
From Arcila to Tangier, 50 km by bus.
From Tangier to Gibraltar, by steamer.
We have to be in Gibraltar on 4 April; today is 28 March.
Our holidays are wonderful, but we're already talking about Liverpool and looking forward to our friends and work. –

I have taken quite a few photographs, and when I have everything developed and printed, I will send you all some pictures. –

We don't know anything at all about what's going on in the rest of the world and we're not even very interested. But I'd like to know how things are back home. – I am alive and

A postcard from Sammer to his brother, Jenda. AMP.

26 March 1933, a postcard from Tétouan

Many greetings from Tétouan.
Frantík. –

Continuation of the letter from p. 161.

well, and would be happy if you all wrote to me in Liverpool, telling me how you're all doing, because it will be a month since I last had news of you. –
Before I left Paris, I arranged everything so that I'd receive replies in Liverpool, and there I will actually see how my affairs are going. – I'm hoping for the best. Of course, I will write to you about all of that and will determine the exact dates.
Because, as you know, the congress is being organized in Moscow and I'd like to play some role in that. – I will definitely manage to. – If not as a member of the Czechoslovak group of architects [within the CIRPAC],[3] then I will definitely arrange something with Le Corbusier or the Association des [écrivains et] artistes révolutionnaires in Paris. – But I will write more about that to you later.
I'll sign off now, because I have to write a few lines home. –

Kisses to you all,
Francek. –

F. S. c/o Gordon Stephenson
Liverpool School of Architecture
Liverpool. –

3| For details, see p. 84.
4| Dámaso Berenguer y Fusté (1873–1953) was a Spanish general and politician, a leading figure in the conquest of Morocco in the reign of Alfonso XIII. In reward for occupying Xauen on 14 October 1920, he was made 1st Count of Xauen.
5| For more about Josef Špalek and Jaromír Krejcar in the Soviet Union, see p. 122.

162

Excursus 2 | Spain and the Maghreb, 1933

A postcard from Sammer to his brother, Jenda. AMP.

29 March 1933

Dear Honza,
We are now in Xauen. This city is interesting because it's hidden in the mountains and populated mostly by Arabs. Until 1920, no Christian had crossed the ramparts that fortify it. No one even knew where it was located. – General Berenguer[4] conquered it with the [Spanish] Foreign Legion. – The only connection by road is to Tétouan. To get to other towns one has to ride on horseback all day over inhospitable mountains. Tomorrow we are going on horseback to EL KSAR KBIR [today's El-Ksar el Kebir, previously mentioned as Alcazar] and will continue to Arcila and Tangier. –
Many greetings Frantík. ––

A letter to Sammer from his parents in Pilsen. SAAA.
(His father's words are here in roman type, his mother's in italics)

Pilsen, 27 March 1933

Dear Franti,
The postcard from your travels in Africa just arrived. The suitcase has been here for about five days. You didn't send the keys for it; we had to force it open at customs and the lock was damaged there. Mum hung out the clothes today and we await word whether something is to be done with those things.
Yesterday, Mr Pávek told me at our shop that some woman there was asking about you, when you would be coming. Her son apparently wrote to Corbus. whether he would see him and received a reply that he should certainly come. She wanted to know the terms and conditions. Apparently she's a Jew. I hope, dear Franti, that you win your 'Liverpool' competition with a lot of money, because it is needed. Have you already written to Professor Soukup? I don't know whether you have your things, your passport and so on, ready for Russia. Mum said that young Špalek, Krejcar's partner in Prague,[5] is unemployed so he is also going to the congress in Russia and already has his passport. Aunt Anči visited us for a few days. She had been ill and was on sick leave.
It is already lovely here now, and the sun is warming everything up. You're probably baking in Africa. Last week your dad and I went to a talk about Africa; there were 200 pictures; before that, an employee of Alliance gave a talk on the same subject for a while, so we have some idea. We wish you much success in Liverpool and are looking forward to seeing you.
Greetings, Mum

<< Agnes Larsen in a hotel room. Photograph 5.4 × 8.4 cm. SAAA.
< Valencia. Contact print, 3 × 4 cm. SAAA.

'Just now in the street below our hotel windows, a Gypsy girl is dancing to the rhythm of a drum beat'.

Agnes Larsen, in a letter from Valencia to Honolulu, 11 March 1933. Quoted in Larsen, *Graffiti*, p. 216 (see n. 122).

'In the afternoon: from Madrid to the Escorial […] Again, travelled by train, which was very amusing, with merry people. Before they begin to eat, they ask if their neighbour would like to have a taste'.

Sammer in a letter to Pilsen, 15 March 1933. AMP.

< Madrid and a journey to the surrounding area, 1933. Contact prints, 2.6 × 4 cm. SAAA.

Excursus 2 | Spain and the Maghreb, 1933

^ Sierra de Guadarrama, 1933. Contact prints, 2.6 × 4 cm. SAAA.

'There is still snow in the Sierras. – In the evening we ran through the Escorial. In the morning, up at six o'clock and run straight into the mountains. – I ran up in three hours, waded through the snow, and ran down before the clock struck ten. –'

Sammer in a letter to Pilsen, 15 March 1933. AMP.

v Sierra de Guadarrama and El Escorial, 1933. Photographs, 7.5 × 5.1 cm. SAAA.

165

∧ Toledo, 1933. Contact prints, 2.6 × 4 cm. SAAA.

'I'll remember three small boys we made friends with while rambling through the crooked streets. They wanted to practice French, so became our guides, pointing out El Greco's house, a Catholic church built as a synagogue centuries ago, and other interesting places'.

Larsen, *Graffiti*, p. 217 (see n. 122).

∨ Córdoba, Plaza del Potro and a boy in the street. Contact prints, 2.6 × 4 cm. SAAA.

'Once upon a time, Córdoba must have been glorious. […] Today, in 1933, beggars are everywhere. The poverty and lack of sanitation is appalling. Every third person seems to have some illness. Little children with sores follow us constantly, and old people stand silent, with cheerless expressions and palms held out'.

Agnes Larsen, in a letter from Córdoba to her family in Honolulu, 16 March 1933. Quoted in Larsen, *Graffiti*, p. 218 (see n. 122).

Excursus 2 | Spain and the Maghreb, 1933

'Granada is famous for two things: the Gypsies living in comparative luxury in caves dug into the rocky hillside, and the Alhambra, a Moorish palace and fortress built 700 years ago'.

Agnes Larsen in a letter from Córdoba to Honolulu, 19 March 1933. Quoted in Larsen, *Graffiti*, p. 219 (see n. 122).

> Agnes Larsen in Granada, 1933. Contact print, 5.5 × 8.1 cm. SAAA.

The Port of Algeciras, 1933.
∧ Contact prints, 3 × 4 cm, and a photograph, 5.3 × 8.3 cm. SAAA.
∨ Contact prints, 5.7 × 8.6 cm. SAAA.

Excursus 2 | Spain and the Maghreb, 1933

Photographs from the trip through north Morocco.
∧ Photograph, 5.2 × 8.2 cm, and contact prints, 5.4 × 8.4 cm. SAAA.
∨ Contact prints, 5.4 × 8.3 cm. SAAA.

'We sketched, and painted watercolors, and gaped in awe at the scenery. Hills of brilliant green vegetation showed patches of bare earth, the color of red lead, cut by winding, unpaved roads of the same red; seascapes of wave-beaten crags, towns and hamlets of simple blue or white houses, hardly touched by our so-called "progress" – all of it under that enormous vault of sapphire sky'.

Agnes Larsen's recollection in Larsen, *Graffiti*, pp. 220–21 (see n. 122).

169

Excursus 3 | Japan 1935

František Sammer was in Japan two times. His first visit was in 1935; his second in late 1937 and early 1938. From there he moved on to Pondicherry, India, for work. He sent letters with his first vivid descriptions of Japan to his family in Pilsen and to Le Corbusier and Charlotte Perriand. He was probably the first architect of Le Corbusier's circle, with the exception of the two Japanese architects, Junzo Sakakura and Kunio Maekawa, of course, to see Japan. He arranged his visit with the help of his friends from the Paris atelier, and his observations of the country he was discovering were made in relation to the shared worldview of this social network – the 'Le Corbusier galaxy'. In this respect, Sammer's letter to Perriand of 22 July 1935, which is published here for the first time, is exceptional.

A letter from Sammer to his aunt. AMP.

The *Siberia Maru*[1] – the Sea of Japan, 2 July 1935

^ Photo from Japan. Negative, 6 × 9 cm. SAAA.

Dear Auntie,
I hope that in your goodness you will forgive me for not having written to you for so long. – You know, Auntie, that our life in Moscow is so intense that even Dad rarely gets reports from me about all my activities. – Now I am on holiday and enjoying a few days of rest on a ship, so I can write to Milča, Dad and you about our experiences, which will definitely interest you – judging from myself, because I cannot stop being ecstatic. – Auntie, it began when Agnes Larsen, the girl whom I was in Paris and Moscow with, left last year for Honolulu to be with her mother, who was ill. – In December, I think it was, her mother died. – Because Agnes wants to keep working here in Moscow, we decided to meet this summer in Japan. – And so it happened that on 19 June I left Moscow, travelled for nine days by the Trans-Siberian Express to Vladivostok, and on 30 June we sailed for Japan. – Today is the second day of our voyage. Tomorrow morning we will be in Tsuruga, a Japanese port, and in the evening we'll be in Tokyo at our Japanese friend's, a professor of art history at Tokyo University. –[2]
Agnes left Honolulu, Hawaii (in the Pacific) on 30 June, and will be in Yokohama on 7 July. – We'll remain together (it's been 11 months since we last saw each other) in Japan until the end of the month and during that time we hope to see many, many interesting things. So – you see, Auntie, one merry, beautiful time of my life has begun. –
It begun, that is, on the 19th. – in the afternoon we departed Moscow and on the third day we were travelling over the Urals until Siberia started – a marvellously beautiful land full of forests and meadows, of a very different character. – The main reason is that in various places the Siberian railway goes through different latitudes – in the south it was already summer but when we headed in a more northerly direction summer was only just beginning. – There were days when we didn't leave the taiga at all (the old-growth forest of Siberia), where the only signs of civilization, apart from our train, were the signalman's cabins and workers along the railway line. – We travelled through large, lively towns and over enormous Siberian rivers. – By the way, exploiting those huge bountiful fields with black earth began a long time ago and now one can see the vast, superbly organized state-owned farms and collectives, and tractor stations with large stocks of tractors. – At the stations we drank baked milk (it is baked in an oven and looks and tastes like condensed milk (like we have back home in tins). – We ate eggs and rye bread with butter. It had become quite a bore in the restaurant car and one didn't feel much like eating, because, after all, being in a railway carriage all day is imprisonment – albeit splendidly comfortable. – And so we were very glad when we could finally sense the end in Vladivostok.
And that is actually where the Orient began, because there are many Koreans, Chinese and Japanese in the city. – And then, every city like that – especially an oriental port (I recall Tangier)[3] – has its own exotic character. – You know, Auntie, everything was new to me and I was having such a good time that I didn't even notice how weary I'd become. – My legs hurt even now. – On the evening of the second day, we set off. – Again, there

1| A steamship that sailed between Vladivostok (USSR) and Tsuruga (Japan).
2| Professor Tominaga (see pp. 114 and 133).
3| See Excursus 2.

∧ Photos from Japan, saved in an envelope with 6 × 9 cm negatives developed in Ginza, Tokyo, on 22–24 July 1935. SAAA.

were many things to explore and experience. – On every ship one is very well taken care off, but especially on that Japanese ship it seemed to me one is even more pampered. You know, for more than two years now I haven't been in an environment like this, and so everything is new again. ---

The Japanese are marvellous – so clean that they seem like birds to me. – I also really like how they move amongst themselves. – Most of them still wear the kimono, but also European clothes. And Japanese women – they are so charming, Auntie, that it is quite difficult to imagine – I mean of course girls in the kimono. – Also how they conduct themselves with such politeness. – I spent a day as the only passenger in second class. – The boy waiting the table always laid it so extremely beautifully, watered the beautiful flower in the pot and went to look for me to tell me that my meal was ready. During the second day, we dropped anchor in two ports in Korea – Yuko [*sic*] and Shinsen [*sic*]. – We took on a few passengers and a bit of cargo. I saw how the Japanese say farewell – music was played on a steamship and it echoed in the mountains. Between the steamer and the shore, strips of paper were stretched out, extremely long, and as the steamer set sail, boys on the shore kept tying additional strips on until, by their weight, they tore. – The Japanese bowed, and waved handkerchiefs, and children waved pennants. – Simply magnificent. –

And now we are resting – for one day – I bathe in the evening in a Japanese bathroom with terribly hot water, and admire the Japanese who eat terribly beautiful things. – Rice and every kind of vegetable possible, fish and other things. – And how beautifully they lay the table – when I am in Tokyo I will also eat only with Japanese people. –

Now, they are still feeding us English style – very well. – You know, Auntie, as soon as Agnes and I meet up, we want to visit all the big cities in Hondo [the historical name for

^ Photos from Japan, saved in an envelope with 6 × 9 cm negatives developed in Ginza, Tokyo, on 22–24 July 1935. SAAA.

Honshu]: Tokyo – Yokohama, Kobe, Kyoto, Osaka – and many others, which have some importance in the history of art. – We'll be able to do it easily in a month, and we'll have lots of time left for excursions to Mount Fuji, and for swimming and sport. – Well, and then we will return home to Moscow – to work. Agnes will sculpt and I will build. – But I will write to you again before that. – You know, Auntie, I have one book[4] with me, which you once gave me for Christmas when I was nine or ten years old. – It is a book about Japan and Dad sent it to me. – But it was written in 1913 and in those 22 years everything has changed so much that the book makes me smile when I read it. – And now I also see that Mr Svojsík, who wrote the book, didn't understand Japan very well. – But there are things in the book, which, as documents, are still of value. – And so it is nice to be informed. – What is interesting is that I found a whole essay about Japanese art that Svojsík translated from a Baedeker [guidebook] and other sources. – That suggests he is quite pitiful, because there are many other better authorities. –
Well, that's the end of my gossip and the end of this letter. –
Many greetings, Auntie,
Frantík. –

A letter from František Sammer to Charlotte Perriand. AChP.

Tokyo, 22 July 1935

My dear Charlotte,
This country of 1,001 Sakakuras[5] is amazing. You have made a big mistake by not coming, and you should realize that it's something you must experience! We have been here a number of days already and we're still discovering things and are afraid that when

4| Alois Svojsík, *Japonsko a jeho lid*, Prague: A. Svojsík, 1913.
5| Junzo Sakakura, a colleague and friend from the Paris atelier, who was Japanese and thus a representative of his country in the Le Corbusier circle. See pp. 52–54 onwards in this book.
6| Sammer was one of the first architects from 35 rue de Sèvres, apart from the Japanese assistants of course, who had been to Japan, and he wrote about the country in letters to Le Corbusier and to Perriand. For context, see pp. 114–119.

Excursus 3 | Japan 1935

> A letter from Sammer in Japan to Perriand in Paris, 22 July 1935. AChP. See pp. 114–119.

we leave we'll be more ignorant than when we arrived. – We decided that we'll come here one more time. – What can I tell you? – You know I came here with Agnes. We're having a great time. And Japan? It's fabulous. – We're experiencing the landscape (yes, the landscape chiefly), then the fish, which we are stuffing ourselves with, the architecture, all the people we meet, mainly in the countryside. – Everything here has its inner life, and it is nature where it all takes place. – One is almost afraid to modify nature (parks, site surveys for temples and houses, the people themselves, with their dwellings and kimonos, wooden shoes and so on and so forth). It is truly moving to see it now and to imagine all the good work one Sakakura [Japanese modern architect] can do, but, at the same time, how many horrible things the others have done. – There are remarkably good things in the area of modern equipment, but so much has to be changed. Japan is the land of purity and a country where architecture – such as we [architects from Le Corbusier's circle] understand it – is only a very natural development of one remarkable tradition. –[6] I am quite curious to know how Saka will reply to all my comments and observations, which I am prepared to tell him or write to him one day. – I also have a certain idea about resemblances between the Greek and the Japanese [cultures]. – I notice it only in some things – not in general, because I know very little about Japan. – I'd like to study all of this a bit more seriously as soon as I return to Moscow. –

◁ A letter from Sammer in Japan to Perriand in Paris, 22 July 1935. AChP. See pp. 114–119.

But, dear friend, despite all these good folks – many good friends – mainly Tominaga and Maekawa!!![7] – what a decent man!!!
P.T.O.
I feel good when I think about being among the Bolsheviks again. Honestly!
And listen to this: I am invited to Mr Raymond's – the one who copied the Errázuriz house for himself.[8] For about five days I will work with Maekawa and his team on a housing unit in Pondicherry. –[9] I think that it will also give me new strength and energy in architecture – oh, how I need it, dear friend. – And, as it's in a beautiful house and we can do sports, swim and so on, I shall be very happy. – I would like to write to Corbu from there. – It concerns an invitation from Mr Raymond. – And I am going to get involved in this because I think that it is very important that Corbu see Japan[10] – and because I have an idea that we could link Japan with his trip to the congress in Moscow[11] – what do you think, dear friend? And perhaps, if this seems good to you, I can tell you that Raymond is a first-rate fellow – truly. – But I will write all of that to Corbu in a more orderly way. If you wish to tell him before he receives my letter, think about it carefully!! But I don't believe that it's a bad idea, especially considering that Sakakura will also be in Japan!! Tell this to Saka!! Corbu could do some good work in Japan and since Raymond will want to arrange all this, I think that our dear Corbu could take a good rest, which he needs, I believe. – You see, dear friend, there are ideas that could, in my opinion, work. – We will talk about all this in Moscow. –[12]

Many greetings to Pierre Jeanneret, and hugs and kisses to you. –
F.–

[7] Kunio Maekawa (1905–86) was an important Japanese architect and a colleague from the atelier in Paris. See 'The Le Corbusier Galaxy' part of this publication and p. 114 onwards in the book.
[8] Sammer is referring to the disagreement between Le Corbusier and Raymond about Le Corbusier's project for the Errázuriz house in Chile and the house Raymond built for himself and his wife in Karuizawa, Japan. See 'The Le Corbusier Galaxy' part of this publication, pp. 114–119.
[9] The first phase of work on the Golconde dormitory.
[10] For quotations from Sammer's letters to Le Corbusier, in which he urges him to visit Japan, see pp. 116–119.
[11] Here it is unclear what congress in Moscow he means. It is of course possible that Sammer was by this time already acquainted with the preparations for the First All-Union Congress of Soviet Architects, which eventually took place in 1937. See 'The Le Corbusier Galaxy' part of this publication, p. 116.
[12] Perriand visited the Soviet Union for the last time in 1934; despite Sammer's repeated urgings she never returned there.
[13] Chronologically this idea appears backwards, but Sammer is probably saying from his point of view the development seems like this because he knew the modern architecture of Europe first.
[14] The painter Sato, see 'The Le Corbusier Galaxy' part of this publication, p. 114.

Excursus 3 | Japan 1935

A letter from Sammer to his father. AMP.
(Sammer's words are printed here in roman type and Agnes's, translated from French, are in italics)

SS *Siberia Maru*, 27 July 1935

Dear Dad,
We are returning from our Japanese holidays.
It was really lovely. – Agnes and I were reunited and we explored [Japan] for almost a month, still surrounded by lots of friends. – We knew three of them from Paris and made a few new ones, Japanese, in Tokyo, as well as Mr. Raymond, his wife and their young son. – Mr. Raymond is Czech with American citizenship, the Honorary Consul of the Czechoslovak Republic in Tokyo – Mrs. Raymond is French. – We had a great time at their place and spent many lovely days with them in Tokyo, especially at their home in Hayama, by the sea, where we were their guests for a few days. – We were invited to Karuizawa for a longer stay – it is the Raymonds' second home, in the mountains. – But the visa could not be extended and we were forced to leave Tokyo on 25 July. –
Our Japanese friends were also doing their best to make sure we experienced as many nice things as possible, so we didn't have to worry about what to do next during our whole stay in Japan. – We saw many lovely things – in museums and outside Tokyo, in Kamakura, Nikko and other places. We weren't bored for a second. – And yet we had a good rest and a change of air, and are returning to the Soviet Union with nice memories. – I am already looking forward to working again. – Now things will go even better because there are two of us. –
Japan is a very lovely country and the people are great. – I am really glad that I had the good fortune to see all of that. I will go once again at the next opportunity. –
It's somewhat of a pity that we could not reach an agreement with Píďa [a relative from the family], because I think that he would be happy with us in Japan. – Well, he'll still get to go one day. – You'd also like it, Dad.
<u>Too bad we didn't have more money</u>. But without money, it was still really, really lovely. – I wrote a bit to Milča and Pepa [Sammer's siblings] about what I saw, because the first few days I had a bit of time. – But afterwards there was no time. – We travelled around Japan, visiting friends, museums, theatres, even the cinema, bathed in the sea, merged with the Japanese landscape, made discoveries in architecture – in short, we lived extremely intensely and <u>we will never forget it</u>. – You know, Dad, I'm unable to write to you about everything we saw and experienced, because you and I haven't seen each other for so long that I simply cannot imagine whether you'd be interested in the form I'd use to do that. – In general, you probably know my first impressions of Japan. And they are roughly the kind of impressions that I am leaving with from Japan. – We were here too briefly to have more genuine impressions. – Of course we saw many things that we didn't like – but those were things that stem directly from the Japanese political system and from the capitalist regime that rules here like in other countries.
The nation itself is marvellous!! Culture at a high level. – Modern Japan is equipped with superb technology, made a reality by people who know their jobs. – The artistic tradition of Japan is exceedingly rich and [illegible, perhaps enabled] modern Japan to experience a superb transformation. With its purity of intention and purity of forms, the traditional architecture follows directly on from the modern architecture of Europe.[13] – Thanks to my friends Sato,[14] a painter, Maekawa, an architect and Tominaga, a professor and critic, we saw a great deal of beautiful modern art. –
Well then – greetings to you, Dad, and write to me in Moscow. – I will be very happy if you're interested in our trip and if I can write to you in a way that will please you. –
Frantík. –

Dear František's Father, I am absolutely happy to be together with František again, and to be able to return to Moscow with him. Our holidays in Japan were so lovely, the country and our Japanese friends too.
Sincerely, Agnes

Excursus 4 | The Caucasus, summer 1936

In 1936, František Sammer, Agnes Larsen and a group of friends set out for the Caucasus Mountains with the aim of climbing Mount Elbrus and spending a few days at the Black Sea. At one point on the journey, Larsen, the only woman on the trip, left the group and travelled by herself via Tbilisi to Batumi, Georgia, where she again met up with the group at the end of the trip. Evidence of the intensity of the experiences from this journey appears in Larsen's recollections and also in Sammer's description of the trip in a draft of a letter to his friend Timofei Ignatevich Makarychev, that he wrote more than 30 years later. In 1968, he wrote about his vivid memories of the summer 1936, as he had been telling them as a bedtime story to his little son Petr.

A draft of a letter from Sammer to T. I. Makarychev, spring 1968. AMP.

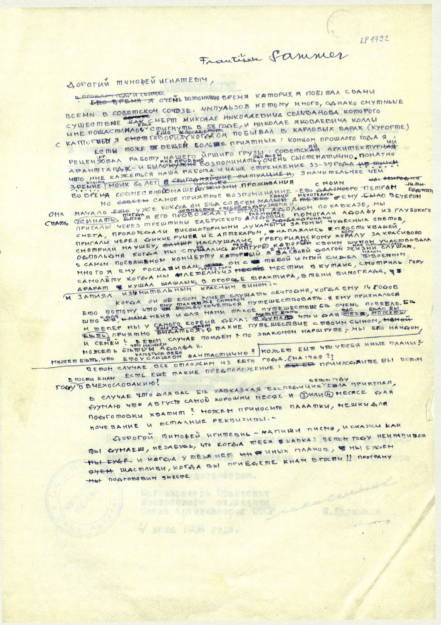

But the most pleasant memory is with my [son] Petr. It began when he was really small and didn't want to sleep in the evening. And so I took him, together with you and friends and the donkey Adolf, across the Caucasus. We were leaping over the crevices of an Elbrus glacier, and were helping Adolf [a donkey] out of the deep snow. We walked through alpine meadows with rhododendrons and magical flowers. We leapt over white-water rapids, and drank prostokvasha [thick soured milk] with Aptekar[1], looked at [Mount] Ushba, listened intensely to Gregorian chants on the beautiful afternoon while we were going down to the River Enguri, which, with its roaring, participated in the most sacred concert I have ever heard in my long life. I told him a great deal. He sat with you and I in a little military aircraft as we flew over the mountains from Mestia to Kutaisi, looking at Mount Ararat, ate shashlik and washed it down with superb red wine in the garden of a tavern in the shade of a vineyard.

1| Aptekar, a rare surname, may be a nickname, suggesting perhaps that this travelling companion was a pharmacist.

˄ Photos from the trip to the Caucasus. In the third photo, Mount Kazbek and a view across the town of Stepantsminda, with the Gergeti Trinity Church on the mountain ridge to the left, August 1936.
Contact prints, 2.9 × 4 cm. SAAA. Photo: Agnes Larsen. SAAA.

'Out on the street the sun shone hot and bright. Women wore colorful print dresses. A newsboy hurried up the sidewalk calling out the names of his papers. I'd never seen that before in the Soviet Union. A fountain in a square shot its water spout high into the air. Men tipped their hats to women [...] Some men on the sidewalk sold articles from glass-topped boxes'.

Agnes Larsen recalling a visit to Tbilisi in summer 1936. Larsen, *Graffiti*, pp. 385–86 (see n. 122).

˅ View of the old streets of Tbilisi, August 1936.
Contact prints, 2.9 × 4 cm. Photo: Agnes Larsen. SAAA.

177

Excursus 4 | The Caucasus, summer 1936

'The road ascended. At a point where I could see across the river, I had to stop. From the rushing yellow water, the precipice on the opposite bank rose several hundred feet straight up to buildings constructed at its very edge. It looked as though they were an extension of the cliff. Into the sheer rock wall steps had been dug. I could see people walking up and down them. To the left, at the bend in the river, an ancient church with a golden, cone-shaped roof on its tower, seemed to have sprouted from the earth'.

Agnes Larsen recalling a visit to Tbilisi in summer 1936. Larsen, *Graffiti*, pp. 386–87 (see n. 122).

^ View of the old town of Tbilisi, August 1936.
Contact prints, 2.9 × 4 cm. Photo: Agnes Larsen. SAAA.

v Agnes Larsen, František Sammer and Antonín Urban(?) at the Black Sea, probably in Batumi.
Contact prints, 3 × 4 cm. SAAA.

178

Timeline

1907	27 October	František Jan Sammer is born in Pilsen, the youngest of three children (he has a sister, Miloslava and a brother, Josef). His father, Jan Sammer (1867–1943), is the son of a miller; he is a business man and member of the National Democratic Party. His mother, Růžena, née Hlavatá, is the daughter of a miller.
1914	28 July	Austria-Hungary declares war on Serbia, thus starting the First World War.
1918		František Sammer's mother dies.
	28 October	The Czechoslovak Republic is formed.
	11 November	The Armistice is signed, ending the First World War.
1920		Jan Sammer, František's half-brother (from his father's second marriage), is born. (In the correspondence referred to in this publication he appears as 'Honza' or 'Jenda'.)
1923–27		František Sammer attends the Czech School of Civil Engineering (a secondary technical school for architecture) in Pilsen. From 1926, his form teacher is Karel Lhota, Adolf Loos's right-hand man. In the summer months, Sammer gains practical experience at the firms of several architects and civil engineers, including those of František Fajer in Hořovice, František Strnad in Prague and the Prague branch of Pittel & Brauswetter.
1924		Le Corbusier publishes his most influential book, *Vers une architecture*. In Czechoslovakia, too, architects soon become acquainted with the original French edition and with excerpts published in periodicals. (A complete Czech edition will not be published until 2005.)
1927	21 June	Sammer graduates from the Czech State Technical School in Pilsen.
1927–28		Sammer completes two semesters at the Faculty of Architecture and Civil Engineering of the Czech Technical University in Prague (today, the Czech Technical University in Prague – ČVUT), while working at the architectural practices of Vojtěch Krch and Josef Záruba-Pfeffermann in Prague.
1928–30		During his 18 months of military service, Sammer makes the acquaintance of the architect Jindřich Krise (1908–89). He graduates from the school for reserve officers in Košice (Slovakia) and an army engineers course in Komárno (Slovakia) and Litoměřice (Bohemia). He was promoted to the rank of sergeant with an officer's exam and was a member of the 5th Mountain Battalion, Ružomberok (Slovakia).
1928		Le Corbusier first visits the Soviet Union and, in the same year, wins the competition for the design of the Centrosoyuz, the building of the Central Union of Consumer Cooperatives in Moscow.
1929		Dziga Vertov makes the experimental documentary film *Man with a Movie Camera*.
	October	The stockmarket crashes on Wall Street and the Great Depression begins.
1930–31		Sammer works as a road construction foreman at the Prague firm of Václav Kratochvíl.
1930		Ernst May leaves Germany for Moscow with his team of architects to design newly-established Soviet cities.
1931		Walter Benjamin publishes *Kleine Geschichte der Photographie* (A Short History of Photography).
	April	František Sammer arrives in Paris.

1931

May	Sammer begins to work at the 'atelier', the architectural practice of Le Corbusier and Pierre Jeanneret at 35 rue de Sèvres.
6 July–14 August	Sammer completes a French course at the Sorbonne.
3 August	Sammer registers his work for the first time in the 'Livre noir', a record of the drawings made at the atelier, with a perspective drawing of the Swiss Pavilion, no. FLC 15334.
August	On his way to Great Britain, Sammer, from land-locked Czechoslovakia, encounters the sea for the first time in his life.
October	Together with Charlotte Perriand, Junzo Sakakura and Edmond Wanner, Sammer travels to Cologne to install an interior at the Internationale Raumausstellung (International Interior Design Exhibition – IRA).
October–December	The team at 35 rue de Sèvres works intensively on a competition design for the Palace of the Soviets in Moscow.
	Sammer befriends other members of the atelier, particularly Gordon Stephenson, Alex Adam and Jane West.
	Sammer makes the acquaintance of an American sculptress of Norwegian descent, Agnes Larsen.

1932

January	Sammer joins in work on urban plans for Algiers.
1 March 1932	The Le Corbusier–Jeanneret atelier begins paying him a salary of 1,000 francs a month.
17 March 1932	Perriand travels to the Soviet Union for the first time, returning before 2 May. Together with Sammer, she plans to leave for work in the Soviet Union and create the 'Le Corbusier Group'.
29 May	An interview with Le Corbusier, conducted by Zdenka Watterson, is published in the *Prager Presse*. The interview was in fact held with Sammer standing in for Le Corbusier.
Summer	Alone at 35 rue de Sèvres, Sammer supervises work at the sites of three main projects: the Swiss Pavilion in the Cité internationale universitaire de Paris, the Salvation Army building and the apartment building at 24 rue Nungesser-et-Coli.
	Sammer and Larsen's intimate relationship begins.
Autumn	At the atelier, Sammer participates in projects for Algeria and in a competition entry for an urban plan of Stockholm.

1933

March–April	Sammer leaves the Le Corbusier–Jeanneret atelier.
	With Larsen, he travels to Spain and the Maghreb.
April–May	During his stay in West Kirby, England, Sammer works with Gordon Stephenson, Alex Adam and William Holford on a competition entry for an urban plan for Antwerp.
June–July	After a visit to his native Pilsen, Sammer leaves for the Soviet Union.
Late July	Sammer joins the architectural office of Nikolai Kolli in Moscow.
29 July–11 August	The CIAM IV congress is held on the SS *Patris II* and in Greece. The main topic is urban planning and the 'functional city'.
	During the congress, László Moholy-Nagy shoots footage for his film *Architects' Congress*.
November	Larsen is accepted to the All-Russian Academy of Art in Moscow.
11 November	Sammer and Larsen wed, agreeing between themselves that this will be a civil marriage that will only last as long as they are living together in the Soviet Union.
December	For her bust of Karl Marx, intended for mass production, Larsen is awarded First Prize at the All-Russian Academy of Art in Moscow.

1934

January–February	Perriand visits Moscow for a second time.
	At Kolli's office, Sammer works on a competition entry for the Trade Unions Theatre in Moscow.
Spring	Kolli and Sammer win the competition for the Kirovskaya Metro station (today Chistye Prudy), in Moscow.

1934	May	Josep Lluís Sert visits Moscow
	30 July	Stephenson visits Sammer in Moscow. Together, they visit Leningrad (today St Petersburg).
	8 August	Larsen leaves the Soviet Union to look after her ill mother in Honolulu for almost a year.
		At the First Congress of Soviet Writers in Moscow, socialist realism is prescribed as the style artists must follow in the Soviet Union.
	September–October	For their holidays, Sammer and Stephenson set off together to explore some Soviet republics and Greece.
1935	April	Larsen wins the Grand Prize of the Honolulu Academy of Arts for her sculpture *Torso*.
	15 May	The first line of the Moscow Metro is opened.
	June–July	Sammer visits Japan, where he again meets up with Larsen. They meet Antonin and Noémi Raymond and stay at the Raymonds' homes in Karuizawa and in Hayama.
		Sammer tries to arrange a visit by Le Corbusier to Japan and also tries to persuade Perriand to visit.
		H. Girsberger of Zurich publishes the second volume of Le Corbusier and Pierre Jeanneret's *l'Œuvre complète*, which includes an overview of their projects from 1929 to 1934. A number of the drawings and plans reproduced in the volume were made by Sammer while working in the Paris atelier.
1936		The Great Terror begins in the Soviet Union.
		Sammer leaves Kolli's office and begins to work at the Narkomzdrav (People's Commissariat of Public Health) under Moisei Ginzburg.
		Sammer works with Viktor Valeryanovich Kalinin on a project for a sanatorium in Gagra.
	July–August	With Larsen, T. I. Makarychev and other friends, Sammer goes on holiday in the Caucasus and the Black Sea.
	September–October	Sammer travels on business to the 'Soviet Riviera', on the eastern shores of the Black Sea. He visits Yalta and the building site of the Ordzhonikidze Sanatorium in Kislovodsk, a project in which two Czech architects, Josef Špalek and Jaromír Krejcar, took part.
		Sammer plans to move permanently from Moscow to work in Yalta in spring 1937.
	December	Larsen visits her family in Norway for the Christmas holidays.
1937	January–February	Sammer visits Paris, where he again meets up with Larsen and with his friends from Le Corbusier's circle.
	March	Sammer visits his family in Pilsen for the first time in four years.
	April	Sammer takes part in the completion of the first phase of the Gagra sanatorium project.
		Stephenson visits Sammer again in Moscow.
	May	Shortly before her Soviet visa expires, Larsen and Sammer divorce, as they had originally agreed to do.
		Larsen leaves the Soviet Union for Vienna.
	25 May––25 November	The Exposition internationale des arts et techniques dans la vie moderne is held in Paris.
	7 June	Sammer receives a telegram from Antonin Raymond with an offer of employment in Tokyo, and he quickly prepares to leave the Soviet Union.
	15–28 June	In Moscow, the first All-Union Congress of Soviet Architects is held. Despite the tense political situation and the Soviet regime's tight control over the architectural profession, a number of architects from the West take part in the congress, including Frank Lloyd Wright from the United States, Sven Markolius from Sweden and Josef Gočár and Pavel Janák from Czechoslovakia.
	28 June–2 July	The CIAM V congress is held in Paris, with the main topic being 'Dwelling and Recreation'.
	12 July	Sammer arrives in Vienna, where he spends a few days with Larsen, who has remained in Europe for work. Before travelling on to Japan, he stops in Pilsen and Paris.

13 August	Sammer sails from Marseille for Yokohama via Suez and Singapore.	**1937**
September	Sammer begins to work in the office of Antonin Raymond in Tokyo on the project of the Golconde dormitory for the Sri Aurobindo ashram in Pondicherry (at that time part of French India).	
January	Together with Antonin and Noémi Raymond, Sammer travels from Japan to India.	**1938**
February	Sammer and the Raymonds arrive in Pondicherry, joined, shortly after them, by Larsen.	
12–13 March	The Anschluss begins: the Third Reich sends troops to Austria and annexes the country.	
29–30 September	The Munich Agreement is signed, whereby Germany, Italy, France and Great Britain force Czechoslovakia to cede border areas to Germany.	
7 March	Larsen leaves Pondicherry, marking the end of her partnership with Sammer.	**1939**
15 March	The Germans occupy the rump of Czechoslovakia and proclaim the area the Protectorate of Bohemia and Moravia.	
1 September	Together with the Soviets and the Slovaks, the Germans invade Poland, beginning the Second World War in Europe.	
18 October	In a written statement to the Czechoslovak Consulate in Marseille, Sammer volunteers to fight for his country.	
14 June	The Germans enter Paris unopposed.	**1940**
15 June	Perriand sails from Marseille for Japan, where she will live and work until the winter of 1942. (She will maintain her links with Japan until the end of her life.)	
27 September	The Tripartite Pact is signed for the allegedly defensive military alliance of Japan, Nazi Germany and Fascist Italy.	
10 October	In Pondicherry, Sammer fills in and signs an enlistment form for the Czechoslovak Army.	
7 December	The Japanese attack Pearl Harbor, leading the United States to declare war on Japan and to enter the Second World War.	**1941**
22 June	Nazi Germany invades the Soviet Union.	
4 September	Sammer's sister, Miloslava Gschwindová (in the correspondence that appears in this publication she is referred to as 'Milča' or 'Milána'), is guillotined in Berlin for her participation in the anti-fascist resistance.	**1942**
30 October	Sammer joins the East Yorkshire Regiment of the British Army in India. He goes through training at the Royal School of Military Engineering for reserve officers of the Royal Engineers at Khadki in Poona (Pune).	
	Sammer's father dies.	**1943**
5 June	Sammer joins a training battalion of the Corps of Royal Engineers in Lahore, Pakistan.	
5 December	Sammer is promoted to the rank of lieutenant.	
1 November	Sammer goes into battle, commanding a company of engineers in Arakan, Bengal and in Rangoon, Burma.	**1944**
8 May	The Second World War in Europe ends.	**1945**
2 September	The surrender of Japan is signed.	
10 September	Sammer joins in operations to drive out the last of the Japanese Army in Malaya, and is promoted to the rank of captain.	
5 November	Sammer is hospitalized in Singapore for a neglected war wound and lung damage.	
24 December	Sammer is transferred from Singapore to Great Britain, where he is given specialist medical care.	

1946		14 February	Sammer undergoes a lung operation, and then convalesces at Osborne House, a former summer residence of Queen Victoria on the Isle of Wight, in the South of England.
		February	Sammer begins to search for his friends from the Le Corbusier circle, finds out some of their current addresses or telephone numbers and gets in touch with them again when possible.
		June	Sammer begins to design a house with a studio for Larsen in Honolulu. Their correspondence, until December 1947, includes consultation about the project and variant designs.
1947		15 Feburary	Sammer returns to Czechoslovakia.
		4 March	Sammer joins the Czechoslovak Communist Party.
		21 April	Sammer is discharged from the British Army with a pension of £240 a year and the honorary rank of Captain of the British Army.
			For his service in the British Army, Sammer is awarded the Star, the Burma Star, the Defence Medal and the War Medal 1939-45.
		15 August	British rule in India ends, and India declares independence.
1948		25 Feburary	The Communist Party seizes power in Czechoslovakia.
		February	Sammer works on the Master Plan for the Development of Pilsen (Směrný územní plán města Plzně) of the Integrated National Committee of the City of Pilsen, in collaboration with Krise.
		6 March	Sammer marries Ludmila Müllerová, a physician at the Institute of Railway Workers' Health in Pilsen.
		Summer	With Krise, Sammer completes the first draft of the Master Plan for the Development of Pilsen, which will become the basis of their long-term project and of the work of the next generation of town planners.
1949		February –mid-1954	Sammer is employed as an architect and town planner at the Pilsen branch of Stavoprojekt, a state-run system of architecture and engineering offices. His major works include: the Study for the housing estate of Slovany I in Pilsen (1953-56, with other Stavoprojekt architects); a housing complex in the socialist realist style, called the Superblok (c. 1951-55, with Otakar Gschwind, Marta Chvojková, Miloslav Sýkora and Miloslav Volráb); and the Lochotín Amphitheatre in Pilsen (1951-61, together with Stanislav Suda).
1950			Political trials begin in Czechoslovakia.
1954			After more than 280 years of French rule, Pondicherry, together with other French possessions in India, is de facto transferred to the Indian Union.
		July-March 1957	Sammer leaves Stavoprojekt, and has limited opportunities to see his architectural ideas carried out. He continues to focus on town planning, and will devote himself to it in his next places of employment. He is hired as chief architect at the Institute of Military Engineering (Vojenský projektový ústav) in Pilsen.
			Sammer is increasingly persecuted by the regime for having worked with leading figures of the international avant-garde and for having served in the British Army. He breaks off contact with friends abroad.
		14 July	A son, Petr, is born to Ludmila and František Sammer.
1955		October	Le Corbusier makes his one and only visit to Japan.
1956		February	At the 20th Congress of the Communist Party of the Soviet Union, Khrushchev states that Stalin, dead for three years, fostered a 'cult of personality' and a dictatorship; this marks the beginning of the Thaw in the Soviet Union.
		3 November	Sammer writes to the British Embassy in Prague, renouncing, for political reasons, his British Army pension.

March–July 1960	Sammer is employed at the Office of Consulting Engineers for Housing in Pilsen (Generální investor bytové výstavby Plzeň).	1957
July–August	Sammer represents the Union of Architects of the Czechoslovak Republic at the Fifth Congress of the UIA (International Union of Architects), held in Moscow. The success of the Czechoslovak Pavilion at Expo 58, in Brussels, reflects the gradual relaxation of the regime in Czechoslovakia.	1958
July–April 1963	The Czechoslovak Communist regime declares an amnesty for some political prisoners. Sammer is employed in the construction department of the Municipal National Committee in Pilsen.	1960
June–September 1965	Sammer is employed at the School of Mechanical and Electrical Engineering in Pilsen.	1963
October–December 1970 27 August	Sammer is employed at the Office of the Chief Architect of Pilsen, where he again devotes himself to his projects, particularly town planning. He draws up a study for the rebuilding of the centre of Pilsen. Le Corbusier dies.	1965
	Sammer resumes contact with friends abroad.	1966
30 June–6 August 4 December	The Ninth Congress of the UIA is held in Prague and Bratislava. Sammer visits England at the invitation of William Holford and Gordon Stephenson. He then visits France. Pierre Jeanneret dies.	1967
5 January 28 February 21 August	The democratization process known as the Prague Spring begins. Sammer resumes correspondence with friends in Pondicherry and inquires into job opportunities for himself in India. Auroville, an experimental township designed by the architect Roger Anger (1923–2008), and located near Pondicherry, is founded. The Soviet Union leads the Warsaw Pact military intervention in Czechoslovakia.	1968
	The post-Prague Spring leadership introduces 'normalization' policy, that is, the restoration of hard-line Communist rule in Czechoslovakia, including purges, increased censorship, further restrictions on freedom and the infringement of basic human rights.	1969
1 January	Sammer takes his retirement. In post-war Czechoslovakia, Sammer was a founding member of the Association of Czechoslovak Architects (Svaz architektů ČSSR); a member of the Association of Czechoslovak Artists, Chairman of its Pilsen branch; and a member of the examination board for the final exams at the Czech Technical University in Prague, sometimes entrusted with writing up reader's reports for final theses, including those of architects and urban planners from abroad.	1970
Summer	Larsen visits Sammer in Czechoslovakia.	1972
January, March	Sammer corresponds with Pierre-André Emery, Vice President of the newly-established Association Internationale Le Corbusier (AILC) in Geneva.	1973

1973	18 October	Sammer dies in Pilsen and is buried in Letařovice near Český Dub pod Ještědem, in the grave of his wife's family. His name is not engraved on the tombstone.
	17 November	Mirra Alfassa, known as Mère and the Mother, the head of the ashram in Pondicherry, dies.
1989		The Velvet Revolution and the end of the Communist regime in Czechoslovakia occurs.
1992		In Fremantle, Australia, Stephenson's semi-autobiographical *On a Human Scale* is published. In it he recalls, among other things, his Paris years and friendship with Sammer.
1994		In Seattle, Washington, Larsen self-publishes the autobiographical *Graffiti on My Heart*, in which she recalls her life in the inter-war years and with Sammer.
1998		Perriand's autobiography, *Une vie de création*, is published; it will become the main source of information about her life and work. In it, she describes her years at the Le Corbusier–Jeanneret atelier, whose milieu she calls the 'Galaxie Le Corbusier', and she recalls Sammer.
2013		The Museum of Modern Art, in New York City, mounts the first major Le Corbusier exhibition in the United States, *Le Corbusier: An Atlas of Modern Landscapes*.
2016		At the Centre Georges Pompidou, in Paris, a conference is held on Le Corbusier's controversial attitude to politics. The Maison de la culture du Japon, also in Paris, mounts a Junzo Sakakura exhibition.
2019		The new Fondation Louis Vuitton art museum, in Paris, designed by Frank Gehry, mounts its first exhibition of a woman artist, presenting a major overview of the life and work of Charlotte Perriand.

Acknowledgements

This book is a result of a very long process, and it would be impossible to write and publish it without the significant assistance of many people and institutions. Their contribution is so fundamental that my expression of gratitude is not only out of duty, but is deeply sincere. First and foremost, I thank the people who were present at the key moments of my research that I describe in the Research Diary. Here I must mention the significant role of the Fulbright Commission in the process. Thanks to their support I gained a year's experience in the academic environment of the United States, met with great colleagues and with leading experts in my field of studies and had entirely new horizons opened to me. Other of my research stays outside of the Czech Republic were made possible thanks to the support of the Charles University Grant Agency, a French Government Scholarship and the Canadian Centre for Architecture in Montreal. Indispensable support on my travels was provided by my family, colleagues and friends, both at home and abroad. I could critically process the information obtained during my research in the Czech Republic and other countries and turn it into a manuscript thanks to a post-doctoral fellowship at the Institute of Art History at the Czech Academy of Sciences in Prague.

For their continuous willingness to provide consultation, their constructively critical approach, their generosity in sharing information and documents, and their help in identifying a number of documents, I am indebted to Mary McLeod, Tim Benton, Jean-Louis Cohen, Irena Žantovská Murray and Chris Long.
My great thanks go to Richard Hartz of the Sri Aurobindo Ashram Archive in Pondicherry, not only for his help in finding the František Sammer Papers amongst the ashram holdings, but also for his support during my stay in India. For their help in research while I was in India I also thank Peter Heehs, Bob Zwicker, Kiran Kakad, Barbie Dailey, Vilas, Gauri Pinto, Samata (of the Art Gallery), Gilles Guigan (of the Auroville Archives), Benedetta Zaccarello and Eda Kriseová.

Special thanks are owed to Petr Sammer, the son of František Sammer, for his generous support, sharing information and willingness to answer a seemingly infinite number of my questions.

For their willingness to oblige and superb collaboration in researching the František Sammer Papers, I am indebted to the Pilsen City Archive (Archiv města Plzně – AMP), particularly Štěpánka Pflegerová.

To the Fondation Le Corbusier, especially Brigitte Bouvier, Isabelle Godineau and Arnaud Dercelles, I owe thanks for their continuous assistance and support while I conducted research in the archives of Le Corbusier and the atelier at 35 rue de Sèvres in Paris.

To Jacques Barsac and Pernette Perriand-Barsac of the Archive Charlotte Perriand, I am indebted for their generosity, advice and willingness to share information about Charlotte Perriand.

To Marco Iuliano I am indebted for his invaluable and inspiring advice during my research in Great Britain. And I thank Robyn Orr of the University of Liverpool Special Collections & Archives for her superb collaboration and assistance while I was researching the Gordon Stephenson Papers there. For his assistance in searching for further information about Stephenson, I am indebted to David Massey, an editor of the *Town Planning Review,* and to David Gordon of Queen's University in Canada. For their assistance in searching for documents in the University of Western Australia Library Special Collections, I owe a debt of gratitude to Deanne Barrett and Jenny Gregory. For her willingness to help and for the valuable information she provided about Gordon Stephenson, I thank Ann Peluso, the youngest of Stephenson's three children.

To Valeria Carullo, Curator of the Robert Elwall Photographs Collection at the Royal Institute of British Architects (London), I am indebted for inspirational advice, assistance in identifying people and places in photographs and valuable collaboration in my searches (not only those related to the architect Alex Adam).

I thank William Whitaker and Heather Isbell Schumacher for consultation and assistance while I was researching in the Antonin Raymond and Noémi Pernessin Raymond Collection in the Architectural Archives of the University of Pennsylvania.

My great thanks for inspirational conversations, expanding my horizons and providing a professional base during my study stay at the Canadian Centre for Architecture (Montreal) go to Phyllis Lambert, Rafico Ruiz, Louise Désy, Richard Pare, Martien de Vletter and Tim Klähn.

For exceptional meetings, valuable conversations and her generosity while I was researching the life and works of Jane West Clauss, I am indebted to Carin Clauss.

My great thanks go to everyone who helped to identify people and places in the photographs in the Sammer collection and to reveal the content of various archive materials. In addition to everyone I have mentioned so far, I must also thank Jurrien van Duijkeren, Inara Nevskaya, Klara van Duijkeren, Vincent Schipper, Kateřina Štěpánková, Marie Sýkorová, Pavla Beranová and Petr Klíma.

For the graphic design and overall look of the book I am indebted to Jiří Příhoda and Jakub Hrab.

For his precious translation of the Czech manuscript into English, careful work with the text and a fine editing work, I thank Derek Paton. For her compiling the bibliography and index, I thank Magda van Duijkeren-Hrabová, and for her valuable advice while working with the text I thank Irena Lehkoživová.

For their unflagging support and providing a base, repeated reading and continuous reflection, I thank to Jana Hrabová, Ondřej Hrab, Danuše Svobodová, Antonín Marián Svoboda and Libuše Hrabová.

For their continuous support to me while I was working on this book, I owe a debt of gratitude to Jindřich Vybíral and Zdenka Heroutová.

I am grateful to the Institute of Art History (at the Czech Academy of Sciences) and Artefactum Press for publishing the Czech edition of the book in 2021.

The English edition of the book would not have been possible in this form without the enthusiasm and support of Fran Ford, a senior editor, and the professional assistance of the Routledge Press.

Special thanks go to Swetlana Heger Davies, the Head of the Department of Fine Arts at the Zurich University of Fine Arts, who significantly supported the English edition of the book and made the translation of the manuscript possible.

Special thanks are due to the archive of the Sri Aurobindo Ashram and to Petr Sammer for their having generously provided me with their rich written and pictorial documents, the essence of which is communicated in this book, and for their permission to reproduce them here.

In conclusion I again must thank Irena Žantovská Murray, Mary McLeod and Chris Long, without whose constant support this book would never have been written or published.

Bibliography

Alexander, A. H., 'Blueprint for Happiness: Teamwork in Marriage', *The Philadephia Inquirer*, 19 February 1950, p. 18.

'Alfred e Jane West Clauss, un villaggio in cooperativa', *Domus: La casa dell'uomo* 210, June 1946, pp. 4-8.

Altherr, Alfred, *Three Japanese Architects: Maekawa-Tange-Sakakura/Drei japanische Architekten: Maekawa-Tange-Sakakura*, New York: Architectural Book Publishing Co., 1968.

Aujame, Roger, et al., *Le Corbusier, Moments biographiques: XIVe Rencontres de la Fondation Le Corbusier,* Paris: La Villette, 2008.

Auroville Architecture: Towards New Forms for a New Consciousness, 5th edn, (2004) Auroville: Prisma, 2014.

Bacon, Mardges, 'Le Corbusier and Postwar America: The TVA and Béton Brut', *Journal of the Society of Architectural Historians* 74, 2015, no. 1, March, pp. 13-40.

—, *Le Corbusier in America: Travels in the Land of the Timid*, Cambridge (MA), London: MIT Press, 2001.

Baird, George, 'Introduction to Karel Teige's Mundaneum' (1929) and Le Corbusier's 'In Defense of Architecture' (1933), in *Oppositions 4*, 1974, pp. 80-81.

Barsac, Jacques, (ed.), *Charlotte Perriand et la photographie: l'œil en éventail*, Paris, Milan: 5 Continents, 2011.

—, *Charlotte Perriand et le Japon*, introd. Germain Viatte, contribution by Sôri Yanagi; postface Yvonne Brunhammer; in collaboration with Pernette Perriand-Barsac, Paris: Norma, 2008.

—, *Charlotte Perriand: L'Œuvre complète*, 4 vols, Paris: Éditions Norma, Archives Charlotte Perriand, 2014–19.

—, *Charlotte Perriand: Un art d'habiter 1903-1959*, Paris: Norma, 2005.

Bauchet-Cauquil, Hélène and Françoise-Claire Prodhon, *Le Corbusier, Pierre Jeanneret: Chandigarh, India 1951-66*, Paris: Galerie Patrick Seguin, 1987.

Baudin, Antoine, (ed.), *Photography, Modern Architecture and Design. The Alberto Sartoris Collection: Objects from the Vitra Design Museum*, Lausanne: EPFL Press and the Vitra Design Museum, 2005.

Baudouï, Rémi, (ed.), *Le Corbusier 1930-2020: Polémiques, histoire et mémoire*, collaboration scientific Arnaud Dercelles, Paris: Tallandier, 2020.

Bédarida, Marc, 'Rue de Sèvres 35: L'Envers du décor', in Lucan, Jacques, (ed.), *Le Corbusier: Une Encyclopédie*, Paris: Centre Georges Pompidou, 1987, pp. 354–59.

—, 'Une journée au 35S', in Roger Aujame et al., *Le Corbusier, Moments biographiques: XIVe Rencontres de la Fondation Le Corbusier,* Paris: La Villette, 2008, pp. 26–51.

Benjamin, Walter, 'Small History of Photography', in id., *On Photography*, ed., transl. and introd. by Esther Leslie, London: Reaktion Books, 2015, pp. 59-105.

—, 'The Work of Art in the Age of Mechanical Reproduction', in

—, *Illuminations*, ed. with an introd. by Hannah Arendt, preface by Leon Wieseltier, transl. by Harry Zohn, New York: Schocken Books, 2007.

Benton, Charlotte, 'From Tubular Steel to Bamboo: Charlotte Perriand, the Migrating "Chaise-longue" and Japan', 'Craft, Modernism and Modernity', special issue, *Journal of Design History* 11, no. 1, 1998, pp. 31-58.

Benton, Tim, 'Atlantic Coast: Nature and Inspiration', in Jean-Louis Cohen (ed.), *Le Corbusier: An Atlas of Modern Landscapes* (exh. cat.), New York: The Museum of Modern Art, 2013, pp. 163-67.

—, 'Drawings and Clients: Le Corbusier's Atelier Methodology in the 1920s', *AA Files*, no. 3, January 1983, pp. 42-50.

—, *LC FOTO: Le Corbusier Secret Photographer*, Zurich: Lars Müller, 2013.

—, *Le Corbusier conférencier*, Paris: Moniteur, 2007.

—, *The Villas of Le Corbusier and Pierre Jeanneret, 1920-1930*, revised and expanded from the original French version, (1987) Basel, Berlin: Birkhäuser, 2007.

—, and Bruno Hubert, *Le Corbusier, mes années sauvages sur le bassin 1926-1936,* Le Petit Piquey: Tim Benton & Bruno Hubert, 2015.

Billing, Joan, and Samuel Eberli, et al., *Alfred Altherr Junior: Protagonist der Schweizer Wohnkultur* (exh. cat.), Baden: Design+Design, 2013.

Bjažić Klarin, Tamara, *Ernest Weissmann: Društveno angažirana arhitektura, 1926-1939/Socially Engaged Architecture, 1926-1939*, Zagreb: Architectonica, Hrvatska akademija znanosti i umjetnosti/Croatian Academy of Sciences and Art, 2015.

Blencowe, Chris, and Judith Levine, *Moholy's Edit. CIAM 1933: The Avant-Garde at Sea, August 1933*, Zurich: Lars Müller, 2019.

Boesiger, Willy, et al (eds), *Le Corbusier et Pierre Jeanneret, Œuvre complète 1929-1934*, vol 2, 18th edn, (1934) Basel: Birkhäuser, 2013.

Bonta, János, 'Functionalism in Hungarian Architecture', in Wojciech Leśnikowski (ed.), *East European Modernism: Architecture in Czechoslovakia, Hungary, and Poland between the Wars, 1919-1939*, with an introd. and essays by Leśnikowski, New York: Rizzoli, 1996, pp. 125-77.

Boukharine, Nicolas, *La théorie du matérialisme historique: manuel populaire de sociologie marxiste*, (1921) Paris: Éditions sociales internationales, 1927.

Bourdieu, Pierre, 'Intellectual Field and Creative Project', in Michael F. D. Young (ed.), *Knowledge and Control: New Directions for the Sociology of Education*, London: Collier-Macmillan, 1971, pp. 161-88.

Bourgeois, Victor, 'Le Concours International pour l'Urbanisation de la Rive gauche de l'Escaut, à Anvers', *La Cité* 11, 1933, no. 8, July-August, pp. 145-68.

Breines, Simon, 'First Congress of Soviet Architects', *Architectural Record* 82, no. 4 (October 1937), pp. 63-65, 94 and 96.

Buchsteiner, Thomas, and Ursula Zeller (eds), *Andreas Feininger: Ein Fotografenleben/A Photographer's Life 1906-1999*, Ostfildern: Hatje Cantz, 2010.

Burniat, Patrick, 'Urbanisme de la rive gauche de l'Éscaut, 1933, Antwerp, Belgium', *Le Corbusier Plans Online*, Echelle 1 Internationale-Fondation Le Corbusier, n.p.

Casciato, Maristella, '35 rue de Sèvres: At Work in the Atelier', in Jean-Louis Cohen (ed.), *Le Corbusier: An Atlas of Modern Landscapes* (exh. cat.), New York: The Museum of Modern Art, 2013, pp. 240-46.

—, *Le Corbusier Album Punjab, 1951*, Zurich: Lars Müller, 2024.

Cauquil, Hélène, and Marc Bédarida (eds), *Le Corbusier: l'atelier 35 rue de Sèvres, Bulletin d'Informations Architecturales*, no. 114, suppl., Paris: Institut français d'architecture, 1987.

Cherry, Gordon E., and Leith Penny, *Holford: A Study in Architecture, Planning and Civic Design,* London: Routledge, Taylor & Francis e-Library 2005.

Cohen, Jean-Louis, *André Lurçat, 1894-1970: L'Autocritique d'un moderne*, Liège: Mardaga, 1995.

—, 'Introduction', in Karel Teige, *Modern Architecture in Czechoslovakia and Other Writings*, transl. from the Czech by Irena Žantovská Murray and from the French by David Britt, Los Angeles: Getty Research Institute, 2000, pp. 1-55.

—, *Le Corbusier et la mystique de l'URSS: Théories et projets pour Moscou 1928-1936*, Brussels: Mardaga, 1987.

—, 'Le Corbusier's Centrosoyuz', *Future Anterior: Journal of Historic Preservation, History, Theory, Criticism* 5, summer 2008, no. 1, pp. 52-61.

—, (ed.), *Le Corbusier: An Atlas of Modern Landscapes* (exh. cat.), New York: The Museum of Modern Art, 2013.

Collignon, Maxime, *Le Parthénon: l'histoire, l'architecture et la sculpture*, introd. by Maxime Collignon, photographs by Frédéric Boissonnas and W. A. Mansell, Paris: Librarie Centrale d'Art et d'Architecture, [1912].

Collins, Christiane Crasemann, 'Le Corbusier's Maison Errázuriz: A Conflict of Fictive Cultures', *The Harvard Architecture Review* 6, 1987, pp. 38-53.

Colomina, Beatriz, 'Le Corbusier and Photography', *Assemblage* 4, October 1987, pp. 7-8.

Cooke, Catherine, 'Beauty as a Route to "the Radiant Future": Responses of Soviet Architecture', *Journal of Design History* 10, 1997, no. 2, pp. 137-60.

Curtis, William J. R., 'Ideas of Structure and the Structure of Ideas: Le Corbusier's Pavillon Suisse, 1930-1931', *Journal of the Society of Architectural Historians* 40, 1981, no. 4, December, pp. 295-310.

Dailey, Victoria, Natalie Shivers, and Michael Dawson, introd. by William Deverell, *LA's Early Moderns: Art, Architecture, Photography*, Los Angeles, CA: Balcony Press, 2003.

Dofková, Jekaterina, 'Avantgarda 20.-30. let: Praha-Moskva', PhD diss., Brno University of Technology, 2016.

'Dokumentace popravených Čechoslováků za druhé světové války v Berlíně – Plötzensee', Institute for the Study of Totalitarian Regimes, Prague, https://www.ustrcr.cz/uvod/popraveni-plotzensee/ Accessed 27 June 2020.

Domanický, Petr, 'Navzdory malomyslné okresní zatvrdlosti: SZVU a architektura', in Petr Jindra (ed.), *Umění českého západu: Sdružení západočeských výtvarných umělců v Plzni 1925-1951*, Řevnice, Pilsen: Arbor Vitae and Západočeská galerie, 2010.

Dumont, Marie-Jeanne, 'Immeuble de la Porte Molitor' and 'Appartement de Le Corbusier, 24 rue Nungesser-et-Coli', in *Le Corbusier: Plans*, DVD, Paris, Tokyo: Codex Images International, 2005-06.

Geyer-Raack, Ruth Hildegard, '"IRA" Internationale Raumausstellung Gebr. Schürmann, Köln', *Moderne Bau-*

formen 30, 1931, pp. 607-16.

Giedion, Sigfried, 'CIAM at Sea. The Background of the Fourth (Athens) Congress', *Architect's Year Book* 3, 1949, pp. 36-39.

Giordani, Jean-Pierre, 'Urbanisme, projets A, B, C, H, Alger, Algérie 1930', in *Le Corbusier: Plans*, DVD, Paris, Tokyo: Codex Images International, 2005-06.

Grunewald, Almut, (ed.), *The Giedion World: Sigfried Giedion and Carola Giedion-Welcker in Dialogue*, Zurich: Scheidegger & Spiess, 2019.

Gupta, Pankaj Vir, Christine Mueller and Cyrus Samii, *Golconde: The Introduction of Modernism in India*, New Delhi: Urban Crayon Press, 2010.

Halík, Pavel, 'Architektura padesátých let', in Rostislav Švácha and Marie Platovská (eds), *Dějiny českého výtvarného umění*, vol. 5: 1939-1958, Prague: Academia, 2005, pp. 324-25.

Heehs, Peter, *The Lives of Sri Aurobindo*, New York: Columbia University Press, 2008.

Helfrich, Kurt, and William Whitaker (eds), *Crafting a Modern World: The Architecture and Design of Antonin and Noémi Raymond*, New York: Princeton Architectural Press, 2006.

Hnídková, Vendula, *Moskva 1937: Architektura a propaganda v západní perspektivě*, Prague: Institute of Art History, Czech Academy of Sciences, 2018.

'Hommage à Pierre Jeanneret', *Werk: Schweizer Monatsschrift für Architektur, Kunst und künstlerisches Gewerbe* 6, 1968, pp. 377-96. House Portfolio: Fifty studies of new houses under $10,000 with plans, interior and exterior photographs, construction data and unit costs', in *Architectural Forum*, April 1940.

Hrabová, Martina, 'Between Ideal and Ideology: The Parallel Worlds of František Sammer', *Umění* 64, 2016, no. 2 , pp. 137-66.

—, 'Mýtus a realita: čeští asistenti Le Corbusiera 1924-1937', PhD diss., Charles University, Prague, 2016.

—, 'The Many Faces of the Master: Le Corbusier and Czechoslovakia', in Irena Lehkoživová and Joan Oackman (eds), *Book for Mary: Sixty on Seventy*, Prague; New York: Quatro Print, 2020, pp. 174-87.

'In Knoxville, Tennessee ... Designed by Alfred Clauss and Jane West Clauss', *Pencil Points: Progressive Architecture* 26, February 1945, pp. 60-62.

Johnson, Donald Leslie, 'Frank Lloyd Wright in Moscow: June 1937', *Journal of the Society of Architectural Historians* 46, no. 1, March 1987, pp. 65-79.

Junzo Sakakura: Une architecture pour homme (exh. cat.), Paris: Maison de la culture du Japon, 2017.

Kofler, Andreas, *Architectures japonaises à Paris 1867-2017*, Paris: Pavillon de l'Arsenal, 2017.

Koukalová, Martina, 'Plzeň – Slovany', in Lucie Skřivánková, Rostislav Švácha, Eva Novotná and Karolina Jirkalová (eds), *Paneláci 1: Padesát sídlišť v českých zemích: kritický katalog k cyklu výstav Příběh paneláku*, Prague: Uměleckoprůmyslové museum, 2016, pp. 108-15.

Kousidi, Matina, 'Through the Lens of Sigfried Giedion: Exploring Modernism and the Greek Vernacular in situ, *RIHA Journal* 0136, 15 July 2016, n.p.

Lahuerta, Juan José, (ed.), *Le Corbusier y España*, [Barcelona]: Centre de Cultura Contemporània, [1997].

—, 'Spain: Travelling to See the Already Seen', in Jean-Louis Cohen, (ed.), *Le Corbusier: An Atlas of Modern Landscapes* (exh. cat), New York: The Museum of Modern Art, 2013, pp. 140-45.

Larsen, Agnessa, *Graffiti on My Heart*, Seattle, WA: Peanut Butter Publishing, 1994.

Le Corbusier et la Méditerranée (exh. cat.), Marseille: Parenthèses and Musées de Marseille, 1987.

Le Corbusier et le mouvement moderne en Belgique 1920-1940 (ex. cat.), Liège: s.n., 1988.

Le Corbusier, *Aircraft*, London: The Studio, 1935.

—, *Des canons, des munitions? Merci! Des logis, s.v.p.*, Boulogne-sur-Seine: Éditions de l'architecture d'Aujourd'hui, 1938.

—, *La Charte d'Athènes*, avec un discours liminaire de Jean Giraudoux, Paris: Plon, 1943.

—, *La Charte d'Athènes*, avec un discours liminaire de Jean Giraudoux, Paris: Éditions de Minuit, 1957.

—, *Les Trois établissements humains*, Paris: Éditions Denoël, 1945.

—, 'Pas la peine de se gêner', in Willy Boesiger et al. (ed.), *Le Corbusier et Pierre Jeanneret, Œuvre complète 1929-1934*, vol. 2, 18th edn, (1934) Basel: Birkhäuser, 2013.

—, *Quand les cathédrales étaient blanches: voyage au pays de timides*, Paris: Plon, 1937.

—, *Sur les quatre routes*, Paris: Gallimard, 1941.

—, *Vers une architecture*, Paris: G. Crès, [1923].

—, *La Ville Radieuse*, Boulogne-sur-Seine: Éditions de l'Architecture d'Aujourd'hui, 1935.

—, *Za novou architekturu* [*Vers une architecture*], transl. from the French by Pavel Halík, Prague: Petr Rezek, 2005.

Johnson, Donald Leslie, 'Frank Lloyd Wright in Moscow: June 1937', *Journal of the Society of Architectural Historians* 46, no. 1, March 1987, pp. 65-79.

Loach, Judi, 'L'Atelier Le Corbusier: Un centre européen d'échanges', *Monuments historiques*, 1992, pp. 49-52.

—, 'Studio as Laboratory', *The Architecture Review,* 1987, January, pp. 73-77.

Lucan, Jacques, (ed.), *Le Corbusier, une encyclopédie*, Paris: Centre Georges Pompidou, 1987.

Maak, Niklas, *Le Corbusier: The Architect on the Beach*, Munich: Hirmer, 2011.

Marzá, Fernando and Josep Quetglas, Palais du Centrosoyuz, in: *Le Corbusier: Plans*, Codex Images International, Paris-Tokyo, [DVD] 2005-2006.

Gautier, Théophile, *Trésors d'art de la Russie ancienne et moderne*, Gide, Paris 1859.

McLeod, Mary (ed.), *Charlotte Perriand: An Art of Living*, New York: H. N. Abrams and the Architectural League of New York, 2003.

—, 'Charlotte Perriand: Her First Decade as a Designer', *AAFiles*, 1987, no. 15 (summer), pp. 3-13.

—, 'Le Corbusier and Algiers', in Kenneth Frampton (ed.), *Le Corbusier 1933-1960*, special issue of *Oppositions*, Winter/Spring 1980, nos. 19/20, Cambridge, MA: MIT Press, 1980, pp. 54-85.

—, 'Le Corbusier, planification et syndicalisme regional', in Rémi Badouï (ed.), *Le Corbusier 1930-2020: Polémiques, mémoire et histoire*, Paris: Tallandier, 2020 pp. 203-23.

—, 'Plans: Bibliography', in Kenneth Frampton (ed.), *Le Corbusier 1933-1960*, *Oppositions*, Winter/Spring 1980, nos. 19/20, Cambridge, MA: MIT Press, 1980, pp. 190-201.

—, 'Urbanism and Utopia: Le Corbusier from Regional Syndicalism to Vichy' PhD diss., Princeton University, Princeton, NJ, 1985.

— and Victoria Rosner (eds), *Pioneering Women of American Architecture*, https://pioneeringwomen.bwaf.org/jane-west-clauss/, Accessed 4 August 2023.

Monnier, Gérard, (ed.), *Le Corbusier et le Japon*, Paris: A. & J. Picard, 2007.

Mumford, Eric, *The CIAM Discourse on Urbanism, 1928-1960*, Forward by Kenneth Frampton, Cambridge, MA, London: MIT Press, 2002.

Murdin, Paul, (ed.), *Encyclopedia of Astronomy and Astrophysics*, vol. 1, Bristol, London: Institute of Physics, 2001.

Oshima, Ken Tadashi, *International Architecture in Interwar Japan. Constructing Kokusai Kenchiku*, Seattle, London: University of Washington Press, 2009.

Pare, Richard, (ed.), *Photography and Architecture: 1839-1939*, catalogue by Catherine Evans Inbusch and Marjorie Munsterberg, with essays by Phyllis Lambert and Richard Pare, Montreal, Quebec: Canadian Centre for Architecture, 1982.

—, *The Lost Vanguard: Russian Modernist Architecture 1922-1932*, introd. by Jean-Louis Cohen, New York: The Monacelli Press, 2007.

—, 'Ginzburg at Kislovodsk: The Ordzhonikidze Sanatorium and the End of Modernism in Russia', lecture, Princeton University, 10 May 2013. https://mediacentral.princeton.edu/media/Ginzburg+at+KislovodskA+The+Ordzhonikidze+Sanatorium+and+the+End+of+Modernism+in+Russia/0_jz0cvvbz/13468701, Accessed 13 July 2023.

Pechar, Josef, *Československá architektura 1945-1977*, Prague: Odeon, 1979.

Pelčák, Petr and Vladimír Šlapeta and Ivan Wahla (eds), *Elly Oehler/Olárová, Oskar Oehler/Olár, Architektonické dílo/Architectural Work* (exh. cat.), Brno, Olomouc: Spolek Obecní dům and Muzeum umění, 2007.

Penkalová, Lenka, 'Rubriky pro ženy v denním tisku 20. let 20. století a jejich autorky: Olga Fastrová, Marie Fantová, Milena Jesenská, Staša Jílovská a Zdena Wattersonová', PhD diss., Charles University, Prague, 2011.

Perriand, Charlotte, *Une vie de création*, Paris: Odile Jacob, 1998.

Perriand-Barsac, Pernette, (ed.), *Charlotte Perriand: Carnet de montagne*, Albertville: Maison des Jeux olympiques d'hiver, 2013.

'**Pierre Jeanneret 1896-1967**', *L'Architecture d'Aujourd'hui,* 1968, no. 136, February-March, pp. V-XII.

Pizza, Antonio, (ed.), *J. Ll. Sert y el mediterráneo/ J. Ll. Sert and Mediterranean Culture*, Barcelona: Colegio de Arquitectos de Cataluña, 1997.

Price, Bill, 'Alfred Clauss, 91, Retired Designer of Many Buildings', *The Philadephia Inquirer*, 11 June 1998, p. 116.

Raymond, Antonin, *An Autobiography*, Rutland, VT, Tokyo: Charles E. Tuttle Co., 1973.
—, 'Autobiography', *The Kentiku: A Monthly Journal for Architects and Designers*, October 1961, pp. 20-22.
Ridpath, Ian, (ed.), *Oxford Dictionary of Astronomy*, Oxford, New York: Oxford University Press, 1997.
Rüegg, Arthur, *Le Corbusier: Furniture and Interiors 1905-1965*, Zurich: Scheidegger & Spiess, 2012.
Sbriglio, Jacques, *Immeuble 24 N. C. et Appartement Le Corbusier/Apartment Block 24 N.C. and Le Corbusier's Home*, Basel: Birkhäuser, 1996.
Sedláková, Radomíra, *Sorela: Česká architektura padesátých let*, Prague: National Gallery, 1994.
Šlapeta, Vladimír and Václav Jandáček, *Český funkcionalismus - Stavební kniha*, Brno: Expo Data, 2004.
Smith, Joel, *Andreas Feininger*, Poughkeepsie, NY: Vassar College, 2003.
Soltan, Jerzy, 'Working with Le Corbusier', in H. Allen Brooks (ed.), *Le Corbusier*, Princeton: Princeton University Press 1987, pp. 1-16.
Stephenson, Gordon, 'Chapters of Autobiography I-III', *The Town Planning Review* 62, 1991, no. 1, January, pp. 7-36.
—, *On a Human Scale: A Life in City Design,* ed. by Christina DeMarco, Fremantle, Western Australia: Fremantle Arts Centre Press, 1992.
Stevens, Russell and Peter Willis, 'Earl De La Warr and the Competition for the Bexhill Pavillion, 1933-34', *Architectural History: Journal of the Society of Architectural Historians of Great Britain* 33, 1990, pp. 135-51.
Švácha, Rostislav, 'Before and after the Mundaneum: Karel Teige as Theoretician of the Architectural Avant-Garde', in Eric Dluhosch and Rostislav Švácha (eds), *Karel Teige 1900-1951: L'Enfant Terrible of the Czech Modernist Avant-Garde*, Introd. Kenneth Frampton, Cambridge, MA, London: MIT Press, 1999 pp. 107-39.
Talesnik, Daniel, 'The Itinerant Red Bauhaus, or the Third Emigration', PhD diss., Columbia University, New York 2016.
Teige, Karel, *Minimum Dwelling*, transl. from the Czech by Eric Dluhosch, Cambridge, MA, Chicago: MIT Press and the Graham Foundation for Advanced Studies in the Fine Arts, 2002.
—, *Nejmenší byt* [*Minimum Dwelling*], Prague: Václav Petr, 1932.
Udovički-Selb, Danilo, 'Between Modernism and Socialist Realism: Soviet Architectural Culture under Stalin's Revolution from Above, 1928-1938', *Journal of the Society of Architectural Historians* 68, no. 4, December 2009, pp. 467-95.
—, 'Le Corbusier and the Paris Exhibition of 1937: The Temps Nouveaux Pavilion', *Journal of the Society of Architectural Historians* 56, no. 1, March 1997, pp. 42-63.
—, *Soviet Architectural Avant-Gardes: Architecture and Stalin's Revolution from Above, 1928-1938,* London: Bloomsbury Visual Arts, 2020.
—, '"C'était dans l'air du temps": Charlotte Perriand and the Popular Front', in Mary McLeod (ed.), *Charlotte Perriand: An Art of Living*, New York: H. N. Abrams and the Architectural League of New York, 2003 pp. 68-89.
Vorlík, Petr, *Meziválečné garáže v Čechách*, Prague: VCPD ČVUT, 2011.
Vybíral, Jindřich, 'The Beacons of Revolutionary Ideas: *Sorela* as Historicism and Rhetoric', *Centropa* I, no. 2, May 2001, pp. 95-100.
Weiss, Peg, *Galka Scheyer and the Blue Four: A Dialogue with America*, Berkeley, CA: University of California Press, 1986.
Wiendlová, Květa, 'Toulavé boty a cesty domů: Rozhovor s Františkem Sammerem', *Pravda,* příloha, 20 February 1971, p. 4.
Wodehouse, Lawrence, 'Houses by Alfred and Jane Clauss in Knoxville, Tennessee', *ARRIS*, vol. 1, 1989, pp. 50-62.
Wright, Frank Lloyd, 'Architecture and Life in the U.S.S.R.', *Architectural Record* 82, no. 4 (October 1937), pp. 58-63.
Žaknic, Ivan, *Klip and Corb on the Road: The Dual Diaries and Legacies of August Klipstein and Le Corbusier on their Eastern Journey, 1911*, Zurich: Scheidegger & Spiess, 2019.
—, *Le Corbusier: Pavillon Suisse: The Biography of a Building/ Biographie d'un bâtiment*, Birkhäuser, Basel 2004.
Zenno, Yasushi, 'Fortuitous Encounters: Charlotte Perriand in Japan, 1940-41', in Mary McLeod (ed.), *Charlotte Perriand: An Art of Living*, New York: H. N. Abrams and the Architectural League of New York, 2003, pp. 90-153.

| **Index**

A

AALC (Association des amis de Le Corbusier) · 150
Acropolis (Athens) · 100, *101*, 102, *102*, *103*, 104, *105*
Adam, Alex (born Kertész, Alek) · 15, 17, 41, 64, 68–70, *70*, 78, *80-83*, 85, 96, 124, 128, 138, 145, 150, 182
Admiralty Building, St Petersburg · 94, *95*
AEAR (Association des écrivains et artistes révolutionnaires) · 88, 162
Ahitouv, Isaac M. (publisher) · *98*
Ahmedabad (India) · 130
AILC (Association Internationale Le Corbusier) · 18, *148*, 150, 186
Alcázar of Toledo · 160
Alcazarquivir, Morocco, see also El-Ksar el Kebir · 161
Alfassa, Mirra (aka Mère or the Mother) · 25, 31, 34, 35, 135, 137, 140, 143, 144, 187
Algeciras (Andalusia, Spain) · 72, *73*, 76, 160, 161, *168*
Algeria · 14, 17, 51, 66, *68*, 70, 74, *75*, 145, 147, 182
    see also Beni Isguen, Durand (entrepreneur), Ghardaïa, Domaine de Badjara, Oued Ouchaïa (project), Plan Obus
Algiers (Algeria) · *42*, 48, 66, 67, *68*, 70, 182
Alhambra, The (Granada, Spain) · 161, 167, *167*
All-Russian Academy of Art, Moscow · 63, *65*, 182
Alps, The · 52–54
Altherr, Alfred · 58, 150
Americans, the · 15, 56, 60–62, 96, 133, 175, 182
America (North/South) · 29, 41, 56, 57, 60, 85, 96
Amsterdam · *86*
Andalusia · 29, 160
Andrievsky, Sergey · *99*
Anger, Roger · *142*, 143, 186
Angkor Wat, Cambodia · 30, 130, 132, *133*
Anna Head School, Berkeley, California · 61
Antwerp · 17, 48, 68, 70, 75, 78, 79, *80–82*, 82, 84, 142, 160, 182
    see also urban plans
Arakan · 184
Ararat, Mount (Turkey) · 176
Architects' Congress, film by László Moholy-Nagy · *85*, *100*, *101*, 182
Arcila (Spanish name for Asilah) (Morocco) · 161, 163
Army, see British Army, Czechoslovak Army, Japanese Army, Red Army
Ashram, Sri Aurobindo, Pondicherry · 13, 25, 28, 29, 31, *31*, 37, 44, 45, 115, 116, *118*, 130, 133–35, *133*, *135*, 137, 143, 144, 146, 184, 187
Association des écrivains et artistes révolutionnaires, see AEAR
ATBAT (Atelier des Bâtisseurs) · 138
Atelier at 35 rue de Sèvres (also known as 35S) · 13–17, 41 46, *42*, 48, 49, 51, 52, 54–60, 62, 66, 68–70, *83*, 84, 85, *85*, 88, 94, 113, 114, 116, 119, 138, 145, 146, 147, *148*, 150, 152, *152*, 160, 172, 182
    see also Le Corbusier–Jeanneret atelier
Atelier of Charlotte Perriand, Paris · 17, 36, 41, 49, 110, *111*, 113, *124*, 128, *128*
    see also Montparnasse
Athens (Greece) · 7, 84, 96, 98, 100, 102, ***100–103***, *105*
Auroville (India) · 34, *34*, *142*, 143, 144, *144*, 186
    see also Matrimandir, Japanese Pavilion, Plan Nebula
Australia · 69, 142, 146, 147, 187
Austria · 181, 184
Avant-garde · 13, 14, 16–18, 25, 30, 35, 43–46, 120, 122, 135, 144, 185

B

Baku (Azerbaijan) · 96, 98
Bangkok (Thailand) · 130
Barbier Saint-Hilaire, Philippe (called Pavitra) · 118, 119, 144
Barcelona · 17, 18, 29, 71–73, *71-73*, 120, 160, 161
    see also Casa Bloc in Calle de Muntaner, Casa Milà, Montjuïc, Moll de Barcelona
Barcelona International Exposition, 1929 · 70, *71*
Barceloneta, La · 70, 71
Barkhin, Grigory Borisovich · *92*, 93
Barkov · 88
Basílica da Estrela, Lisbon · *77*
Baťa (company) · 56
Baťa, Jan Antonín · *56*
Baťa, Tomáš · *56*
Batumi (Georgia) · 98, 176, *178*
Bauhaus · 62, 85, 100
Beaudouin, Eugène · *125*
Bedford Square, London · 157
Beneš, Edvard · 136
Beneš, Vladimír · 42, 43
Bengal, Bay of (India) · 32, *32*, *133*
Beni Isguen (Algeria) · 74
Benjamin, Walter · 93, 181
Benton, Tim · 16, 36, 42, 43, 46, 48
Berkeley (California) · 61
Berlin · 74, 84, *87*, *137*, 184
Bexhill (England) · 17, 79, *83*
Black Book, *see* 'Livre noir'
Blencowe, Chris · 16
Blue Four (artists' group) *see also* Scheyer, Galka · 62
Boba (childhood friend of Sammer's) · 146, *146*
Boissonnas, Frédéric · 102, *103*
Bombay · 136, 137
Boone, Veronique · 16
Bosshardt, Edwin · 51, 56, 57, 156, 158
Bossu, Jean (architect) · 25, 145
Bourdieu, Pierre · 18
Bourgeois, Victor · 54, 70
Bratislava · *142*, 186
Brighton (England) · 142, 158, 159
British, the, *also* English, the · 15, 42, 52, 68, 69, 138, 142, 157, 159
British Army · 13, 28, *30*, 45, *134*, 137, 140, 184, 185
    see also East Yorkshire Regiment, Royal Engineers (RE)
British Malaya (today, Malaysia) · 137, 184
British Museum (London) · 158, 159
Brooks, Marjorie · 78
Brussels · 84, 186
Budapest · 58, 68
Bukharin, Nikolai Ivanovich · 88
Burma (today, Myanmar) · 27, 137, *139*, 184

C

Cahier noir *see* 'Livre noir'
Cairo (Egypt) · *129*, 130, *131*
California · 61, 64, *97*
Canada · 13
Carnarvon, 5th Earl of, George Herbert · 159
Carter, Edward (Librarian, RIBA) · *139*
Casa Bloc (Barcelona, building in Calle de Muntaner) · 18, 72, *72*, *73*
Casa Milà (building in Barcelona) · *71*

Casablanca (Morocco) · 28, 56
Caucasus · 98, 122, 123, *123*, 176, *177*, 183
Central Stadium of the Soviet Union (Stade central) (Moscow, project) · 88, 89
Centre Georges Pompidou (Paris) · 120, 187
Centrosoyuz, aka Centro (building in Moscow) · 14, 85, 89, *89*, 119–21, *121*, 181
Cercle de la Russie neuve · 85, 88
Česká Kubice (Czechoslovakia, now in Czech Rep.) · *64*
Ceuta (North Africa) · 161
Chadwick Fellowship · 102
Chaise Longue · 27, 54, 55
Chandigarh (India) · 130, 139, 145
Charles Bridge, Prague · *87*
Chartres (France) · 51
Chefchaouen (Morocco) · 74, *74*, 161-63
Chermayeff, Serge · 79
Chinese, the · 170
Chistye Prudy, Moscow Metro station, *see* Kirovskaya
Chvojková, Marta · 185
CIAM (Congrès Internationaux d'architecture moderne) · 7, 16, 17, 54, 84, 85, *85*, 88, 98, 100, *100*, *101*, 123, 125, 127, 128, 144, 182, 183
    see also Congresses, *Patris II*
CIRPAC (Comité Internationale pour la Réalisation des Problèmes d'Architecture Contemporaine) · 84, 162
Cité internationale universitaire de Paris · 14, *42*, 52, *52*, 54, 58, *58*, 60, 182
Cité Mondiale, Geneva (urban plan) · 47
Cité de la Muette, Drancy · *125*
Cité de réfuge (Salvation Army building), Paris · 14, *42*, 58–60, 122, 182
Clauss, Alfred · 17, 66, *66*, *67*, 96
Clauss, Carin · 60, 64
Clauss, Jane *see* West, Jane
Clauss, Peter Otto · *67*
Clauss Residence, Knoxville, Tennessee · 17, 66, *66*, *67*
Club of Architects, Moscow · 121
Cohen, Jean-Louis · 25, 29, 42
Cologne (Germany) · 54, *54*, 55, 182
    see also IRA (Internationale Raumausstellung)
Colombo (Sri Lanka) · 130
Congresses:
    CIAM IV, 1933 · 17, 84, 85, *85*, 98, 100, *100*, *101*, 123, 182
    see also *Patris II*
    CIAM V, 1937 · 125, 127, 128, 183
    First Congress of Soviet Writers, 1934 · 120, 183
    First All-Union Congress of Soviet Architects 1937 · 127, 174, 183
    Fifth Congress of the UIA Moscow 1958 · 186
    Ninth Congress of the UIA Prague-Bratislava 1967 · *142*, 143, 186
Corbusier *see* Le Corbusier
Córdoba (Spain) · 72, 160, 161, 166, *166*, 167
Crimea · 122, *123*
Czech Republic · 13, 26, 35, 45
Czechoslovak · 14, 25, 27, 42, 43, 84, 88, 122, 124, 135–37, 140, 141, 162, 184–86
Czechoslovak Association of Socialist Architects · 88
Czechoslovak Army · 137, 184
Czechoslovak Government-in-Exile · 136, 137
Czechoslovak Pavilion (the Exposition internationale des arts et techniques dans la vie moderne, 1937, Paris and Expo 58, Brussels) · 124, 186

Czechoslovak Republic · **136**, 175, 181, 186
Czechoslovakia · 18, 25, 32, **34**, 41-43, 45, 51, 56, **56**, 57, 64, 70, **87**, 88, 122, 124, 135, 137, 140, **141**, 145, 146, 150, 181-87
Czechs, the · 13, 28-30, 35, 42, 44, 47, 59, 114, 117, 127, 137, **148**, 175, 183

D

Dalmatia · 108, **109**
Danda, Josef · 42, 43
Dardanelles, the · 102
Dávid, Károly · 55, 58
Delphi (Greece) · 104, **106**, **107**
Dempo (ship) · 17, 75, 76, **77**
Dieppe (France) · 51, 156, 158
Dnieper (Dnipro, river) (Russia, Belarus, Ukraine) · 98, **99**
Dnipro (formerly Dnipropetrovsk) · 98
Dnipro Dam (also Dnieper Hyrdoelectric Station, Dnipro-HES, Ukraine) · 98, **99**
Doesburg, Nelly van · 54
Doesburg, Theo van · 54
Domaine de Badjara (Oued Ouchaïa) (Algeria) · 58, 66, **68**
Doshi, Shanti · **135**
Drancy (Paris suburb) · **125**
Duiker, Jan · **86**
Durand (entrepreneur) · 66, **68**
Dutch, the · 54, 129, **129**, 132

E

East Yorkshire Regiment · 137, 184
Easton, John Murray · 51, 157, 158
Egypt · 29, **131**, 159
El Greco · 160, 166
El-Ksar el-Kebir *see also* Alcazarquivir (Morocco) · 161, 163
Elbrus, Mount (in the Caucasus) · 98, **123**, 176
Elzas, Abraham · 46
Emery, Pierre-André · 18, 25, 147, **148**, 150, **150**, 152, **152**, 186
Endoh San (manager of A. Raymond's office Tokyo) · 133, **134**, 136
England, *see* Great Britain
English, the, *see* British
English Channel, The (aka La Manche) · 51, 56, 156
Enguri (river in Georgia) · 176
Erechtheion, Athens · 102, **103**
Errázuriz, Maison (project) · 114, 115, **118**, 174
El Escorial · 160, 164, 165, **165**
L'Esprit Nouveau (magazine) · 46
L'Esprit Nouveau, Paris (pavilion) · 55
Exhibitions:
    Le Corbusier: An Atlas of Modern Landscapes, New York, 2013 · 25, 187
    Charlotte Perriand: Inventing a New World, Paris, 2019 · 187
    Dans l'intimité de l'atelier du 35 rue de Sèvres, Paris, 2017 · 16
    Expo 58, Brussels · 186
    Exposición Internacional de Barcelona 1929 (Expo 1929) · 70, **71**
    l'Exposition internationale des arts décoratifs et industriels modernes, Paris, 1925 · 55, 157
    Exposition internationale des arts et techniques dans la vie moderne (L'Exposition universelle de 1937),
    Paris, 1937 · 17, 41, 124, **126**, 128, 183
    Internationale Raumausstellung (IRA), Cologne, 1931 · 54, **54**, 55, 182
    Le Salon d'automne, Paris, 1922 · 55
    Le Salon d'automne, Paris, 1932 · 62, **63**
    Výstava tělesné výchovy a sportu (Exhibition of Physical Training and Sport), Pardubice, 1931 · **56**

F

Fauteuil Grand Confort · 36, **111**, 113
Feininger, Andreas · 17, 62, **63**
Feininger, Lyonel · 62
Finisterre, Cape (Spain) · 77
First All-Union Congress of Soviet Architects *see* congresses
FLC (Fondation Le Corbusier) · 15, 16, 25, 42, 44, 150
Florence (Italy) · 146
Fondation Louis Vuitton, Paris · 187
France · 13, 25, 41, 42, 45, 56, 57, 68, 61, 84, 85, 88, 94, 119, 128, 135, 138, 145, 150, 184, 186
François (František Sammer) · 13, 14, 21, 26, **27**, 52, 54, 73, 76, 117, 120, 137, 143, 146, 147
Frankfurt am Main (Germany) · 85
Fremantle (Australia) · 187
French, the · 57, 88, 94, 117, 132, 134, 138, 143, 157, 175
Fuji, Mount (Japan) · 172
functional city, the · 84, 125, 144, 182

G

Gagra (Georgia) · 121, 127, 183
Gainsborough, Thomas · 159
Gallis, Yvonne (wife of Le Corbusier) · 60
Garches (Paris suburb) · 49
Gaudí, Antoni · **71**
    see also Casa Milà
Gehry, Frank · 187
Geneva (Switzerland) · 18, **46**, 47, 68, 150, 152, 186
    see also Palais de la Société des Nations (League of Nations Building), Mundaneum (project), urban plans
Georgia (then, USSR) · 98, **98**, 121, 123, 176
Germans, the · 62, 66, 137, 184
Germany · 41, 56, 61, 62, 135, 181, 184
Ghardaïa (Algeria) · 74
Gibraltar · 17, 72, 75, 76, **76**, **77**, 160, 161
Giedion, Sigfried · 7, 17, 41, 84, 100
Ginza, Tokyo · 115, **115**, 116, **171**, 172
Ginzburg, Moisei · 14, 121, 127, 183
Giza (Egypt) · **129**, 130, **131**
Glacier National Park (Montana), USA · **61**, **96**
Gočár, Josef · 183
Golconde, Pondicherry (dormitory) · 14, 30, **30**, 31, **31**, 35, 115, 118, **118**, 119, 128, 130, 133, **134**, 136, 140, 143, 174, 184
Graffiti on my Heart, Larsen (autobiography) · 60, 187
Granada (Spain) · 72, 160, 161, 167, **167**
Great Britain, *also* England· 13, 17, 25, 51, 52, 56, 57, 68-70, 75, 78, **78**, 79, **81**, 84, 94, 96, 128, 135, 137, 138, **139**, 140, 142, 145, 156, 160, 182, 184, 186
Greece · 17, 29, 41, 56, 84, **85**, 98, 100, **100**, 104, **106**, **107**, 108, 182, 183
Grenoble (France) · 128, 139
Gropius, Walter · 62, 81, 93
Grunewald, Almut · 17
Gschwind, Otakar · 56
Gschwindová, Miloslava, *see* Sammerová, Miloslava (Milča, Milána)
Gurzuf, Crimea · **123**

H

Hakozaki Maru (ship) · 128, **128**
Hampstead, London · 157, 159
Hanavský pavilon (Hanau Pavilion), Prague (*see also* pavilions) · **146**
Hawaii · 65, **108**, 136, 170
Hayama (Japan) · 17, 116, **116**, 175, 183
Head (statue by Agnes Larsen) · 62, **63**
Head of a Crying Child (statue by Agnes Larsen) · **65**
Heehs, Peter · 135
Hekatompedon temple, Athens · 102
Hermitage Museum, St Petersburg · 94
Herzen, Alexander Ivanovitch · 134
Herzen, Gabriel Monod · 134, 144
Herzen, Olga · 134
Heyneman, Anne · 60, 61, **61**, 64
Hilversum (Netherlands) · 86, **86**
Hlavatá, Růžena *see* Sammerová, Růžena
Holford, William · 17, 68-70, 78, 79, **81**, 82, **83**, 96, 138, 142, 145, 182, 186
Hollywood Bowl, Los Angeles (amphitheatre) · **97**
Honolulu (Hawaii) · 62, 63-65, 73, 81, 82, 86, 98, 108, 114, 115, 117, 120, 123, 127, 139, 147, 164, 166, 167, 170, 183, 185
Honolulu Academy of Arts (Hawaii) · 63, 183
Honshu (Hondo) (Japan) · 172
Hořovice (Czechoslovakia, now in Czech Rep.) · 181
Hoste, Huib · 70
Un hôtel de haute montagne (mountain resort) (project of Charlotte Perriand) · 17, 36, **112**, 113, **113**
Hungarians, the · 51, 55, 69, 85
Hungary · 41, 56, 85, 128, 181
Hyde Park, London · 157, **158**

I

Iberian Peninsula · 70
India · 13, 25-29, 32, 35-37, 45, 62, 128, 130, 132, 133, 135-39, **142**, 144, 147, 170, 184-86
    see also Auroville, Bombay, Madras, Pondicherry
L'Institut d'Urbanisme de l'Université de Paris · 68, 102
Institute of Baking, Moscow (project) · 88
International House, Auroville, Pondicherry · 144
International Union of Architects (UIA) · **142**, 143, 186
    see also congresses
IRA (Internationale Raumausstellung) *see also* exhibitions · 54, **54**, 55, 182
Istanbul, *also as* Constantinople, Stamboul · 96, 98, **98**, 108
Izvestia Building, Moscow · 18, 36, **92**, 93, **93**

J

Janák, Pavel · 183
Jansová, Magda · 42
Japan · 13, 15, 17, 25, 30, 32, 37, 41, 57, 114-16, **116**, 119, 123, 128, 130, 132, 133, **134**, 136, 137, 139, 143, 170-75, **170-74**, 183-85
Japanese, the · 27, 52, 54, 114, 115, 124, 133, 170-75
Japanese Army · 137, 184
Japanese Pavilion, Auroville · 143, 144, **144**

Japanese Pavilion, Paris · 124
Jawlensky, Alexej von · 62
Jeanneret, Pierre · 14, 15, 17, 25, 36, 41, *41*, 45, 48, *48*, 49, 51, *54*, 55, 57-59, *58*, *61*, 70, 72, 110, *110*, *111*, 120-22, 126, *126*, 128, 138, 139, 145, 160, 174, 182-83, 186
Jirásek, Alois · 140
Jourdain, Francis · 56, 85, 88
Jourdain, Frantz · 56

K

Kaganovich, Lazar Moiseyevich · 120
Kalinin, Viktor Valeryanovich · 121, 127, 183
Kamakura (Japan) · 175
Kandinsky, Wassily · 62
Karfík, Vladimír · 42, 43, *57*
Karl Marx (sculpture by Agnes Larsen) · 63, 65, *65*, 182
Karuizawa (Japan) · 114, 116, *118*, 119, 130, 174, 175, 183
Kazansky Station Moscow · *91*
Kazbek, Mount (in the Caucasus) · *177*
Kensington Gardens, London · *159*
Kertész, Alek *see* Adam, Alex
Kharkov (Kharkiv) (Ukraine) · 98
Kirkee (today, Khadki) near Poona (today, Pune) (India) · 137
Kirovskaya Metro station (today, Chistye Prudy) · 14, 88, *89*, 182
Kislovodsk (Russia) · 122, 183
Klabava (river near Pilsen) · 78
Klee, Paul · 62
Klipstein, August · 100, 102
Knoxville, Tennessee · 17, 66, *66*, *67*
  see also Little Switzerland, Clauss Residence
Kobe (Japan) · 136, 172
Kolli, Nikolai D. (*also as* Colley, Colly, Coly) · 14, 21, *41*, 84, 85, 88, 89, *89*, 98, *99*, 108, 120-22, 127, 138, 182, 183
Komárno (Czechoslovakia, now in Slovakia) · 181
Komsomolskaya Square, Moscow · *91*
Korea · 171
Koreans · 170
Košice (Czechoslovakia, now in Slovakia) · 181
Krejcar, Jaromír · 88, 122, 124, 162, 163, 183
Krise, Jindřich · 140, *141*, 143, 181, 185
Kriseová, Eda · *30*, 32, 142, 143
Kutaisi (Georgia) · 176
Kyoto (Japan) · 115, 130, *131*, 172

L

La Rochelle-Pallice (Grand Port of) (France) · 138
Lahore (Pakistan) · 136, 137, 184
Larache (Morocco) · 161
Larsen, Agnes (aka Agnessa) · 15, 17, 27, 60-65, *62-65*, 71-76, *74*, *77*, 78, 79, *78*, 81, 82, 84, 86, *87*, 90-94, *90*, *92*, 108, *108*, 110, 114-17, *116*, 119, 120, 122, 123, *123*, 125, *125*, *126*, 127, 128, *128*, 132, *133*, 134, *135*, 136, 137, 145, 146, *146*, 147, *147*, 160, *161*, 164, *164*, 166, 167, *167*, 169, 170, 176, 177, *177*, 178, *178*, 182-187
  see also Karl Marx, Head, Head of a Crying Child, Torzo (sculptures)
Le Corbusier (born Charles-Édouard Jeanneret-Gris) · 13-18, 21, 25, 27, 29, 35-37, 41-49, *41*, *42*, *47-49*, 51, 52, 54, *54*, 55-59, *58*, 60, *61*, 61-64, 66, 68, *68*, 69, 70, 74, *75*, 79, 81, *83*, 84, 85, 88, 89, *89*, 100, *101*, 102, *103*, 104, 110, 113-16, *118*, 119-21, *121*, 124, 126, *126*, 127, 128, 130, 138-40, *139*, 144, 145, *148*, 150, 152, 156, 162, 170, 172, 173, 181-83, 185-87
  aka Corbík · 70, Corbu · 21, 44, 48, 58, 61, 73, 88, 89, 98, 116, 120, 145, 174
  see also books: *Œuvre complète, Quand les cathédrales étaient blanches, Vers une architecture*
  see also projects and buildings: Centrosoyuz, Cité de refuge (Salvation Army building), Errázuris (project), Mundaneum, National Museum of Western Art, Pavillon des Temps Nouveaux / de L'Espirit nouveau / Suisse, urban plan for Algiers / Antwerp / La Rochelle-Pallice / Ville contemporaine / Stockholm / St-Dié / Cité Mondiale / Ville Radieuse; Oued Ouchaïa, Palace of the Soviets, Palais de la Société des Nations, Unité d'habitation, Villa de Mandrot, Villa Savoye, Wanner, 24 rue Nungesser-et-Coli
Le Corbusier-Jeanneret atelier (inter-war period) · 13-18, 35, 41, *41*, 42, *42*, 44, 45, 46, 48, 55-58, 60, 64, 66, 68-70, 72, 78, 84, 85, 88, 98, 113, 114, 119, 125, 128, 140, 145, 150, 152, 156, 160, 182, 187
  see also Atelier at 35 rue de Sèvres
Le Corbusier archive, Paris *see* FLC
Le Corbusier Group · 84, 85, 88, 182
Léger, Fernand · 49, 57, 70
Leningrad (today, St Petersburg) · 93, 94, *94*, *95*, 183
Leonidov, Ivan · 121, 122
Letařovice u Českého Dubu (Czechoslovakia, now in Czech Rep.) · 187
Levine, Judith · 16
Lhota, Karel · 181
Libra, František Albert · 56
Lisbon · 75, 77, *77*
Litoměřice (Czechoslovakia, now in Czech Rep.) · 181
Little Switzerland, Knoxville (Tennessee) · 66, *66*
Liverpool · 70, 75, 78, 79, 96, 108, 160-63
Liverpool School of Architecture · 68, 69, 75
Livre noir aka *Cahier noir, Log Book, Black Book* · 15, 18, 25, 42, *42*, 43, 44, 54, 58, 60, *61*, 66, 69, 145, 150, *150*, 152, *152*, 182
Loach, Judi · 42, 46
Lochotín, Pilsen (amphitheater) · 185
Lods, Marcel · *125*
Log Book see *Livre noir*
London · 51, 85, 136, 138, *139*, 142, 156-60, *156-59*
Loos, Adolf · 54, 181
Lorenc, Miroslav · *57*
Los Angeles, California · *97*
Louvre, Paris · *127*
Lovegrove, William · *134*
Lurçat, André · 54, 56, 120

M

Madras (today, Chennai) · 29, 32, *32*, 35, 37
Madrid · 72, 160, 164, *164*
Maekawa, Kunio · 114, 119, 170, 174, 175
Maghreb, the · 17, 70, 71, 74, *76*, 160, 182
Maison de la culture de Japon, Paris · 187
Makarychev, Timofei Ignachevich · 122, 176, *176*, 183
Makhachkala (Dagestan, Russia) · 98
Malaya *see* British Malaya
Man with a Movie Camera (film), Dziga Vertov · 93, *93*, 181
Manila (Philippines) · 130

Marathon (Greece) · 100, *100*
Marken (the Netherlands) · 86, *86*
Markolius, Sven · 183
Marseille · 84, 128, *128*, 136, *136*, 138, 184
  see also Unité d'habitation
Master Plan for the Development of Pilsen (Směrný územní plán města Plzně) · 140, *141*, 185
Matrimandir (Mother's Temple), Auroville · 34, *34*, 144
May, Ernst · 85, 181
McClellan, Hugh Derby (also as MacCellan) · 56, 85
McLeod, Mary · 18, 25, 43, 46, 55, 56, 60, 66, 85, 144
Mendelsohn, Erich · 79
Mestia (Georgia) · 176
Metropol, Moscow (hotel) · 120
Meudon-Val-Fleury (France) · 54
Mexerah (Morocco) · 161
Meyer, Hannes · 85, 93
Mies van der Rohe, Ludwig · 66
MIT (Massachusetts Institute of Technology), Boston (USA) · 102
Moholy-Nagy, László · 16, *85*, 100, *100*, *101*, 182
  see also Architects' Congress (film)
Moll de Barcelona (Barcelona Dock) · *73*
Monod-Herzen, Gabriel · 144
Montferrand, Auguste Ricarde de · 94
Montjuïc, Barcelona · 70, 71, *71*
Montparnasse, Paris · 17, 36, 41, 49, 110, *111*, 113, *124*, 128, *128*
Morocco · 17, 51, 56, 70, 72, 74, *74*, *75*, 161, 162, *161*, *169*
Moscow · 14, 18, 36, 37, 48, 56, 59, 63, *65*, 68, 79, 84, 85, 88-91, *89-92*, 93, 94, 96, 98, 108, 114, 116, 119-22, 124, 125, 127, 128, 140, 160, 162, 170, 172-75, 181-83, 186
  see also Centrosoyuz, Central Stadium of the Soviet Union (Stade central), Theatre of the Trade Unions, Institute of Baking, Izvestia Building, Kirovskaya (now Chistye Prudy) Metro Station, Club of Architects, Metropol, Narkomzdrav, Palace of the Soviets
Mother, the *see* Alfassa, Mirra
Mrityunjoy Mukherjee · 115, 127
Müllerová, Ludmila *see* Sammerová, Ludmila
Mundaneum, Geneva (project) · 47, 145
Munich Agreement · 135, 184
Munttoren, Amsterdam · *86*
Museum of Modern Art, New York · 25, 187
Myasnitskaya Street, Moscow *see* Centrosoyuz

N

Nad Ovčírnou, district of Zlín · *57*
Nakashima, George · 133, *135*
Narkomzdrav (the People's Commissariat of Public Health), Moscow · 121, 183
National Gallery, London · 157, 159
National Museum of Western Art, Tokyo · 119
Nejmenší byt (The smallest flat), by Karel Teige · 88
Nelson, Paul · 56, 57
Neue Sachlichkeit · 54
New Mexico · *97*
Newhaven (England) · 51, 156, 158
Nijō Castle, Kyoto · 130, *131*
Nikko (Japan) · 175
Nishta *see* Wilson, Margaret Woodrow
Norway · 125, 183
Nová Huť (village near Pilsen) · 78

O

Odesa (Ukraine) · 98
Œuvre complète, Le Corbusier · 48, 58, **58**, 59, **68**, 114, ***118***, 183
Architectural offices of:
    Le Corbusier and Pierre Jeanneret *see* Atelier at 35 rue de Sèvres, and the Le Corbusier–Jeanneret atelier
    Easton & Robertson (John Murray Easton and Howard Robertson) · 157
    Nikolai Kolli · 14, 84, 88, 89, 98, 108, 120–22, 127, 182, 183
    František Albert Libra · 56
    Narkomzdrav (Narodnyi Komissariat Zdravo-okhra-neniia) · 121
    Paul Nelson · 56
    Antonin Raymond · ***118,*** 119, 128, 130, 133, 136, 184
    Josep Lluís Sert · 73
On a Human Scale (book by Gordon Stephenson, ed. by Christine DeMarco) · 187
Ordzhonikidze Sanatorium, Kislovodsk (Russia) · 122, 183
Oriol (photographer) · **73**
Orlov, Georgy · **99**
Osborne House, East Cowes (England) · 185
Oued Ouchaïa, Algeria (project) *see also* Domaine de Badjara · 58, 66, ***68***
Oxford (England) · 157–59

P

Pakistan · 184
Palace of the Soviets (Palais des Soviets), Moscow · 14, 48, ***48,*** 49, 66, ***83***, 84
Palais de la Société des Nations (League of Nations building), Geneva · 46, ***46,*** 47
Pardubice (Czechoslovakia, now in Czech Rep.) · ***56***
Paris · 13–17, 25, 27, 36, 37, 41, ***42***, 43–45, 47, 49–52, **50,** **52,** 54–58, ***58,*** 59, 60, ***61,*** ***63***, 64, 68–71, 79, 84, 85, ***87,*** 88, 89, 91, 94, 96, 108, 113–15, 119–25, 127, 128, ***124–28***, 134, 139, 140, 145, 150, 152, 156, 157, 159, 160, 162, 170, ***173, 174,*** 175, 181–184, 187
    see also Atelier at 35 rue de Sèvres, Cité de refuge (Salvation Army building), Cité internationale universitaire de Paris, Garches, l'Institut d'Urbanisme de l'Université de Paris, Montparnasse, Villa Savoye, pavilions, urban plans, exhibitions, 24 rue Nungesser-et-Coli
Parthenon, Athens · 100, ***101***, 102, ***102***, ***103***, 104, 159
Patel, Ambu · ***134***
Patris II (ship) · 84, ***85,*** 182
    see also congresses, CIAM IV
Paul, Bruno · 54
pavilions:
    British, Paris, 1925 · 157
    Czechoslovak, Brussels, 1958 · 186
    Czechoslovak, Paris, 1937 · 124
    De La Warr, Bexhill · 79
    l'Esprit Nouveau, de, Paris, 1925 · 55
    Hanavský (Hanau), Prague · ***146***
    Industrial, Pardubice · 56
    Japanese, Auroville · 143, ***143***
    Japanese, Paris, 1937 · 124
    Spanish, Paris, 1937 · 124
    Swiss (Pavillon Suisse or Fondation suisse), Paříž · 14, ***42,*** 52, ***52,*** 54, 58–60, ***58***, 182
    Temps Nouveaux, des, Paris, 1937 · 124–26, ***126,*** 128

Pavitra *see* Barbier Saint-Hilaire, Philippe
Pearl Harbor · 184
Penang Island (Malaysia) · 130
Perret, Auguste · 56, 57
Perriand, Charlotte · 15, 17, 25, 27, 36, 37, 41, ***41***, 42, 49, 52, ***53***, 54, ***54***, 55, 57, 59, 60, 64, 70, 78, ***80***, 84, 85, 88, 89, 96, 98, ***98***, 100, ***101***, 104, 108, ***109***, 110, ***110–13***, 113–16, 119–22, ***124***, 128, ***128***, 138–39, 145, 150, 170, 172, ***173–74***, 182–84, 187
    see also Fauteuil Grand Confort, Chaise Longue, *Une vie de création*, hôtel de haute montagne, exhibitions
Perriand-Barsac, Pernette · 54, 108, 113, 114
Perth (Australia) · 104, 146, ***146***, 147, ***147***
Picasso, Pablo · 124
Pilsen (Czechoslovakia, now in Czech Rep.) · 25–29, ***26***, 31, ***31***, 32, ***42***, 44, 45, ***46***, 48, ***49***, 50–52, ***52***, 54, 56, 61, 71, 75, 78, 84, 96, 98, 99, 114, 122, 124, ***124***, 125, 128, 130, 133, 135–44, ***141***, 156, 163–65, 170, 181–83, 185–87
    see also Slovany, Lochotín
Pinto, Gauri · ***134***
Pinto, Mona · 31, ***134***
Pinto, Udar · 143
Piquey (France) · 58
Plan Obus, Algiers (urban plan) · 66, ***68***, 70, 182
Plan Nebula, Auroville (urban plan) · ***142***, 143
Plan Voisin, Paris (urban plan) · 54, 55
Plans (periodical) · 46, 66, 78, 88
Pleistos (river) (Greece) · ***107***
Poland · 184
Pollak (*also as* Polak), Georges · 128, 146
Pondicherry (India) · 13, 14, ***27***, 28, 30–32, ***30–32***, 34, ***34***, 44, 45, 51, 52, 62, ***64***, 66, 108, 115, 116, ***118***, 119, 122, 130, 132–37, ***133–35***, 140, 143, 144, 146, 147, 170, 174, 184–87
    see also ashram, Golconde, Mirra Alfassa, Nakashima, Raymond, Sri Aurobindo
Poseidon, Temple of, Sounion · 100, ***101***
Prado, the, Madrid (museum) · 160
Prager Presse (newspaper) · 47, ***47***, 182
Prague · 27, 29, 35, 44, 45, 47, 56, 84, ***87***, 140, ***142***, 143, ***146***, 163, 181, 185, 186,
    see also congresses, pavilions
Prélude (magazine) · 88
Procházka, Vítězslav · 89, 127
Pushkin monument, Moscow · 36, 93
Pushkin Square, Moscow · 36, ***92***, 93, ***93***
Pyrenees, the (mountains, Spain) · 138, 160

Q

Quand les cathédrales étaient blanches (book by Le Corbusier) · 138, 139

R

Raadhuisstraat, Amsterdam · ***86***
Rajniš, Václav · 42, 43, 150
Rangoon, Burma · 184
Raymond, Antonin · 14, 17, 25, 28, ***30***, 114–19, ***116***, ***118***, 127, 128, 130, 132, 133, ***134,*** 136, 137, 140, 142, 143, 144, ***144***, 174, 175, 183, 184
Raymond, Noémi Pernessin · 25, 116, 117, 132, 137, 140, 143, 183, 184
Red Army · 137

Red Cross · 74, 135
Red Square, Moscow · ***90***, 93
Regent Street, London · ***156***, 157
Reiner, Jan · 42, 43
Řepa, Karel · ***56***
Répertoire des collaborateurs de Le Corbusier aka List of assistants · 18, 42, 51, 55, 58, 68, 69, 85, 146, 147, ***148***, 152, 156
Rhein, the (river) · 55
RIBA *see* Royal Institute of British Architects
Richebourg, Pierre-Ambroise · 94, ***95***
Richmond (England) · 157, 159
Robert *see* Stephenson, Gordon
Robin Hill (fictitious London location of house in *The Forsyte Saga*) · 157
Rokycany (Czechoslovakia, now in Czech Rep.) · 161
Rome · 78
Rosenberg, Evžen · 42, 43, 59
Rostov-on-Don (Russia) · 98
Roth, Alfred · 58
Roy, Dilip Kumar · ***135***
Royal Engineers (RE) · 137, 184
Royal Institute of British Architects (RIBA), London · 69, 138, ***139***, 157
Russia · 25, 32, 69, 70, 84, 85, 98, 121–23, 125, 127, 135, 163
Russians, the · 62, 84, 85, 120, 124, 127, 134, 138
Rypl, Čestmír · 44, 45

S

Saigon (today, Ho Chi Minh City, Vietnam) · 130
St-Dié (urban plan) · 138
St Isaac's Cathedral, St Petersburg · 93, ***94***, 95
St James's Street, London · 157
St Petersburg · 35, 93, 94, ***94***, ***95***, 183
Sakakura, Junzo (*also as* Saka) · 15, 25, 41, 52–55, ***52***, 114–16, 119, 124, 128, 136, 150, 170, 172–74, 182, 187
    see also Japanese Pavilion, Paris
Salaün, Albin · ***52***, ***61***, ***126***
Salon d'automne, Le, Paris, 1922 (exhibition) · 55
Salon d'automne, Le, Paris, 1932 (exhibition) · 62, ***63***
Samaritaine, La, Paris (department store) · 56
Sammer, Jan (aka Dad) · ***26***, ***32***, 60, 63, 64, ***64***, 70, ***77***, 78, 89, 98, 137, 159, 160, 163, 170, 172, 175, 181, 184
Sammer, Jan (aka Honza, Jenda) · 21, 32, 52, ***52***, 54, 75, 76, ***76***, 84, 122, 160, 162, 163, ***163***, 181
Sammer, Josef (aka Pepa) · ***26***, 137, 175, 181
Sammer, Petr · 27, 28, 140, 176, 185
Sammerová, Ludmila (née Müllerová) · 140, 147, 185
Sammerová, Miloslava (married name Gschwindová) (aka Milča, Milána) · 21, ***26***, 52, 56, 74, 75, ***87***, 122, 130, ***131***, 137, ***136–37***, 156–59, 161, 170, 175, 184
Sammerová, Růžena (née Hlavatá) · ***26***, 181
Sammer's photograph collection · 13, 16–18, 23, ***32***, 44, ***44***, 45, 51, 52, 54, 62, ***64***, 66, 72, 74, 75, 78, 79, 93, 96, 98, ***100***, ***101***, ***103***, 104, 108, ***109***, 110, ***112***, 113, ***113***, 115, 116, 120, 122, 132, ***133***, 137,
Sarkar, Nolini Kanta · ***135***
Sato (painter) · 114, 175
Scheldt (river) · 70, 79, 81, ***81***
Scheyer, Galka *see also* Blue Four · 61, 62
Seine (river) · ***127***
Sert, Josep Lluís · 15, 17, 29, 41, 70–73, ***72***, ***73***, 120, 124, 128, 160, 183
    see also Calle de Muntaner, Spanish Pavilion

Sert, Muncha · 41, *72*, ***125***, 128
Sevastopol (Crimea) · 98
Seville (Spain) · 72, 160, 161
Shafshāwan, (aka Xauen) (Morocco), *see* Chefchaouen
Shugakuin Imperial Villa, Kyoto · 130, ***131***
Siberia · 170
Siberia Maru (ship) · 119, 170, 175
Siemensstadt (Berlin) · 81
Sierra de Guadarrama (mountains, Spain) · 160, ***165***
Sierra Nevada (mountains, Spain) · 161
Simeiz (Crimea) · ***123***
Singapore · 129, 130, 137, 184
SKI (magazine) · 113, ***113***
Slough (England) · 17, 79, ***83***
Slovany, Pilsen (housing complex) · 27, 140, ***141***, 185
socialist realism · 44, 120, 121, 127, 140, 183, 185
Soissons, Louis de · 51, 157, 159
Sokol, Jan · 42, 43
Sorbonne, the, Paris · 156, 182
Sounion (Greece) · 100, ***101***
South Africa, Republic of · 69, 142
Southampton · 75, 76
Soviet Union · 13, 15–17, 54, 56, 57, 59, 62, 64, 69, 81, 84, 85, 87–89, *90*, 91, 93, 94, 96, 108, 113, 114, 119–22, 124, 125, 127, 135, 137, 140, 174, 175, 177, 181–86
Spain · 17, 25, 29, 51, 70, 71, 72, ***73***, 127, 160, ***160***, 182
Špalek, Josef · 88, 122, 163, 183
Spanish, the · 29, 120, 161
Spanish Pavilion, Paris, 1937· 124
Společenský dům (hotel), Zlín (Czechoslovakia, now in Czech Rep.) · ***57***
Sri Aurobindo · 28, 134, 135, 143
   see also ashram, Pondicherry
Stalin, Joseph Vissarionovich · 120, 185
Stam, Mart · 85
Stavoprojekt · 140, 185
Stepantsminda (Georgia) · ***177***
Stephenson, Gordon (aka Robert) · 15, 17, 60, 64, 68–70, *70*, 75, 78, 79, *79*, *80*, 81, *81*, *83*, 84, 85, *91*, 93, 94, *94*, *95*, 96, 98–100, *99*, *101*, 102, *102*, 104, 105, *106*, 107, *107*, 108, 110, 122, 125, 138, 140, 142, 145–47, ***146***, ***147***, 150, 162, 182–83
Stevenson, Robert Louis · 68, 69, 156
Stockholm (urban plan) · 68–70, 182
Stránik, Karel · 42, 43
The Studio (magazine) · 102, 158
Suda, Stanislav · 185
Suez Canal · ***129***, 130, ***131***, 184
Svaz architektů ČSR (Association of Czechoslovak Architects) · 186
Svaz československých výtvarných umělců (Association of Czechoslovak Artists) · 186
Svaz socialistických architektů (Association of Socialist Architects, Czechoslovakia) · 88
Swiss, the · 51, 58, 84, 85, 114, 147, 152, 156, 158
Swiss Pavilion (also as Pavillon Suisse), Paris ·14, *42*, 52, *52*, 54, 58, ***58***, 60, 182
Switzerland · 41, 57, 58, 84, 128, 150
Sýkora, Miloslav · 185

T

Tagus (river in Spain) · 160
Tangier (Morocco) · 161, 163, 170
Taos (New Mexico) · ***97***

Tbilisi (aka Tiflis) (Georgia) · 96, 98, ***98***, 176, 177, ***177***, 178, ***178***
Teige, Karel · 47, 84, 88
Tétouan (Morocco) · 17, 70, 72, 74, 160-63, ***162***
Theatre of the Trade Unions, Moscow (project) · 88, 120, 182
La théorie du *materialisme historique*, by Nicolaï Boukharine (Nikolai Bukharin) · 88
Three-bodied Daemon, Athens (sculpture) · 102, ***103***
Tokyo · 14, 37, 41, 114, 115, 117, 119, 127, 128, 130, 133, ***134***, 136, 170, 171, ***171***, 172, ***172***, 175, 183, 184
   see also National Museum of Western Art
Toledo (Spain) · 17, 72, 160, 161, ***166***
Tominaga (historian) · 114, 133, 136, 170, 174, 175
Torso (sculpture by Agnes Larsen) · 63, 183
Tower of London, the · 158, ***159***
Town Hall, Slough (project) · 17, 79, ***83***
Trans-Siberian Railway · 114, 170
Tsuruga (Japan) · 170
Tuileries, Jardin des, Paris · ***126***
TVA (Tennessee Valley Authority) · 66, 67

U

UIA (Union internationale des Architectes) *see* International Union of Architects
Union of Socialist Architects (Soviet Union) · 121
Unité d'habitation building, Marseille · 138
United States of America (USA) · 13, 29, 56, 57, 60, ***61***, 62, 64, 66, 85, 96, 128, 133, 136–38, 140, 145, 183, 184, 187
Urals, the · 170
Urban, Antonín · ***178***
urban planning · 25, 66, 68, 69, 84, 102, 125, 126, 140, 143, 182, 185, 186
urban plans:
   Antwerp · 17, 48, 68, 70, 75, 78, 79, ***80-82***, 82, 84, 142, 160, 182
   Cité mondiale, Geneva · 47
   Geneva · 68
   Moscow · 68, 84, 124, 125
   Plan Obus, Algiers · 66, ***68***, 70, 182
   Plan Nebula, Auroville · ***142***, 143
   Plan Voisin, Paris · 54, 55
   La Rochelle-Pallice · 138
   Master Plan for Pilsen · 140, ***141***, 185
   St-Dié · 138
   Stockholm · 68–70, 182
   Ville Radieuse · 68, 78, 79, 81, 84
Ushba, Mount (Georgia) · 176

V

Vaculík, Jaroslav · 42, 43
Vaithikuppam, Pondicherry (India) · ***32***
Valencia (Spain) · 29, 72, 160, 161, 164, ***164***
Velázquez, Diego · 160
Vers une Architecture (book by Le Corbusier) · 102, ***103***, 181
Vertov, Dziga · 93, ***93***, 181
Vesnin, brothers (Alexander, Leonid, and Viktor) · 14, 85, ***99***, 121, 127
Une vie de création (Charlotte Perriand's autobiography) · 41, 42, 49, 52–55, 60, 84, 85, 88, 108, 187
Vienna · 119, 127, 128, 146, 159, 183
Villa de Mandrot, Le Pradet · 66

Villa Savoye, Poissy (outskirts of Paris) · 45, 51
Ville contemporaine de trois millions d'habitants (project) · 55
Ville Radieuse (urban plan) · 68, 78, 79, 81, 84
Vladivostok (Russia) · 114, 119, 170
Volendam (Netherlands) · 86, ***86***
Volráb, Miloslav · 185

W

Wanner, Edmond · 51-55, 85, 182
Wanner, Hans (János) · 51, 55, 84, 85
Wanner (project) · 66
De La Warr Pavilion, Bexhill (England) · 79
Warren, Edward Prioleau · 51, 157–59
Warren, Margaret · 157–59
Warsaw · 119
Warsaw Pact, the · 186
Watterson, Zdenka · 47, *47*, 48, 182
Watts, George Frederic · ***159***
Weissmann, Ernest · 16, *41*, 58, 84, 85
Welwyn Garden City (England) · 157–59
West, Jane · 15, 17, 27, 60, ***61***, 64, 66, ***66***, ***67***, 96, ***96***, 138, 150, 182
West Kirby (England) · 17, 70, 78, ***78-81***, 81, 82, 160, 182
Wight, Isle of (England) · 185
Wilson, Margret Woodrow (Nishta) · 134, ***134***
Windsor (England) · 159
Wolker, Jiří (Czech poet) · 140
Wright, Frank Lloyd · 117, 127, 183

X

Xauen *see* Chefchaouen (Shafshāwan)

Y

Yalta (Crimea) · 121, 183
Yokohama (Japan) · 128, 136, 170, 172, 184

Z

Zadkine, Ossip · 62
Zakharov, Andreyan (Adrian) Dmitrievich · 94
Zaknic (Žaknić), Ivan · 59
Zlín (Czechoslovakia, now in Czech Rep.) · ***56***, ***57***
   see also Nad Ovčírnou, Společenský dům
Zurich · 58, 183

24 rue Nungesser-et-Coli (apartment building), Paris · 14, *42*, 58–60, ***61***, 89, 182

Abbreviations

Archives

AAUP	The Architectural Archives of the University of Pennsylvania
ABS	Archiv bezpečnostních složek (Security Services Archive of the Czech Republic)
AChP	Archives Charlotte Perriand, Paris
AIA	American Institute of Architects
AMP	Archiv města Plzně (City of Pilsen Archives)
CCA	Canadian Centre for Architecture, Montréal
FLC	Fondation Le Corbusier, Paris
PNP	Památník národního písemnictví v Praze (Museum of Czech Literature)
RIBA	Royal Institute of British Architects
SAAA	Sri Aurobindo Ashram Archives
UoLL	Special Collections and Archives, University of Liverpool
UWA	Special Collections and Archives of the University of Western Australia, Perth
VHÚ	Vojenský historický ústav v Praze (Military History Institute Prague)

Organizations listed in the text

AALC	Association des amis de Le Corbusier
AEAR	Association des écrivains et des artistes révolutionnaires
AILC	Association internationale Le Corbusier
ATBAT	Atelier des bâtisseurs
CIAM	Congrès internationaux d'architecture moderne
UIA	Union Internationale des Architectes

Image credits

The permission for the reproduction of photographs from Sammer's collection and all documents related to František Sammer was kindly granted by Petr Sammer. Image material related to Jane West and Gordon Stephenson is reproduced with the permission of Carin Clauss, Ann Peluso and John Rose. Eda Kriseová kindly granted premission to publish her photo. Jakub Hrab created a number of reproductions and prepared all the visual material for printing. The author has made every effort to ensure that all illustrations remain copyrighted and to obtain permission for publication from the authors, their heirs, agents or owners. Should any outstanding claims arise, we ask the copyright owner or their representative to contact the publisher immediately.

Illustrations and / or permission for reproduction was kindly provided by:

AKG-Images
© AKG-Images / Walter Limot / ADAGP / DACS 2025
P. 48
The Architectural Archives, University of Pennsylvania
© Antonin Raymond and Noémi Pernessin Raymond Collection, The Architectural Archives, University of Pennsylvania
P. 134
The Architectural Archives of the University of Pennsylvania
© Masanori Sugiyama Collection, The Architectural Archives, University of Pennsylvania
P. 134 (detail)
Archives Charlotte Perriand, Paris
© AChP a Arthur Rüegg / ADAGP / DACS 2025
P. 55
© AChP / ADAGP / DACS 2025
P. 41, 80, 98, 101, 109, 111, 112, 173, 174
Archiv města Plzně, fond Františka Sammera
© Archiv města Plzně / Petr Sammer
P. 26, 27, 46, 49, 53, 73, 76, 77, 87, 124, 136, 137, 138, 141, 161–163, 176
Arxiu Històric del COAC, Barcelona
© Arxiu Històric del COAC / Oriol
P. 73
Canadian Centre for Architecture, Montréal
© Canadian Centre for Architecture, Montréal. Gift of Howard Schickler and David Lafaille.
P. 89
© Canadian Centre for Architecture, Montréal
P. 95
Fondation Le Corbusier, Paris
© FLC / ADAGP / DACS 2025
P. 43, 52, 58, 59, 60, 61, 68, 69, 75, 84, 89, 100, 101, 103, 118, 121, 126, 139, 151, 153
Light Cone, Paris
© Moholy-Nagy Foundation & Light Cone
P. 85, 100, 101
Private archive, Prague
© ADAGP / DACS 2025
P. 139, 148, 149, 151, 153
Special Collections and Archives of the University of Western Australia, Perth
© Special Collections and Archives of the University of Western Australia, Perth. Gordon Stephenson Papers, 1942-1997, MS 144 / John Rose
P. 146, 147
The University of Liverpool Library
© The University of Liverpool Library
P. 79, 107
Sri Aurobindo Ashram Archives, Pondicherry
© Sri Aurobindo Ashram Archives / Petr Sammer
Cover photo and a photo on p. 33, 35, 38, 44, 45, 50, 53, 57, 61– 65, 67, 69–78, 80–83, 86, 87, 90– 92, 94–113, 115–118, 122–132, 134, 135, 156–160, 164–172, 177, 178
© ADAGP / DACS 2025
P. 53, 109–111, 112, 113
Sri Aurobindo Ashram – Art Gallery, Pondicherry
© Sri Aurobindo Ashram – Art Gallery
P. 133

Martina Hrabová | The Le Corbusier Galaxy

z hdk
—
Zürcher Hochschule der Künste
Zurich University of the Arts
—
—

 Univerzita Palackého
v Olomouci